# mindful aging for 100+ living

Strategies for Preserving Brain Function

the 100+ living plan
book seven

## Dr Heinrich Henstock HKin DC

## Dr Graham Jenkins BSc DC

# contents

# neuro-insights

"Maintaining brain health is the key to living a long, successful life. It's not just about preventing disease, but about enhancing cognitive resilience and emotional well-being." – Dr. Mark Hyman, Functional Medicine Expert

"The brain and spinal cord are the central control systems of the body. Protecting them is essential to living a long and vibrant life free of mental decline." – Dr. Daniel Amen, Psychiatrist and Brain Health Expert

# introduction: your brain, your powerhouse

Imagine waking up every day with a clear mind, able to remember details with ease, solve problems swiftly, and stay curious about the world around you. The brain is at the center of everything we experience and do, making it one of the most precious—and powerful—assets we have. Yet, as essential as our brain is, we often overlook how important it is to actively nurture and protect it, even when we are young.

This book takes you on a journey into the world of brain health. You'll learn not only how your brain works but also what you can do to keep it functioning at its best through every phase of life. As we'll see, there's a lot that's within our control when it comes to maintaining and even enhancing our cognitive abilities. Whether you're interested in boosting your memory, sharpening your focus, or simply learning how to age with mental vitality, this book will guide you through practical, science-backed strategies that empower you to take control of your brain health.

**The Science of the Brain: An Amazing Complexity**

The brain is an astonishing organ, composed of approximately 86 billion neurons that work together in a vast network, allowing us to think, learn, feel, and move. Neurons communicate through intricate electrical and chemical signals, forming pathways that support every habit, memory, and skill we develop. This system is also incredibly adaptable, capable of reconfiguring itself in response to new information and experiences—a property known as neuroplasticity.

As we grow older, however, the brain naturally changes. Parts of it, particularly those involved in memory and complex decision-making, may shrink slightly over time. Neurotransmitters, the chemicals that relay signals between neurons, may not flow as quickly as they once did, leading to minor memory lapses or slower reaction times. It's a normal part of aging and not necessarily a sign of cognitive decline. But, for some people, these changes become more severe, progressing into neurodegenerative diseases like Alzheimer's and Parkinson's, where memory, mobility, and even personality can be deeply affected.

**Neuroplasticity: The Brain's Capacity for Change**

The good news is that our brains are remarkably resilient. Even as we age, our brains retain a unique ability to adapt and change—a phenomenon known as neuroplasticity. Neuroplasticity is, in many ways, our brain's superpower. It means that the brain can rewire itself, forming new connections and strengthening existing ones, a process that can be actively encouraged through lifestyle choices.

For instance, learning a new language, playing an instrument, or picking up a hobby can stimulate neuroplasticity and help maintain cognitive flexibility. Physical exercise, particularly aerobic activities, promotes the growth of new neurons and improves blood flow to the brain, supporting its structural and functional health. Even simple actions like engaging in regular social interactions or practicing mindfulness can bolster neuroplasticity, helping the brain stay robust and adaptable.

**What Affects Brain Health? From Daily Choices to Long-Term Habits**

Our brain health is influenced by a complex interplay of factors, some within our control and others less so. Genetics, for instance, plays a role in determining susceptibility to certain neurodegenerative conditions. However, research shows that lifestyle choices—diet, exercise, sleep, stress management, and mental engagement—are powerful determinants of cognitive health and can make a big difference in how our brains age.

One of the most significant threats to brain health is oxidative stress, a process that occurs when there's an imbalance between free radicals (unstable molecules) and antioxidants in the body. The brain, due to its high oxygen consumption, is particularly vulnerable to oxidative stress, which can damage neurons and accelerate cognitive decline. Chronic inflammation is another risk factor, contributing to the wear and tear of neural pathways over time. Additionally, certain types of protein buildup—such as amyloid plaques in Alzheimer's disease—can disrupt neural communication and lead to cell death.

Lifestyle choices can either contribute to or help counteract these processes. Diets high in antioxidants and omega-3 fatty acids, for example, can support cellular health and reduce inflammation, while physical activity can increase blood flow to the brain and stimulate protective growth factors. Sleep, often overlooked, is essential for cognitive health, allowing the brain to consolidate memories and remove metabolic waste. Taken together, these daily choices create an environment that either nurtures brain health or leaves it vulnerable.

**Why Brain Health Matters at Every Age**

When we're young, our brains are remarkably adaptable, quick to learn and absorb new information. But it's a myth to think that cognitive growth and maintenance are only for the young. Brain health matters at every stage of life, from childhood, where foundational skills are built, to adulthood, where stress and lifestyle habits start to impact cognitive function, and into old age, when maintaining mental clarity becomes essential for quality of life.

In fact, brain health is now a topic of interest for people of all ages. Young adults are finding value in learning strategies that enhance focus and reduce stress. Middle-aged adults seek ways to improve memory and prevent age-related decline. And older adults are increasingly interested in preserving cognitive function as they age. The exciting part is that regardless of age, there are concrete actions we can take to support our brains. The right habits can make a difference, not only in prolonging cognitive vitality but also in enriching our lives with greater clarity, creativity, and connection.

**Looking Forward: A Path to a Healthier Mind**

In the chapters that follow, we'll explore the fascinating science of brain health and how you can apply it to your own life. Each chapter will dive into key areas that affect the brain, from diet and exercise to mental engagement and stress management. We'll look at specific strategies and lifestyle changes that research has shown can help maintain and even improve cognitive function over time. You'll learn how simple, everyday choices can help keep your mind sharp, your memory strong, and your mood balanced.

Taking care of our brain is not about staving off inevitable decline but about empowering ourselves to lead fulfilling, mentally vibrant lives. Whether you're starting young or beginning later in life, the brain's adaptability and potential for growth mean that it's never too late to benefit. This journey to brain health is an invitation to invest in your mind—an investment that will pay off in greater resilience, clarity, and well-being throughout life.

**Why a book on Brain Health?**

Writing a book on brain health felt like a natural next step for me, driven by my deep belief that the brain is the foundation of overall health and longevity. Having experienced the importance of physical and mental resilience firsthand, I understand how essential it is to care for our brain as we age. My own journey—from a life of intense physical activity to overcoming health challenges through chiropractic care—has fueled my passion for helping others achieve not just recovery, but optimal brain health. I believe the brain is at the core of everything we do, and its health impacts every aspect of our lives, from cognition to emotional well-being. This book is my way of sharing the knowledge and insights I've gathered over the years, with the goal of empowering others to maintain their brain health and unlock lifelong vitality. My mission is to inspire people to take control of their health and live the vibrant, successful life I believe everyone deserves.

# neuro-insights

"**We often think of our muscles and heart as the most important parts of the body. But without a healthy brain, nothing else works well.**" – Dr. Sanjay Gupta, Neurosurgeon

"**Longevity isn't just about years lived; it's about quality of life. The key to a long, healthy life is to care for your brain and nervous system, the body's command center.**" – Dr. David Perlmutter, Neurologist and Author

one
# understanding the brain – from neurons to networks

**THE BRAIN: A Quick Overview**

The human brain, a marvel of biological complexity, contains around 86 billion neurons that create a vast, interconnected network responsible for everything we experience and do. These neurons aren't alone in their work; they're supported by glial cells, which outnumber neurons and play essential roles in maintaining brain health. While neurons transmit electrical signals to communicate, glial cells provide structural support, deliver nutrients, clean up waste, and defend the brain against pathogens. Together, neurons and glia form a resilient system that allows us to think, feel, move, and react to the world around us. It's a finely balanced partnership, ensuring the efficient processing of information and keeping the brain flexible and adaptable throughout life.

**Anatomy of the Brain: Key Parts That Matter**

The brain's structure is incredibly organized, with specific regions dedicated to distinct functions, much like different departments within a company. At the brain's surface, the cerebral cortex acts as the control center for higher-level thinking, decision-making, and problem-solving. When we make a choice or solve a puzzle, the cortex is hard at work. Beneath the cortex lies the hippocampus, which plays a key role in forming, organizing, and storing memories. It's like a personal filing system, helping us remember experiences and recall information as needed. The basal ganglia, located deeper within the brain, manage movement and motor learning. They're the reason we can perform complex physical tasks, like riding a bike, almost automatically after practice.

Another essential player is the cerebellum, often called the "little brain" due to its shape and structure. It's responsible for balance and coordination, allowing us to walk, stand, and move gracefully. Finally, the brainstem connects the brain to the spinal cord and regulates vital functions, such as breathing, heart rate, and sleep cycles. Each of these parts works in concert with the others to help us navigate the world. When this system begins to age or malfunction, the harmony among these regions may falter, affecting everything from memory to movement.

**How the Brain Ages**

Aging naturally affects the brain, bringing changes that range from subtle slowdowns in processing to occasional forgetfulness. Many of these shifts are part of normal aging and don't necessarily signal cognitive decline. As we get older, brain volume gradually decreases, especially in areas like the prefrontal cortex and hippocampus, which are involved in complex thought and memory. This reduction in volume, along with a slower rate of neurotransmission, can make it seem like our thoughts aren't as quick or sharp as they once were. However, it's important to note that while certain skills like multitasking may feel harder, accumulated knowledge and wisdom often remain intact and can even improve with age.

Normal cognitive aging might show up as slower thinking or mild forgetfulness. You might find it takes a bit longer to recall a word, remember someone's name, or multitask as efficiently. These changes don't necessarily indicate a problem but reflect the brain's natural aging process. Yet for some, these shifts become more pronounced, crossing into the territory of neurodegeneration. This more severe decline often signals diseases like Alzheimer's or Parkinson's, where the brain doesn't just slow down—it begins to lose critical neurons and connections, leading to memory loss, changes in movement, and other impairments.

**What Causes Brain Aging and Neurodegeneration?**

Aging impacts every part of the body, but the brain faces unique challenges that can lead to both normal wear and tear and more serious neurodegenerative conditions. One major factor is oxidative stress. The brain requires a lot of oxygen to function, which unfortunately leaves it vulnerable to oxidative damage from free radicals. These unstable molecules can damage cells over time, contributing to inflammation and a gradual decline in cognitive abilities. Antioxidants, which we get from foods and natural bodily processes, usually neutralize these free radicals. However, as we age, our natural antioxidant defenses weaken, leading to an accumulation of cellular damage.

Chronic inflammation is another culprit. Just as inflammation in a joint can lead to pain and damage, inflammation in the brain can harm neurons and their connections. This inflammation is often driven by immune cells in the brain that become overactive, attacking healthy cells and potentially leading to conditions like Alzheimer's. Additionally, certain neurodegenerative diseases involve a buildup of harmful proteins in the brain. For instance, in Alzheimer's disease, amyloid plaques form, interrupting communication between neurons and leading to cell death. These protein deposits can clog the brain's intricate communication network, making it harder for neurons to relay signals, which ultimately affects memory, learning, and even physical abilities.

The interplay of oxidative stress, inflammation, and protein buildup leads to cell death, which gradually reduces brain function, causing symptoms to become more noticeable over time.

.   .   .

**Neuroplasticity: The Brain's Superpower**

While the aging process may seem daunting, there's an incredible silver lining: neuroplasticity. Neuroplasticity refers to the brain's ability to reorganize itself by forming new neural connections. This adaptability doesn't stop in childhood but can continue throughout life, even into old age. Studies show that engaging in mentally stimulating activities, staying physically active, and fostering social connections can encourage neuroplasticity, helping the brain retain its flexibility.

Learning a new language, playing an instrument, or simply staying curious can help maintain brain health. Physical activities like walking or dancing increase blood flow to the brain, promoting growth factors that stimulate the creation of new neurons and strengthen existing ones. Even social engagement has been shown to reduce cognitive decline, as conversations and interactions challenge the brain to stay sharp. So, although aging may bring challenges, the brain's remarkable adaptability means it's never too late to strengthen its connections and keep it functioning at a high level.

**Early Signs of Neurodegeneration: It Can Start Early**

Contrary to common belief, neurodegenerative diseases like Alzheimer's and Parkinson's don't only affect the elderly. In fact, these conditions can begin their quiet development years, even decades, before noticeable symptoms arise. In Alzheimer's disease, for example, amyloid plaques may start to accumulate in the brain as early as one's 30s or 40s. For many, these changes occur silently, with no outward signs of memory loss or confusion until much later.

In Parkinson's disease, early signs may appear long before the well-known tremors or movement difficulties. Instead, subtle issues like a loss of smell, sleep disturbances, or digestive problems might show up 10 to 20 years before more pronounced symptoms. Recognizing these early, less obvious signs can be crucial, as early intervention through lifestyle changes or emerging treatments has the potential to slow the progression of neurodegenerative diseases. By paying attention to these warning signs, we can empower ourselves to take proactive steps for brain health.


**Looking Forward: Protecting Your Brain**

Aging is inevitable, but how we experience it is partly within our control. Understanding how the brain functions and what factors impact its health gives us valuable tools for maintaining cognitive well-being throughout our lives. From adopting a diet rich in antioxidants to staying active and mentally engaged, there are numerous strategies to protect brain health. And while neurodegeneration may seem like an unavoidable part of aging, research increasingly suggests that through these lifestyle adjustments and early interventions, we can mitigate many of its effects.


In later chapters, we'll explore specific methods to support the brain, strengthen its functions, and potentially counter some effects of aging. The journey to protecting our cognitive health is a lifelong endeavor, but with knowledge and action, we can foster a vibrant, active mind well into our golden years.

# chapter 1 summary:
our introduction to the brain

**The Brain: A Quick Overview**

- The brain contains around 86 billion neurons forming a complex network.
- Neurons communicate via electrical signals; glial cells provide structure, nutrients, waste cleanup, and protection.

**Anatomy of the Brain: Key Parts That Matter**

- **Cerebral Cortex:** Responsible for decision-making, problem-solving, and higher-level thinking.
- **Hippocampus:** Manages memory formation, organization, and retrieval.
- **Basal Ganglia:** Coordinates movement and motor learning.
- **Cerebellum:** Controls balance and coordination.
- **Brainstem:** Regulates vital functions (e.g., breathing, heart rate, sleep).

All regions work in harmony; dysfunction can impact memory, movement, and cognition.

### How the Brain Ages

- Normal aging causes gradual decreases in brain volume and slower processing.
- The prefrontal cortex and hippocampus shrink, affecting complex thought and memory.
- Cognitive skills may slow, but accumulated wisdom remains steady or improves.
- Severe declines lead to neurodegeneration, affecting memory, movement, and function.

### What Causes Brain Aging and Neurodegeneration?

- **Oxidative Stress:** High oxygen use makes the brain vulnerable to free radicals, causing cellular damage.
- **Chronic Inflammation:** Overactive immune cells in the brain harm neurons and connections.
- **Protein Buildup:** Diseases like Alzheimer's involve protein deposits (e.g., amyloid plaques), disrupting neural communication.
- These factors collectively cause cell death and declining brain function.

### Neuroplasticity: The Brain's Superpower

- Neuroplasticity allows the brain to form new connections, even in old age.
- Activities like learning, physical exercise, and socializing promote neuroplasticity.
- Mental and physical activities increase blood flow, support neuron growth, and reduce cognitive decline.

### Early Signs of Neurodegeneration: It Can Start Early

- Conditions like Alzheimer's and Parkinson's can begin decades before symptoms.

- Early signs of Alzheimer's include silent amyloid plaque buildup; Parkinson's may show subtle issues like loss of smell or sleep disturbances.
- Early recognition enables proactive lifestyle changes and potential treatments.

**Looking Forward: Protecting Your Brain**

- Lifestyle changes (antioxidant-rich diet, activity, mental engagement) help protect brain health.
- Understanding brain function and health factors empowers better aging experiences.

# afterword

The brain is a highly complex organ, with around 86 billion neurons working together to manage everything from memory and cognition to movement and balance. As we age, the brain naturally experiences gradual changes, including a decrease in volume and slower processing speeds. However, the brain's remarkable ability to adapt through neuro-plasticity offers hope for maintaining cognitive function even in older age. Understanding the causes of brain aging and neurodegeneration—such as oxidative stress, inflammation, and protein buildup—helps us take proactive steps to protect brain health. By incorporating healthy lifestyle choices, including a nutrient-rich diet, physical activity, and mental engagement, we can support brain health and mitigate the effects of aging, leading to a better quality of life and enhanced cognitive resilience.

# neuro-insights

"The brain, with its intricate network of neurons, is the organ most crucial to our ability to thrive, adapt, and grow. It's the control center for both the mind and the body." – Dr. Jill Bolte Taylor, Neuroanatomist

"Your brain holds the key to your future. The better you take care of it today, the sharper and more resilient you will be in your later years." – Dr. Andrew Huberman, Neuroscientist

two

# neuro-
# degenerative
# diseases

## WHAT HAPPENS IN NEURODEGENERATIVE DISEASES?

Neurodegenerative diseases are fundamentally about the gradual and often irreversible death of neurons, the cells responsible for communication within the brain and between the brain and body. When these neurons die, the brain's ability to perform essential functions like memory storage, movement control, and behavior regulation declines. The symptoms we associate with each neurodegenerative disease depend on which brain areas and types of neurons are most affected.

In Alzheimer's disease, memory and cognitive skills are primarily impacted. As neurons in the hippocampus and other memory-related areas begin to die, people may experience confusion, disorientation, and memory loss. In Parkinson's disease, the neurons that produce dopamine—a neurotransmitter critical for smooth, coordinated movement—are affected, resulting in tremors, stiffness, and slowed movements. ALS (Amyotrophic Lateral Sclerosis) targets motor neurons, which control voluntary muscle movements. As these motor neurons die, muscle control becomes increasingly difficult, making everyday tasks, speaking, and even breathing challenging.

. . .

What drives this cellular breakdown? Although each neurodegenerative disease has unique features, they share several underlying processes that lead to the death of neurons.

## The Brain's "Garbage Disposal" Problem: Protein Build-Up

One of the central issues in neurodegenerative diseases is the accumulation of toxic proteins. Imagine the brain as a bustling city that generates waste as it functions. Normally, the brain has systems that act as "garbage disposal" units, clearing away this waste to keep neurons working smoothly. However, in neurodegenerative diseases, this disposal system falters, leading to the buildup of proteins that disrupt cellular function.

In Alzheimer's disease, this waste includes two major protein types: amyloid and tau. Amyloid proteins clump together to form **amyloid plaques** outside neurons, interfering with communication between them. Inside the neurons, tau proteins form twisted tangles, disrupting the cells' internal structure and transport system. These combined effects prevent neurons from functioning properly, leading to cell death and brain shrinkage over time, which manifests as memory loss and confusion.

Parkinson's disease involves a different toxic protein called **alpha-synuclein**, which forms clumps known as Lewy bodies within dopamine-producing neurons. Dopamine is vital for regulating movement, so as these neurons die, symptoms like tremors, rigidity, and slowness appear. In both Alzheimer's and Parkinson's, the inability to clear out these harmful proteins creates a toxic environment that gradually poisons the brain, leading to worsening symptoms.

## The Energy Crisis: Mitochondrial Dysfunction

Neurons, like all cells, need energy to function, which they derive from mitochondria, often referred to as the "power plants" of cells. Mitochondria produce ATP (adenosine triphosphate), the molecule that powers cellular activities. However, in neurodegenerative diseases, mitochondria become less efficient, leading to an energy shortfall that affects neuron function and survival.

Think of it like a home with an inconsistent power supply; at first, some appliances may work sporadically, but eventually, as the power becomes even less reliable, nothing functions correctly.

This energy deficit is especially damaging to neurons, which require high levels of energy to send messages across the brain and body. In diseases like Parkinson's and ALS, where muscle control relies heavily on high-energy neurons, mitochondrial dysfunction can quickly lead to cell death and muscle weakness.

Mitochondrial dysfunction is a crucial factor in neurodegeneration because it compromises neurons' ability to carry out even basic tasks, hastening their decline. Research into protecting and restoring mitochondrial function has shown promise, offering potential avenues to slow neurodegenerative processes.

**Oxidative Stress: The Brain's "Rust"**

Oxidative stress is another significant factor in neurodegeneration. Neurons, due to their high energy demands, produce many by-products, including free radicals—unstable molecules that can damage cells. In a healthy brain, antioxidants neutralize these free radicals, but in neurodegenerative diseases, the balance is disrupted. When free radicals outpace antioxidants, oxidative stress occurs, damaging neurons similarly to how rust damages metal.

. . .

This oxidative stress not only harms individual neurons but also creates a cycle of further damage. Damaged neurons release even more free radicals, which harm nearby cells and escalate cellular breakdown. In conditions like Alzheimer's and Parkinson's, oxidative stress plays a dual role: it damages neurons directly and increases vulnerability to other degenerative processes, accelerating cell death across affected brain areas.

Oxidative stress highlights the importance of antioxidant-rich diets and lifestyle choices that support cellular health. While no diet or supplement alone can prevent neurodegenerative disease, antioxidants may help counteract oxidative stress, potentially slowing disease progression and supporting overall brain health.

**The Immune System Gone Wrong: Chronic Inflammation**

The brain's immune response plays a complex role in neurodegenerative diseases. Immune cells in the brain, called **microglia**, are responsible for clearing away damaged cells and proteins. However, when neurodegeneration begins, microglia can become overactive, initiating a chronic inflammatory response. This persistent inflammation damages healthy neurons, accelerating cell death.

In Alzheimer's, for example, the brain's reaction to amyloid plaques triggers microglial activation, leading to inflammation. Instead of clearing away harmful proteins, these overactive immune cells release chemicals that harm healthy neurons. This inflammatory response doesn't just fail to solve the problem; it exacerbates the damage, speeding up cognitive decline and worsening symptoms.

Chronic inflammation is like a fire that's meant to cleanse but instead scorches everything around it. While the body uses short lived inflammation to fight infections and heal injuries, chronic inflammation in the brain becomes destructive, breaking down neurons and worsening the effects of neurodegeneration.

## The Role of Genetics

Genetics plays a pivotal role in neurodegenerative diseases, with certain genetic variants increasing susceptibility. In Alzheimer's disease, for instance, individuals carrying a specific variant of the APOE gene, known as **APOE ε4**, have a higher risk of developing the disease. However, genetics alone doesn't determine fate. Many people with this gene variant never develop Alzheimer's, and others without it do, indicating that lifestyle, environment, and other factors also play a significant role.

Parkinson's disease is similarly linked to certain genetic mutations, including those in the **LRRK2** and **SNCA** genes, though these mutations are rare. Most cases of Parkinson's are "sporadic," meaning they occur without a clear genetic cause, underscoring that environmental exposures, lifestyle, and even aging itself contribute to disease development.

While genetic predispositions are beyond our control, understanding them can empower individuals to make informed lifestyle choices. For those with a family history of neurodegenerative diseases, regular cognitive assessments, a balanced diet, and an active lifestyle can be proactive steps toward reducing risk.

## Neurodegeneration Starts Long Before Symptoms Appear

One of the more troubling aspects of neurodegenerative diseases is that they begin long before any symptoms surface. In Alzheimer's disease, for example, amyloid plaques can start forming 20 years before memory loss is noticeable. This means that by the time a diagnosis is made, significant brain damage has already occurred.

. . .

Parkinson's disease also has a long pre-symptomatic phase, often marked by subtle, non-motor symptoms like a reduced sense of smell, sleep disturbances, and digestive issues. These early indicators can appear a decade or more before tremors or stiffness are evident.

This "silent phase" of neurodegeneration presents both a challenge and an opportunity. Since the disease process begins so early, catching it at this stage could offer a window for intervention, potentially slowing or even halting progression before severe symptoms appear. Although we currently lack routine early-detection methods, researchers are exploring biomarkers and imaging techniques that could identify these diseases in their initial stages.

**Why Neurodegenerative Diseases Get Worse Over Time**
Neurodegenerative diseases are progressive, meaning they worsen over time as more neurons die. Initially, the brain can often adapt to the loss of neurons by rerouting connections, allowing certain functions to be maintained despite damage. However, as neuron loss continues, the brain's ability to compensate diminishes, and symptoms become more pronounced.

In Alzheimer's disease, for instance, the degeneration often begins in the hippocampus, the region associated with memory. This is why memory issues are usually the first symptom. But as the disease spreads to other parts of the brain, cognitive abilities such as reasoning, language, and emotional regulation become impaired, eventually affecting basic life functions.

Parkinson's disease follows a similar pattern, starting with the motor areas of the brain responsible for movement. As these areas lose neurons, physical symptoms like tremors and stiffness emerge. Over time, other parts of the brain are affected, leading to mood changes, cognitive issues, and sleep disturbances.

This progressive nature underscores the need for treatments that can slow or stop neuron loss, ideally preserving brain function as long as possible.

**Looking Ahead: Can We Stop Neurodegeneration?**

Although there is currently no cure for neurodegenerative diseases, research is advancing rapidly in areas aimed at slowing, stopping, or even preventing neuron death. Scientists are developing various approaches, including medications, lifestyle strategies, and therapeutic interventions. Some promising areas of research include:

1. **Protein Clearance**: Developing treatments that prevent toxic protein buildup or improve the brain's ability to clear these proteins. Experimental drugs targeting amyloid and tau proteins in Alzheimer's are examples of this strategy.

2. **Mitochondrial Protection**: Therapies aimed at improving mitochondrial function to ensure neurons have the energy needed for survival. By enhancing mitochondrial health, researchers hope to protect neurons from premature death, especially in energy-intensive diseases like ALS and Parkinson's.

3. **Oxidative Stress Reduction**: Interventions that reduce oxidative stress in the brain, such as diets high in antioxidants, may help protect neurons from damage. Some studies are exploring whether supplements or specific foods can provide additional support against oxidative damage.

4. **Inflammation Control**: Managing chronic inflammation in the brain through drugs or lifestyle adjustments could help protect neurons from the harmful effects of overactive immune responses. Anti-inflammatory treatments,

combined with lifestyle changes that reduce inflammation, are being studied for their potential to slow disease progression.

In upcoming chapters, we'll explore these research areas in more detail, examining both current treatments and experimental therapies. We'll also cover lifestyle strategies that individuals can adopt to potentially reduce their risk of neurodegenerative disease, providing a comprehensive look at how we can work to protect the brain as it ages.

# chapter 2 summary: neurodegenerative diseases

**What Happens in Neurodegenerative Diseases?**

- Neuron death leads to a decline in memory, movement, and behavior.
- Different diseases affect specific neurons:
- **Alzheimer's:** Memory and cognitive areas.
- **Parkinson's:** Dopamine-producing neurons (movement).
- **ALS:** Motor neurons (muscle control).

**Protein Build-Up: Brain's "Garbage Disposal" Problem**

- Toxic proteins (amyloid, tau in Alzheimer's; alpha-synuclein in Parkinson's) accumulate due to malfunctioning disposal systems, disrupting cell function and leading to cell death.

**Mitochondrial Dysfunction: Energy Crisis**

- Mitochondria, the cell's "power plants," become inefficient, leading to energy deficits that impact neuron survival.

## Oxidative Stress: Brain's "Rust"

- Free radicals damage neurons; antioxidants help but are often insufficient in neurodegenerative diseases.

## Chronic Inflammation: Immune System Misfire

- Overactive immune cells in the brain cause inflammation, harming neurons and worsening disease progression.

## Genetics and Risk

- Genetic predispositions (e.g., APOE ε4 in Alzheimer's) increase risk, though lifestyle factors also play a significant role.

## Early Neurodegeneration

- Damage often begins years before symptoms (e.g., amyloid plaques in Alzheimer's), suggesting early detection is crucial for intervention.

## Progression and Worsening Symptoms

- As neuron loss continues, the brain's ability to adapt diminishes, and symptoms worsen over time.

## Future Approaches to Stop Neurodegeneration

- Potential therapies focus on: Clearing toxic proteins, supporting mitochondrial function, reducing oxidative stress and controlling inflammation.
- Lifestyle changes (e.g., diet, physical activity) may complement treatments to help reduce the risk of neurodegeneration.

# afterword

Neurodegenerative diseases, characterized by the death of neurons and a decline in cognitive, motor, and behavioral functions, present significant challenges to brain health. The accumulation of toxic proteins, mitochondrial dysfunction, oxidative stress, and chronic inflammation all contribute to the progression of these diseases. While genetic factors play a role, lifestyle choices are also crucial in managing risk and slowing degeneration. Early detection and intervention are key to preventing or delaying symptoms, and emerging therapies offer hope in clearing toxic proteins and supporting brain function. Incorporating healthy lifestyle changes, such as diet and physical activity, can complement medical treatments and provide a proactive approach to maintaining brain health and reducing the impact of neurodegenerative diseases.

# neuro-insights

"To age well and live free of disease, we must prioritize the health of our brain. It is where our memories, thoughts, and actions are created, and it needs nourishment, stimulation, and care." – Dr. David J. Linden, Neuroscientist

"The health of our spine and brain are the cornerstones of our well-being. When we protect and nurture these structures, we protect our vitality and longevity." – Dr. Joe Dispenza, Chiropractor and Neuroscientist

# how exercise supercharges your brain

**WE'VE** all heard that exercise is good for our bodies. It keeps our heart strong, our muscles toned, and our waistlines in check. But did you know that moving your body is one of the best things you can do for your brain too? In fact, research over the past few decades has uncovered some remarkable connections between exercise and brain health. If you want to keep your brain sharp, ward off mental health issues, and even reduce your risk of dementia as you age, exercise is like a miracle drug.

In this chapter, we'll break down exactly how exercise benefits your brain and why you should lace up your sneakers if you want a mental boost.

**Exercise: Fuel for Brain Growth**

Your brain is a dynamic organ, constantly evolving and adapting, and remarkably, physical exercise plays a significant role in this process. This adaptability, known as **neuroplasticity**, is how your brain can reorganize itself by forming new neural connections throughout life. While you may think of exercise primarily as a way to improve your physical health, its impact on your brain is just as profound.

. . .

When you engage in aerobic activities—like running, swimming, or cycling—a cascade of biological processes is triggered that supports neuroplasticity. At the heart of this is a powerful protein called **brain-derived neurotrophic factor (BDNF)**. Think of BDNF as brain fertilizer; it promotes the growth of new neurons and strengthens the connections between them, particularly in the **hippocampus**, the brain region essential for learning and memory.

BDNF plays a crucial role in neurogenesis, the process of creating new neurons. Studies have shown that exercise significantly increases BDNF levels, which enhances brain plasticity. During exercise, your body increases oxygen and blood flow to the brain, which in turn stimulates neurons to release more BDNF. The result? New brain cells grow, and existing ones become more robust, improving your overall cognitive abilities. The boost in BDNF from consistent aerobic activity helps protect your brain from stress and allows it to respond more flexibly to new challenges. This means that if you exercise regularly, your brain stays sharper, you can learn new skills faster, and your memory works better.

But BDNF is just one piece of the puzzle. Exercise also boosts other growth factors, such as **insulin-like growth factor 1 (IGF-1)** and **vascular endothelial growth factor (VEGF)**. Both IGF-1 and VEGF help sustain the brain's plasticity. IGF-1, for example, promotes the growth and differentiation of neurons, making them more capable of forming and maintaining connections. Meanwhile, VEGF encourages the formation of new blood vessels in the brain, a process known as **angiogenesis**. This improved vascular network ensures that the brain gets a steady supply of oxygen and nutrients, which further supports the growth and survival of neurons.

**Exercise Grows the Brain**
     All of these changes significantly impact the hippocampus, a region

of the brain crucial for memory formation and spatial navigation. Over time, particularly as we age, the hippocampus naturally shrinks, contributing to memory loss and cognitive decline. However, aerobic exercise has been shown to counteract this shrinking. In fact, studies found that older adults who engaged in regular walking for a year actually increased the size of their hippocampus by about 2%. Those who did not exercise experienced the typical age-related decline, showing that physical activity can protect and even enhance the brain's structure.

The benefits of exercise on brain growth go beyond just the structure. The increase in BDNF, IGF-1, and VEGF also boosts cognitive function. Learning, memory, and problem-solving abilities all improve with regular aerobic activity. In animal studies, for instance, mice that had access to running wheels grew more new neurons in the hippocampus and performed significantly better on memory tests than those that didn't exercise. Similarly, in human studies, individuals who regularly engage in aerobic exercise show marked improvements in tasks requiring memory retention, attention, and cognitive flexibility.

The takeaway? Regular aerobic exercise stimulates brain growth by enhancing neuroplasticity through BDNF and other growth factors. This results in the production of new neurons and the preservation of the hippocampus, leading to better memory, faster learning, and overall cognitive resilience. Whether you're looking to stay sharp, protect against age-related decline, or improve your ability to learn new things, exercise is one of the most powerful tools you can use to fuel your brain's growth.

**Fighting Inflammation: A Brain Saver**

Inflammation is a natural response of the immune system, meant to protect the body from infection or injury. However, when inflammation becomes chronic, it can turn into a slow, silent assault on various organs—including the brain. Chronic inflammation is now understood to be a major driver of cognitive decline and a contributing factor to neurodegenerative diseases like Alzheimer's and Parkinson's. But here's where exercise comes in as a powerful defense.

Regular physical activity acts as a natural anti-inflammatory agent. When you exercise, your body undergoes a host of physiological changes that modulate the immune response, reducing levels of harmful **pro-inflammatory cytokines**—molecules that promote inflammation—and increasing the production of **anti-inflammatory** substances. This shift in the immune balance helps keep inflammation in check, particularly in the brain.

Chronic inflammation in the brain can damage neurons and interfere with the brain's ability to communicate effectively. One of the reasons inflammation is so harmful is that it disrupts the signaling of growth factors like **BDNF**. As we mentioned earlier, BDNF is crucial for neuroplasticity, and when inflammation levels are high, BDNF signaling gets impaired, reducing neurogenesis (the formation of new neurons) and hampering cognitive function.

Inflammation also affects the brain's **microglia**, which are the primary immune cells of the central nervous system. In a healthy brain, microglia are like the brain's housekeepers, clearing away damaged cells and keeping things running smoothly. But chronic inflammation can make these cells overactive, leading them to attack healthy neurons and synapses. This is particularly dangerous in older adults, where excessive inflammation and overactive microglia have been linked to increased risk for neurodegenerative diseases.

Exercise helps regulate these processes. By reducing inflammation, it allows the brain's growth factors to do their job more effectively, fostering neuroplasticity and neuron survival. Moreover, exercise calms the activity of the microglia, preventing them from causing unnecessary damage to healthy brain tissue. This neuroprotective effect is why people who engage in regular physical activity tend to have a lower risk of developing conditions like Alzheimer's and dementia later in life.

## A Whole-Body Defense for Brain Health

The anti-inflammatory effects of exercise extend beyond the brain and involve systemic changes throughout the body. When you engage in physical activity, your muscles release specific proteins called **myokines** into the bloodstream. One of these, **interleukin-6 (IL-6)**, acts as a signal to reduce inflammation not just in the muscles but across the entire body, including the brain. IL-6 has a dual role, initially increasing inflammation to initiate repair processes but later promoting an anti-inflammatory response. It achieves this by stimulating the release of anti-inflammatory cytokines and suppressing the production of pro-inflammatory cytokines, helping to create a healthier environment for brain cells to thrive.

Research backs this up. Studies have shown that people who engage in regular exercise have lower levels of inflammatory markers in their blood compared to sedentary individuals. Even moderate physical activity—like brisk walking for 30 minutes a day—can significantly lower inflammation. In older adults, this can make a big difference in maintaining cognitive function and slowing the progression of neurodegenerative diseases.

In addition, exercise promotes a healthier gut, which may indirectly reduce inflammation in the brain. Emerging research suggests that the gut-brain axis—the complex communication network between the gut and the brain—plays a crucial role in regulating inflammation. Regular physical activity promotes a more diverse and balanced gut microbiome, which can reduce systemic inflammation, thereby benefiting brain health.

. . .

In short, chronic inflammation is a major risk factor for cognitive decline, but regular exercise acts as a powerful countermeasure. By reducing proinflammatory markers, calming overactive immune cells like microglia, and promoting the release of protective molecules, exercise helps safeguard the brain against inflammation-related damage. This is particularly important as we age, making regular physical activity one of the most effective ways to preserve brain health and function over the long term.

## Strengthening the Brain's Wiring

One of the most remarkable ways exercise benefits the brain is by enhancing its wiring—the intricate network of connections that allows brain cells (neurons) to communicate with each other. This process, called **synaptic plasticity**, refers to the brain's ability to strengthen or weaken the connections between neurons in response to experience, learning, or environmental changes. When these connections are strong and efficient, our brains function at a higher level—we can think more clearly, solve problems more quickly, and remember things more easily.

Exercise, particularly aerobic exercise, plays a pivotal role in promoting synaptic plasticity. At a basic level, exercise increases **synaptic transmission**, meaning that neurons communicate more effectively. This enhanced communication is key to a variety of cognitive functions, including memory formation, learning, problem-solving, and attention. The stronger the synapses, the more efficiently the brain processes information and adapts to new challenges.

A critical region of the brain that benefits from enhanced synaptic plasticity is the **hippocampus**. As we've discussed, the hippocampus is vital for memory formation, but it's also deeply involved in spatial navigation and learning. Studies have shown that exercise, especially aerobic activities like running, increases the density of synapses in the hippocampus, leading to better memory and cognitive performance.

But how exactly does exercise enhance synaptic plasticity? One of the key mechanisms is through the increased production of **neurotrophic factors** like **BDNF** (brain-derived neurotrophic factor). BDNF is not only crucial for neurogenesis, as we discussed earlier, but it also plays an essential role in strengthening synapses. When BDNF is present in higher levels—such as after regular aerobic exercise—neurons form stronger connections, and new synapses are created. This is particularly important for memory consolidation, where the brain transforms short-term memories into long-term ones.

### Increased Communication

Another factor that contributes to stronger brain wiring during exercise is the release of **neurotransmitters**, the chemicals that transmit signals between neurons. Exercise increases the levels of key neurotrans-mitters like **dopamine**, **serotonin**, and **norepinephrine**, all of which improve mood, focus, and attention. More importantly for synaptic plasticity, these neurotransmitters help optimize the environment for neurons to communicate more effectively. For example, dopamine plays a significant role in reward-based learning and motivation, while sero-tonin contributes to mood regulation and emotional stability, both of which are essential for clear, focused thinking.

Furthermore, research indicates that physical activity stimulates the formation of new synaptic connections through a process called **long-term potentiation (LTP)**. LTP is the brain's way of increasing the strength of synapses through repeated activation. It's essentially how your brain "learns" to become more efficient. When you exercise, you activate neural circuits that are involved in movement, coordination, and even cognitive tasks, reinforcing those pathways through LTP. This is one reason why athletes and people who regularly engage in physical activities often have faster reaction times and better coordination—not only are their muscles stronger, but their brain's synapses are better wired.

Beyond strengthening individual synapses, exercise also improves **brain connectivity**—the way different regions of the brain communicate with each other. One fascinating area of research has shown that exercise enhances **functional connectivity** between regions of the brain responsible for attention, memory, and executive function. In particular, it improves the connection between the **prefrontal cortex** (the part of the brain responsible for decision-making and complex thought) and the **hippocampus**. This improved communication allows for better integration of memory, learning, and decision-making, leading to enhanced cognitive performance.

A study published in 2020 demonstrated how aerobic exercise increases hippocampal volume in older adults, which is closely linked to improved memory function. This finding is particularly exciting because it suggests that regular physical activity may not only preserve cognitive abilities but also improve brain structure in aging populations. Even in people at risk for Alzheimer's disease, exercise has been shown to increase connectivity between brain regions, slowing cognitive decline and improving quality of life.

## Structural Changes and Everyday Benefits

Exercise also promotes the development of **white matter** in the brain, which consists of bundles of axons (the long fibers that carry signals between neurons) covered by a fatty substance called myelin. White matter is crucial for fast communication between brain regions, much like a highway system that allows traffic to flow smoothly between cities. As we age, white matter tends to deteriorate, slowing down communication between neurons. However, studies show that regular physical activity can help maintain or even improve the integrity of white matter, allowing the brain to maintain fast, efficient communication pathways.

The improvements in synaptic plasticity, connectivity, and white matter integrity translate into practical, everyday benefits. People who engage in regular aerobic exercise tend to perform better on tasks that require memory, attention, and executive function. For example, they may be able to focus on complex tasks for longer periods, switch between tasks more easily, and solve problems faster than their sedentary counterparts.

As you can see, exercise doesn't just benefit your muscles—it strengthens the very wiring of your brain. By enhancing synaptic plasticity, improving connectivity between brain regions, and preserving white matter integrity, regular physical activity helps your brain communicate more effectively and respond more quickly to challenges. These changes translate into better memory, faster thinking, and greater mental agility —benefits that can last a lifetime.

**Muscle-Brain Crosstalk: The Role of Myokines**

You might think of your muscles and brain as two separate systems in your body, but recent discoveries show that they are intricately linked, especially during exercise. In fact, your muscles aren't just responsible for moving your body—they also play a critical role in keeping your brain healthy. This communication between muscles and the brain happens through signaling molecules called **myokines**, which are released into the bloodstream during physical activity. These myokines can cross the **blood-brain barrier** (the protective membrane that shields the brain from harmful substances) and have powerful effects on brain health and function.

One of the most fascinating myokines involved in this muscle-brain crosstalk is **cathepsin B**. This protein is released by muscles during exercise and travels to the brain, where it stimulates the production of **BDNF**, the brain's key growth factor. As discussed earlier, BDNF is crucial for neuroplasticity (the brain's ability to change), neurogenesis (formation of new neurons), and overall cognitive function. The discovery that muscles can indirectly boost BDNF production through cathepsin B underscores the systemic benefits of exercise. It means that every time you move your muscles, you're not just strengthening your body—you're also sending signals to your brain that promote the growth of new neurons and stronger synaptic connections.

But cathepsin B is just one piece of the puzzle. Another important myokine, **irisin**, plays a major role in brain health. Irisin is produced when your muscles contract during exercise, and it has been shown to increase BDNF levels, especially in the **hippocampus**, which is essential for learning and memory. Once released, irisin travels to the brain, where it enhances neurogenesis, particularly in areas involved in memory formation. Animal studies have shown that increased levels of irisin lead to improvements in memory and cognitive function, making it one of the key mediators of the exercise-brain connection.

**Muscles, Mood, and Mental Health**

In addition to these brain-boosting effects, myokines also play a role in regulating mood and mental health. For example, the myokine **interleukin-6 (IL-6)**, which is released by muscles during exercise, has been shown to have both pro- and anti-inflammatory effects depending on the context. While chronic inflammation is detrimental to brain health, the controlled release of IL-6 during exercise helps regulate the body's immune response, reducing harmful inflammation and protecting the brain from inflammatory damage. This is particularly relevant for conditions like depression and anxiety, where inflammation in the brain can worsen symptoms. By modulating the immune response and promoting a healthier inflammatory balance, exercise-induced IL-6 helps support better mood regulation and mental resilience.

· · ·

This muscle-brain crosstalk is part of what makes exercise such a potent tool for combating mental health disorders. Research has shown that people who engage in regular physical activity have lower rates of depression, anxiety, and stress. Part of this benefit comes from the increased production of neurotransmitters like **serotonin** and **dopamine**, which we'll discuss in more detail later, but another key factor is the ability of myokines to create a healthier, more balanced environment in the brain. By reducing inflammation and promoting neuroplasticity, these muscle-derived molecules help the brain cope better with stress and improve overall emotional well-being.

**How Exercise-Activated Myokines Guard the Aging Brain**

The impact of myokines on brain health also has long-term implications for aging and neurodegenerative diseases. As we age, our muscles tend to weaken, a process known as **sarcopenia**, and this decline in muscle mass can reduce the levels of myokines in the body. This is one reason why older adults who are sedentary tend to have a higher risk of cognitive decline and dementia. However, regular physical activity can help counteract this process. By maintaining muscle mass and promoting the release of myokines like cathepsin B and irisin, older adults can preserve cognitive function and protect against neurodegenerative diseases.

In fact, studies have shown that exercise can slow the progression of diseases like **Alzheimer's** and **Parkinson's** by upregulating neuroprotective factors and reducing harmful inflammation. In animal models of Alzheimer's disease, exercise has been found to increase BDNF levels and improve memory, while also reducing the buildup of amyloid-beta plaques, one of the hallmark signs of Alzheimer's. Similarly, in Parkinson's disease, regular exercise has been shown to enhance dopamine signaling and reduce neurodegeneration, suggesting that muscle-brain crosstalk plays a crucial role in protecting against these conditions.

. . .

The concept of muscle-brain crosstalk also challenges the traditional view of exercise as purely a physical activity. It underscores the fact that the benefits of exercise extend beyond muscle strength and cardiovascular fitness—they also encompass profound changes in brain health. This muscle-brain communication highlights the interconnectedness of the body's systems and shows how exercise creates a cascade of beneficial effects that influence not just one part of the body, but the entire organism.

In short, when you exercise, your muscles do more than just move your body—they send critical signals to your brain that promote neuroplasticity, reduce inflammation, and support mental health. Through the release of myokines like cathepsin B, irisin, and IL-6, your muscles and brain engage in a dialogue that strengthens both systems. This muscle-brain crosstalk is one of the many reasons why regular physical activity is so essential for maintaining cognitive health, particularly as we age.

**Improved Cerebral Blood Flow and Vascular Health**

One of the most immediate effects of exercise is an increase in blood flow throughout the body, including the brain. This enhanced blood circulation is not just a short-term benefit; over time, it leads to lasting improvements in the brain's vascular system, promoting better cognitive function, protecting against age-related decline, and even reducing the risk of vascular-related cognitive issues like strokes.

The brain depends on a continuous supply of oxygen and nutrients to perform optimally, and blood is the vehicle that delivers these essential resources. During exercise, your heart pumps more blood, boosting circulation to the brain. This increase in **cerebral blood flow** is beneficial for all areas of the brain, but it is especially helpful for regions involved in higher-order cognitive functions, such as the **prefrontal cortex** (responsible for decision-making and complex thinking) and the **hippocampus** (essential for memory and learning).

. . .

Regular exercise doesn't just increase blood flow temporarily; it leads to long-term changes in the brain's blood vessel network. When you exercise consistently, your body promotes **angiogenesis**, the formation of new blood vessels. This process creates a denser, more robust network of blood vessels in the brain, ensuring that every region has access to the nutrients and oxygen it needs. Over time, this improved vascular network can help maintain brain health, supporting both short-term cognitive performance and long-term resilience against age-related decline.

One fascinating study published in the journal *Frontiers in Aging Neuroscience* in 2019 examined how both short-term and long-term exercise affect brain blood flow. The researchers found that people who exercised regularly not only had better circulation during and after physical activity but also showed greater vascular density in key brain areas over time. This change in vascular density helps keep the brain healthier and can even increase **functional connectivity** between different brain regions, which improves cognitive flexibility—the brain's ability to switch between tasks, adapt to new information, and manage complex decision-making.

**Preventing Cognitive Decline and Reducing Stroke Risk**

The benefits of improved blood flow from exercise also extend to the prevention of cognitive decline and the reduction of stroke risk. As people age, blood vessels can harden or become blocked by fatty deposits, reducing blood flow to the brain. This process, known as **atherosclerosis**, increases the risk of both strokes and vascular dementia, a type of cognitive decline caused by poor blood circulation to the brain. Regular physical activity helps prevent this by keeping blood vessels more flexible and reducing the buildup of harmful plaques, essentially "cleaning up" the vascular system and allowing blood to flow freely.

. . .

Exercise also helps improve the function of **endothelial cells**, which line the blood vessels and control the release of substances that regulate blood pressure, clotting, and immune response. With regular exercise, these cells work more effectively, contributing to a healthy vascular environment in the brain. For example, endothelial cells produce **nitric oxide**, a molecule that relaxes blood vessels and increases blood flow. When you exercise, nitric oxide levels rise, reducing blood pressure and ensuring that oxygen-rich blood can reach the brain without obstruction. This improved endothelial function lowers the risk of conditions like hypertension, which is known to accelerate cognitive decline.

The impact of enhanced cerebral blood flow and vascular health on cognitive function is substantial. People who engage in regular aerobic exercise often perform better on cognitive tasks that require memory, attention, and problem-solving skills. For instance, older adults who maintain an active lifestyle typically score higher on tests of executive function—abilities crucial for managing daily life, such as planning, organizing, and multitasking. This is because exercise not only improves the physical structure of the brain's blood vessels but also promotes **functional connectivity** among different brain regions, allowing them to work together more efficiently.

Furthermore, enhanced blood flow from exercise may have neuroprotective effects against diseases like **Alzheimer's**. Poor cerebral blood flow is associated with an increased risk of Alzheimer's, as decreased blood supply limits the brain's ability to clear toxic proteins, like beta-amyloid, which can accumulate and form plaques. Studies suggest that regular physical activity can increase blood flow to brain areas affected early by Alzheimer's, possibly slowing disease progression or delaying the onset of symptoms.

. . .

For those at risk of stroke, exercise's role in maintaining vascular health is equally crucial. A healthy vascular network helps prevent blockages and reduces the risk of small strokes, which can cause damage over time and lead to cognitive impairments. In fact, research shows that individuals who engage in regular physical activity experience fewer mini-strokes (also known as transient ischemic attacks), which, though often symptomless, can silently contribute to cognitive decline.

In summary, exercise acts like a long-term investment in the brain's vascular health. By promoting cerebral blood flow, encouraging the growth of new blood vessels, and improving the function of existing vessels, exercise creates a healthier brain environment. These changes not only enhance cognitive function in the short term but also offer significant protection against age-related decline and vascular-related cognitive issues. In other words, by moving your body, you're ensuring that your brain is well-nourished and resilient, capable of withstanding the challenges of aging.

**Regulation of Neurotransmitter Systems**

When you exercise, you're not just working your muscles; you're also setting off a wave of chemical changes in your brain. These changes primarily involve **neurotransmitters**—the brain's chemical messengers that play a major role in regulating mood, motivation, and mental clarity. Among these, **serotonin**, **dopamine**, **norepinephrine**, and **γ-aminobutyric acid (GABA)** are some of the most affected by exercise, and they're also essential to mental health and cognitive function.

Let's start with **serotonin**, often called the "feel-good" neurotransmitter. Serotonin helps regulate mood, anxiety, and happiness, and low levels are linked to depression. When you engage in physical activity, your body increases the availability of tryptophan (the amino acid needed to produce serotonin) in the bloodstream, which then enters the brain and boosts serotonin production. This is one reason why exercise is often recommended as a complementary treatment for depression. Physical activity essentially acts as a natural antidepressant by increasing serotonin, helping improve mood and reduce feelings of anxiety. For those with mild to moderate depression, exercise can sometimes be as effective as medication.

**Dopamine** is another critical neurotransmitter influenced by exercise. Often associated with the brain's reward system, dopamine plays a key role in motivation, attention, and learning. It helps us feel pleasure and satisfaction when we achieve goals or engage in enjoyable activities. When you exercise, your brain releases dopamine, giving you a sense of accomplishment and pleasure, which many people refer to as the "runner's high." But dopamine's effects go beyond just making you feel good —it's also essential for focus and drive. Regular exercise maintains healthy dopamine levels, which is especially beneficial in managing conditions like ADHD, where dopamine balance is often disrupted. By helping regulate dopamine, exercise boosts motivation, attention span, and overall cognitive resilience.

**Norepinephrine**, another key neurotransmitter affected by exercise, enhances alertness, energy, and focus. When you engage in physical activity, norepinephrine levels increase, preparing your brain for attention-demanding tasks. This makes exercise particularly beneficial if you're looking to improve your mental clarity or sharpen your focus before a challenging day. Higher norepinephrine levels can also improve emotional regulation, making you more resilient to stress. Studies have shown that people who exercise regularly tend to handle stress better than sedentary individuals, partly due to more stable norepinephrine levels.

Exercise also boosts **GABA**, an inhibitory neurotransmitter that acts as the brain's natural calming agent. GABA helps regulate overactive brain activity, which can contribute to stress and anxiety. When you exercise, especially in activities like yoga or rhythmic movement exercises such as running or cycling, GABA production increases, calming the brain and reducing symptoms of anxiety. This is why people often feel a sense of calm and mental clarity after exercising; GABA helps soothe the nervous system, creating a balanced mental state. For people who struggle with anxiety, this GABA boost from exercise can provide significant relief, acting as a natural stress-reducer.

**Practical Changes In Real Life**

What's interesting is how these neurotransmitter changes translate into real-life mental health benefits. Research shows that regular exercise can reduce the severity of symptoms in anxiety and mood disorders. For instance, a study from the *American Journal of Psychiatry* found that people who engage in regular physical activity have a 12–17% lower risk of developing major depression compared to those who are inactive. For people already dealing with depression, exercise helps alleviate symptoms by lifting serotonin and dopamine levels, while simultaneously calming the brain with GABA. These combined effects help to elevate mood, decrease anxiety, and promote a more balanced mental state.

In addition to immediate boosts in neurotransmitters, regular exercise also helps **regulate the brain's response to stress** over the long term. When you exercise, your body produces **cortisol**, the primary stress hormone, in a controlled way. This controlled cortisol release trains your body to manage stress more effectively, reducing the overproduction of cortisol during daily challenges. Over time, this "stress resilience" becomes one of the most valuable psychological benefits of regular physical activity. It can help lower the risk of stress-related mental health issues, such as chronic anxiety or burnout, by maintaining a more balanced hormonal response to stress.

Another fascinating area of research highlights how exercise can improve sleep quality, further enhancing mental health. Quality sleep is essential for maintaining balanced neurotransmitter levels, particularly serotonin and dopamine, which are replenished during deep sleep. Physical activity helps regulate sleep-wake cycles by enhancing the production of **adenosine**, a neurotransmitter that promotes sleepiness and recovery. This means that people who exercise regularly tend to have more restful, uninterrupted sleep, which amplifies the positive effects on mood and cognitive function. For people with insomnia or other sleep disturbances, exercise can be an effective non-medication approach to improving sleep quality, ultimately benefiting mental well-being.

The positive changes in neurotransmitter levels and stress resilience are also critical in conditions like **post-traumatic stress disorder (PTSD) and addiction recovery**. For example, dopamine and serotonin are often dysregulated in these conditions, and exercise can help restore balance, making it a valuable component of treatment. In the case of addiction, exercise can replace some of the pleasure-driven dopamine spikes that people once sought from addictive substances, reducing cravings and improving overall mood stability.

As you can see, exercise doesn't just strengthen your body—it also balances your brain's chemical environment, providing a natural boost to mental health. By increasing serotonin, dopamine, norepinephrine, and GABA, exercise improves mood, reduces anxiety, enhances focus, and builds stress resilience. These effects contribute to a more balanced emotional state, better cognitive performance, and, ultimately, a healthier mind. Whether you're managing a mental health condition or simply aiming to boost your mood and mental clarity, regular exercise offers a powerful, drug-free way to enhance your brain's chemistry and overall well-being.

**Brain Development**

The effects of exercise on brain development are particularly powerful during critical periods, such as childhood and adolescence.

These years are marked by rapid brain growth and structural changes, where experiences and environmental factors can shape the architecture of the brain in profound and lasting ways. Regular physical activity during these formative years plays an essential role in establishing a solid foundation for cognitive health and resilience that can last a lifetime.

During childhood, the brain is incredibly **plastic**, meaning it's highly responsive to change and capable of forming new connections quickly. This plasticity is what allows children to learn languages, develop motor skills, and absorb vast amounts of information. Exercise enhances this natural plasticity by increasing the production of **neurotrophic factors** —especially **BDNF** (brain-derived neurotrophic factor). As we've discussed, BDNF is essential for neuron growth and synaptic strength, but during childhood, it's even more impactful. Higher BDNF levels from regular physical activity help accelerate neurogenesis, laying down a strong neural foundation for skills like memory, focus, and problem-solving.

Research shows that children who engage in regular physical activity tend to perform better academically. Studies have linked higher levels of fitness with improvements in cognitive tasks that require memory, attention, and processing speed. This is partly because exercise enhances **synaptic plasticity** and **cerebral blood flow**, allowing children's brains to process and retain information more effectively. In particular, aerobic exercises—like running, swimming, or cycling—have been associated with increased hippocampal volume in children, which translates into better memory function. For a developing brain, this enhanced hippocampal growth sets the stage for improved academic performance and greater cognitive flexibility, allowing children to adapt to new information more easily.

During adolescence, the brain undergoes another significant growth period, marked by extensive **synaptic pruning** and **myelination**.

Synaptic pruning is the brain's way of refining its neural connections by eliminating those that are not frequently used, making the brain's network more efficient. Myelination, on the other hand, involves the formation of a fatty sheath around nerve fibers, allowing faster transmission of signals between neurons. These processes are essential for complex thinking, impulse control, and emotional regulation, functions managed by the **prefrontal cortex**. This brain region, responsible for decision-making, planning, and risk assessment, undergoes extensive development during adolescence.

## Building a Resilient Mind Through Exercise

Exercise positively influences these processes by promoting synaptic plasticity and increasing myelination, especially in regions involved in executive function. Physical activity during adolescence has been shown to increase **white matter integrity** in the prefrontal cortex, which enhances connectivity within the brain's decision-making networks. This development translates into real-world skills—teens who exercise regularly may exhibit better impulse control, higher resilience to stress, and more effective decision-making. These are not just immediate benefits; the structural enhancements that happen during adolescence due to exercise create a lasting impact, contributing to cognitive resilience in adulthood.

Another remarkable benefit of exercise for adolescents is its impact on **emotional regulation** and **mental health**. This period is often accompanied by heightened emotional responses due to hormonal changes and increased stressors. Regular physical activity has been found to reduce the risk of mental health issues like depression, anxiety, and even symptoms of ADHD. This is partly because exercise supports the balance of neurotransmitters, such as dopamine and serotonin, which play significant roles in mood regulation. For teens, this boost in emotional stability is critical, as it helps them navigate the often-turbulent adolescent years with greater confidence and psychological resilience.

. . .

Exercise during these developmental stages also builds habits that contribute to long-term cognitive health. Adolescents who are active are more likely to maintain a lifestyle of physical activity into adulthood, which provides lasting benefits to brain health, particularly as we age. Studies have shown that people who engage in physical activity during their youth have a reduced risk of developing neurodegenerative diseases like Alzheimer's and dementia later in life. By cultivating physical activity as a regular habit early on, children and teens are setting themselves up for a healthier brain over their entire lifespan.

One notable study, published in *The Journal of Pediatrics*, followed a group of adolescents over several years and found that those who were more physically active had better cognitive performance and mental health outcomes in adulthood than their sedentary peers. The researchers concluded that early physical activity didn't just benefit short-term academic performance; it established a neurological advantage that endured into adulthood, highlighting how crucial exercise is during these formative years.

In summary, exercise plays an essential role in brain development during childhood and adolescence by enhancing neuroplasticity, supporting synaptic pruning and myelination, and promoting emotional resilience. Regular physical activity during these years not only boosts academic performance and mental health but also builds a strong neurological foundation that supports long-term cognitive health. For children and teens, exercise isn't just about physical fitness—it's a fundamental investment in their brain's growth, resilience, and adaptability.

## Benefits for Longevity

When we think about longevity, it's easy to focus solely on living longer. However, health experts now emphasize the concept of

**healthspan**—the number of years we live in good health, free from major physical or cognitive decline. Regular physical activity is one of the most effective ways to not only increase lifespan but also to enhance healthspan, particularly when it comes to maintaining brain health. By supporting brain function and resilience, exercise helps ensure that we can enjoy those extra years with mental clarity and independence.

Exercise promotes longevity through several well-documented mechanisms, many of which contribute directly to brain health. One significant factor is the **reduction in systemic inflammation**. Chronic inflammation is linked to a variety of age-related diseases, including Alzheimer's, cardiovascular disease, diabetes, and even some cancers. Regular physical activity lowers markers of inflammation throughout the body, reducing the overall "wear and tear" on cells and organs. In the brain, this reduction in inflammation helps protect neurons and supports cognitive longevity, lowering the risk of age-related diseases that can impair quality of life.

Another key to exercise's longevity benefits is its role in **mitochondrial health**. Mitochondria, often called the "powerhouses" of cells, are responsible for energy production. As we age, mitochondrial function tends to decline, leading to reduced cellular energy and increased oxidative stress—a process that damages cells, including neurons. Exercise has been shown to boost mitochondrial biogenesis, which is the production of new, healthy mitochondria. By enhancing mitochondrial health, physical activity helps maintain energy levels and resilience within cells, slowing the aging process and supporting cognitive function. This mitochondrial boost is especially important for the brain, which is highly energy-dependent.

Exercise also promotes **telomere health**, which is directly related to cellular aging. Telomeres are protective caps on the ends of chromosomes that shorten as cells divide over time. Shorter telomeres are associated with aging and a higher risk of age-related diseases. Interestingly, research has shown that people who engage in regular physical activity tend to have longer telomeres, suggesting that exercise may slow cellular aging and support longevity. By maintaining telomere length, exercise helps protect not only physical health but also cognitive health, as healthier cells are less prone to age-related dysfunction.

One of the most visible ways exercise supports longevity is by enhancing **vascular health**, which is essential for delivering oxygen and nutrients to the brain. Aging naturally impacts blood vessels, leading to a greater risk of strokes and other vascular issues that can impair cognitive function. However, regular exercise strengthens the cardiovascular system, promoting the elasticity and function of blood vessels. By keeping the brain's vascular system healthy, exercise reduces the risk of vascular-related cognitive decline, ensuring that the brain remains nourished and resilient even as we age. This vascular benefit is particularly relevant in reducing the risk of **vascular dementia**, a common form of cognitive impairment in older adults.

**Benefits The Physical**

Exercise also supports mental and social factors that contribute to longevity. Physical activity is known to reduce stress levels and improve mood, both of which are crucial for long-term health. Stress, when chronic, can accelerate aging by elevating cortisol levels and promoting inflammation. Exercise acts as a natural stress reliever, reducing cortisol and promoting a more balanced hormonal environment. This stress resilience supports brain health, as prolonged high cortisol levels can impair memory and increase the risk of cognitive decline.

Additionally, many forms of exercise foster social interaction and mental engagement, which are both linked to a longer life and healthier aging. Group activities, such as dance classes, team sports, or even community walking groups, provide opportunities for socialization, which is shown to lower rates of depression, improve emotional well-being, and enhance cognitive reserve. Social engagement stimulates the brain in unique ways, reinforcing neural connections and further protecting against cognitive decline. In essence, exercise doesn't just benefit the brain in isolation—it reinforces healthy lifestyle habits, including social interaction and mental engagement, that support longevity.

The combined effects of exercise—improved neuroplasticity, reduced inflammation, enhanced vascular health, and stress resilience—create a foundation for **healthy aging**. Numerous studies underscore this, showing that individuals who engage in regular physical activity tend to experience slower cognitive decline, lower rates of neurodegenerative diseases, and even increased overall lifespan. One long-term study published in *JAMA Network Open* followed participants for decades and found that those who were regularly active had a significantly lower risk of mortality, with a stronger impact on reducing the risk of dementia and age-related cognitive impairments.

Exercise contributes to both longevity and healthspan by promoting cellular health, reducing inflammation, supporting vascular function, and fostering mental and social engagement. These benefits work together to protect brain function, allowing people to live longer, healthier, and more mentally vibrant lives. By making physical activity a regular part of our routine, we invest not only in adding years to life but in ensuring that those years are rich with mental clarity, independence, and well-being.

# chapter 3 summary: supercharging our brain with exercise

**Exercise: Fuel for Brain Growth**

- Exercise promotes **neuroplasticity** and **neurogenesis** (new neuron growth), particularly in the hippocampus, which is essential for memory and learning.
- **BDNF** (brain-derived neurotrophic factor) increases with aerobic exercise, acting as "brain fertilizer" to grow and strengthen neurons.
- Other growth factors, **IGF-1** and **VEGF**, support brain plasticity and encourage blood vessel growth, enhancing oxygen and nutrient supply to the brain.

**Fighting Inflammation**

- Regular exercise reduces chronic brain inflammation, lowering levels of harmful pro-inflammatory cytokines.
- Exercise helps keep brain immune cells (microglia) balanced, preventing them from damaging healthy neurons, which is especially protective against neurodegenerative diseases.

## Strengthening Brain's Wiring

- Exercise enhances **synaptic plasticity**, improving neuron communication and cognitive abilities such as memory and learning.
- Boosts neurotransmitters like dopamine, serotonin, and norepinephrine, improving mood, focus, and resilience to stress.

## Muscle-Brain Crosstalk: Myokines

- Muscles release **myokines** during exercise (e.g., cathepsin B, irisin) that cross to the brain and stimulate neuroplasticity, neurogenesis, and anti-inflammatory effects.
- Myokines help regulate mood, protect against mental health disorders, and support cognitive resilience.

## Improved Cerebral Blood Flow

- Exercise promotes **cerebral blood flow** and **angiogenesis** (new blood vessel formation), delivering more oxygen and nutrients to brain regions essential for cognitive function.
- Enhances vascular health, reducing risk of strokes and vascular-related cognitive decline.

## Regulation of Neurotransmitter Systems

- Increases levels of **serotonin**, **dopamine**, and **GABA**, which improve mood, attention, stress resilience, and mental clarity.
- Exercise helps maintain balanced neurotransmitter levels, aiding in mental health conditions like depression, anxiety, and PTSD.

## Brain Development in Youth

- During childhood and adolescence, exercise supports brain plasticity and builds a foundation for lifelong cognitive health.
- Encourages **synaptic pruning** and **myelination** in teens, refining neural networks for decision-making and emotional regulation.

## Benefits for Longevity

- Exercise reduces systemic inflammation, supports mitochondrial health, and protects telomeres, slowing cellular and brain aging.
- Improved vascular health and stress resilience from exercise help sustain cognitive function and lower dementia risk, enhancing both lifespan and healthspan.

# afterword

In summary, exercise not only strengthens the body but supercharges the brain, enhancing neuroplasticity, reducing inflammation, and promoting longevity. Regular physical activity provides foundational benefits for memory, learning, mood, and mental clarity, supporting a healthier brain at every life stage.

# neuro-insights

"The health of the nervous system, which starts with the brain, determines our ability to function physically, emotionally, and mentally." – Dr. Peter Attia, Physician focusing on longevity

"Neuroplasticity is one of the brain's greatest assets. By engaging in healthy habits and thought patterns, we can actually rewire the brain to be healthier, sharper, and more resilient." – Dr. Norman Doidge, Psychiatrist

four

# the role of diet in brain health and cognitive longevity

**HOW DIET SHAPES Cognitive Health and Longevity**

Imagine waking up each day with a sharp mind, a mind that remembers, learns, and adapts with ease. Yet, for many of us, those capabilities can begin to fade over time, seemingly without cause. What we often overlook is the powerful, everyday influence that diet has on our cognitive health. It's easy to think of our brains as separate from what we eat, but recent science paints a different picture: our brain and diet are inextricably linked, with every bite affecting how well we think, remember, and even age.

The concept is straightforward, but the mechanisms are incredibly complex. Unlike other parts of our body, our brain demands constant nourishment and stability. It's an organ that uses about 20% of our body's total energy at rest, and it primarily relies on glucose. But here's the twist—our brain needs glucose in just the right amounts. A diet high in sugar or processed foods can throw this balance off-kilter, creating a cascade of effects that impact not only our brain's structure but also its daily performance.

· · ·

For years, we considered "brain food" to mean little more than a balanced meal or a few specific nutrients, like fish oil. But mounting evidence has shown that there's much more at play. Today, scientists understand that our brains are highly sensitive to dietary patterns. An overload of refined sugars, trans fats, and processed foods doesn't just lead to poor physical health; it initiates biochemical shifts in our brain that make it vulnerable to inflammation, oxidative stress, and even neurodegeneration. Over time, these changes can dull memory, slow learning, and increase susceptibility to conditions like Alzheimer's disease and dementia.

One of the most compelling discoveries in modern neuroscience is how dietary choices impact neuroinflammation—a silent but potent disruptor of brain health. Chronic inflammation affects neurotransmitter function, reduces synaptic plasticity, and contributes to the degeneration of brain cells, all of which are key to maintaining a healthy mind. When we consume diets high in sugars and unhealthy fats, we inadvertently stoke the fires of neuroinflammation, placing our brains under a near-constant state of stress. As a result, cognitive abilities like focus, memory, and problem-solving become compromised, and over time, these cumulative effects make it harder to maintain mental clarity.

However, not all dietary choices lead down this path. Just as there are foods that damage, there are also foods that heal. Certain nutrients—like omega-3 fatty acids, antioxidants, and complex carbohydrates—have proven to be powerful tools in supporting brain health. For example, antioxidants help counteract oxidative stress, a harmful process that accelerates brain aging. Omega-3s, on the other hand, act as anti-inflammatory agents, supporting cellular integrity and promoting neuroplasticity, the brain's ability to adapt and form new connections. When we choose a diet that supports the brain's health, we protect its cellular structure, enhance its function, and give ourselves the best chance at cognitive longevity.

. . .

In this chapter, we'll explore how specific dietary components—sugars, trans fats, and processed foods—affect the brain, altering its chemistry and function. We'll uncover the pathways through which poor dietary choices lead to memory loss, impaired learning, and accelerated cognitive decline. But more importantly, we'll highlight the powerful, positive impact that a nutrient-rich diet can have. By the end, you'll see that our brains thrive not just on calories but on quality—quality in the foods we choose to fuel our minds.

Let's begin by examining the brain's complex relationship with diet and how critical the right nutrients are to preserving our mental sharpness and resilience.

**An Overview of the Importance of Diet in Brain Health**

Our brains are intricate, interconnected systems, made up of billions of neurons that communicate with each other through electric impulses and chemical signals. Yet, this highly sophisticated organ is vulnerable to the effects of something as simple as our daily meals. The brain's immense energy needs, its dependence on a stable environment, and its sensitivity to metabolic changes make it uniquely affected by diet. The link between what we eat and how our brain performs is rooted in both energy supply and the prevention of cellular damage.

**Glucose: The Brain's Fuel and the Hidden Risks of High-Sugar Diets**

To start, let's explore the brain's reliance on glucose. Glucose is the primary fuel source for brain cells, and the brain alone uses about 120 grams of glucose daily—almost half of the body's total sugar intake. While glucose is essential, problems arise when we consume too much or too little. Diets high in refined sugars and simple carbohydrates flood the body with glucose, leading to dramatic spikes in blood sugar. This rapid influx strains the body's regulatory systems, eventually causing metabolic disturbances, such as insulin resistance, that impair the brain's ability to absorb glucose effectively.

When brain cells can't access the glucose they need, they can't function optimally, and we may experience symptoms like brain fog, poor concentration, and even mood swings. But the impact goes deeper: over time, high-sugar diets contribute to neurodegeneration, eroding the brain's structural integrity and putting us at risk for cognitive decline. It's a hidden danger that many of us encounter daily, as we unwittingly choose foods high in sugar and low in nutritional value.

**Fats and Brain Health: The Power of Omega-3s vs. the Dangers of Trans Fats**

Alongside glucose, fats play an equally critical role in brain health, but the type of fat matters immensely. Omega-3 fatty acids, found in foods like fish, flaxseeds, and walnuts, are considered essential for brain health because they support cellular structure and reduce inflammation. Unlike saturated and trans fats, which can stiffen cellular membranes and clog arteries, omega-3s promote flexibility in cell membranes. This flexibility is crucial for neurons to send and receive signals efficiently, enabling smooth cognitive function and supporting memory formation.

Meanwhile, trans fats and processed fats are a different story. These fats can interfere with neuron integrity, reducing the brain's ability to adapt to new information, a quality known as neuroplasticity. Neuroplasticity underpins all learning and memory processes, and when it's compromised, so is our cognitive adaptability. High-fat diets, particularly those rich in trans fats, have also been linked to low levels of brain-derived neurotrophic factor (BDNF), a protein that stimulates the growth of new neurons and strengthens existing connections. Reduced BDNF levels lead to a decrease in brain plasticity and resilience, essentially accelerating brain aging.

. . .

## Antioxidants: The Brain's Protector

The role of antioxidants in brain health is another critical area of research. Our brains are highly susceptible to oxidative stress, a process where free radicals damage cells. Oxidative stress is part of normal cellular metabolism, but when it becomes chronic, it overwhelms the brain's defense mechanisms. Antioxidants, like those found in berries, green leafy vegetables, and nuts, help neutralize free radicals, protecting brain cells from damage. Studies show that people who eat antioxidant-rich diets perform better in memory and reasoning tasks, likely because their brains are better shielded from age-related wear and tear.

The impact of diet on brain health is more than the sum of its parts. The interaction of these nutrients—glucose, healthy fats, antioxidants—affects the brain's resilience and adaptability, influencing everything from cognitive performance to emotional health. When we choose a diet rich in complex carbohydrates, lean proteins, and healthy fats, we're not only nourishing our bodies but also fortifying our minds. A balanced, nutrient-dense diet provides a foundation upon which our brain can thrive, safeguarding memory, learning ability, and overall cognitive function.

## Sugar and Its Effects on the Brain

Sugar, particularly Glucose, is the brain's preferred energy source, fueling neurons and supporting cognitive processes. Yet, when consumed in excess, sugar transforms from an energy hero into a stealthy saboteur, infiltrating the brain's delicate balance and initiating processes that damage cells and impair function. While occasional indulgence in sugar isn't the culprit, modern diets often expose us to unprecedented levels of refined sugars and sweeteners, overwhelming the brain's regulatory systems and leading to long-term consequences.

. . .

One of sugar's most immediate impacts on the brain is its influence on blood glucose levels. When we eat foods high in refined sugars, blood glucose levels spike, triggering a rush of insulin to move the glucose into cells. But the brain is highly sensitive to these spikes and subsequent crashes. Each fluctuation in blood sugar can alter mood, focus, and energy, leading to what many people recognize as "sugar highs" and "crashes." This roller-coaster effect isn't just an inconvenience; it gradually wears down the brain's capacity to regulate emotions and cognitive function.

Over time, consistently high blood sugar levels contribute to a condition known as "brain glycation." Glycation is a process where sugar molecules attach to proteins, causing them to become "sticky" and form harmful compounds called **advanced glycation end products (AGEs)**. These AGEs accumulate over time, accelerating aging and impairing brain function. AGEs can directly damage neurons and are particularly harmful to the hippocampus, the region of the brain responsible for memory formation and retrieval. Studies reveal that high blood glucose levels are correlated with hippocampal shrinkage, which leads to poor memory and cognitive decline. Even in people without diabetes, higher blood sugar levels have been linked to memory impairment and decreased brain volume.

**Sweet Inflammation**
Beyond glycation, high-sugar diets can also initiate neuroinflammation, a process with profound effects on brain health. Neuroinflammation occurs when the brain's immune cells, called microglia, become overactive. This heightened state can interfere with neurotransmitter function, specifically impacting serotonin and dopamine levels, the chemicals that help regulate mood and motivation. In this inflamed environment, the brain struggles to manage information flow and memory formation effectively, impairing the brain's ability to think clearly and retain information. Neuroinflammation has also been impli-

cated in the development of mood disorders, with research linking high-sugar diets to an increased risk of depression and anxiety.

Animal studies add another layer of insight into sugar's impact on the brain. In experiments, animals fed high-sugar diets for just a few weeks showed significant reductions in hippocampal function. These animals exhibited more difficulty with learning and memory tasks than their counterparts on balanced diets. The studies further reveal that sugar stimulates chronic inflammatory responses in the brain, making it harder for neurons to forge new connections. The brain's neuroplasticity—its capacity to adapt, learn, and recover—is hindered when exposed to an overload of sugar.

Moreover, insulin resistance, a condition commonly associated with excessive sugar intake, can extend to the brain. Known as "type 3 diabetes" or "brain insulin resistance," this condition affects the brain's ability to use glucose effectively. Insulin resistance in the brain impairs neuronal energy production, contributing to cognitive decline and creating an environment conducive to neurodegenerative diseases. Alzheimer's disease, in particular, has shown links to insulin resistance, suggesting that chronically elevated blood sugar may be a driving factor in its progression.

The science is clear: while the brain needs some glucose, it does best with a steady, controlled supply rather than an onslaught of refined sugars. Shifting away from high-sugar diets and opting for complex carbohydrates—such as whole grains, legumes, and fiber-rich vegetables—can help stabilize blood sugar levels. This stability allows the brain to function more smoothly, reducing the risk of inflammation, glycation, and insulin resistance. By keeping sugar in check, we can give our brains the chance to function optimally, supporting memory, mood, and long-term cognitive health.

. . .

**Trans Fats and Their Impact on Cognitive Function**

For decades, trans fats have been present in a wide array of processed foods, from margarine and baked goods to fried fast foods. These fats emerged as a convenient, shelf-stable alternative to healthier oils, but we now understand they pose a significant threat not only to heart health but also to the brain. Unlike other fats, trans fats have a unique chemical structure that disrupts the brain's cellular function, leading to both immediate and long-term consequences.

One of the most concerning effects of trans fats is their impact on neuroplasticity, the brain's ability to form and reorganize synaptic connections in response to learning and new experiences. Trans fats are known to lower levels of brain-derived neurotrophic factor (BDNF), a protein crucial for neuroplasticity. When trans fats lower BDNF levels, it becomes more challenging for the brain to adapt and learn, reducing cognitive flexibility and memory function over time.

The mechanism here is both fascinating and alarming: trans fats become integrated into cell membranes, including those in the brain. Our brain cells, or neurons, rely on flexible, healthy membranes to communicate effectively. When trans fats are incorporated into these membranes, they create a "stiffening" effect that hampers cellular flexibility. This rigidity in cell membranes disrupts the flow of neurotransmitters, the brain's chemical messengers, leading to slower processing speeds, weakened memory recall, and impaired communication between brain regions.

**Fatty Inflammation**

Inflammation is another destructive effect of trans fats. When consumed in high amounts, trans fats trigger a pro-inflammatory response, not only in the body but also in the brain. Chronic neuroin-flammation is increasingly recognized as a root cause of cognitive decline and dementia, creating an environment where the brain's immune cells, microglia, remain in a persistent state of activation. While these immune cells are essential for protecting the brain, prolonged activation causes them to damage healthy brain cells and hinder their ability to repair, thus accelerating the aging process and increasing vulnerability to neurodegenerative diseases like Alzheimer's.

Research in this area reveals a strong link between high trans fat intake and increased dementia risk. In one study, participants who consumed a diet high in trans fats were found to be significantly more likely to develop dementia than those who minimized trans fat intake. This heightened risk is attributed to the inflammation and oxidative stress that trans fats initiate. The damage goes deep, impacting brain structures like the hippocampus, essential for memory and spatial navigation, and the prefrontal cortex, which is critical for decision-making and complex thought.

In addition to direct effects on brain structure and function, trans fats also interfere with cardiovascular health, indirectly affecting the brain. Since the brain relies on a steady flow of oxygen and nutrients delivered by blood, any impairment in blood flow due to clogged arteries or cardiovascular inflammation will reduce brain function. A diet high in trans fats can contribute to this reduced blood flow, depriving the brain of the resources it needs to maintain peak performance. This reduction in blood flow, known as **cerebral hypoperfusion**, can lead to symptoms like mental fog, impaired memory, and a decrease in executive function, which includes skills like problem-solving, planning, and impulse control.

**The cumulative effects of trans fat consumption on the brain are clear:**

- decreased BDNF levels
- heightened neuroinflammation
- stiffened cell membranes

- reduction in blood flow.

Together, these changes create an environment where cognitive decline becomes more likely. The good news is that trans fats are avoidable. Replacing these harmful fats with brain-supportive options like **monounsaturated** and **polyunsaturated fats**, particularly omega-3 fatty acids, can provide both immediate and long-term benefits. Foods rich in these healthier fats, such as salmon, olive oil, avocados, and nuts, help maintain cellular flexibility, reduce inflammation, and support the brain's natural plasticity, allowing it to adapt and thrive.

In summary, the lesson from trans fats is simple but profound: what we consume on a daily basis has the power to either weaken or strengthen our brain's resilience. By minimizing trans fats and choosing fats that support neuroplasticity, we are giving our brain the tools it needs to learn, adapt, and fend off age-related decline.

**Processed Foods and the Gut-Brain Connection**

The human gut, often referred to as the "second brain," has a profound impact on our cognitive and emotional well-being. This connection, known as the gut-brain axis, involves a complex communication network that links the gastrointestinal tract with the brain. While it may seem surprising, the foods we consume influence our gut microbiome—a diverse community of trillions of microorganisms that play essential roles in digestion, immunity, and, as we're discovering, brain health.

Processed foods, laden with refined carbohydrates, added sugars, artificial ingredients, and unhealthy fats, wreak havoc on the gut microbiome, disrupting the delicate balance required for optimal brain function. A diet high in processed foods reduces microbial diversity in the gut, allowing harmful bacteria to dominate and reducing beneficial species that are crucial for maintaining brain health. This disruption can lead to a phenomenon known as "leaky gut," where the intestinal barrier weakens, allowing unwanted particles and toxins to enter the bloodstream and, eventually, reach the brain.

When harmful substances from the gut enter circulation, they activate the immune system, prompting an inflammatory response. This process, known as **systemic inflammation**, does not stay confined to the body—it extends to the brain, leading to neuroinflammation. Neuroinflammation, in turn, disrupts the production and regulation of neurotransmitters, such as serotonin and dopamine, which are essential for mood stability, motivation, and cognitive performance. This pathway is one reason why processed foods are associated with a higher risk of mood disorders, such as depression and anxiety.

Studies have shown that people who consume high levels of processed foods are more likely to experience cognitive impairment, likely due to these changes in the gut-brain axis. In experiments, animals fed a processed diet exhibited not only changes in gut microbiota but also memory and learning deficits. These animals showed increased levels of inflammatory markers in the brain, as well as disrupted synaptic plasticity—the brain's ability to form new connections. This plasticity is essential for learning and adapting, and when compromised, the brain struggles to retain information and perform complex tasks.

## How Processed Foods Influence Neurodegeneration and Mental Health

One of the most intriguing aspects of the gut-brain connection is its role in the formation of proteins associated with neurodegenerative diseases. Processed foods are linked to the accumulation of beta-amyloid plaques and tau proteins, the hallmark proteins of Alzheimer's disease. Research suggests that inflammation stemming from a disrupted gut microbiome may accelerate the buildup of these proteins, increasing the risk of neurodegeneration and memory loss. These findings underscore that a diet high in processed foods doesn't just affect the gut; it has long-term consequences on brain health as well.

To further understand the link between processed foods and cognitive decline, we can look at how the gut microbiome influences neurotransmitter production. Certain bacteria in the gut produce neurotransmitters directly, while others help synthesize precursors for neurotransmitters like serotonin and GABA, which are crucial for emotional stability and stress regulation. When the microbiome is disturbed by processed foods, the production of these brain chemicals declines, contributing to mood dysregulation and increased susceptibility to stress, anxiety, and depression.

Improving gut health, therefore, is an essential part of preserving cognitive function and emotional well-being. Shifting away from processed foods and embracing a diet rich in fiber, probiotics, and prebiotics can promote a healthy gut microbiome, leading to enhanced brain health. Fiber-rich foods, such as fruits, vegetables, legumes, and whole grains, fuel beneficial gut bacteria, helping them thrive and multiply. Probiotic-rich foods, like yogurt, kefir, and fermented vegetables, add helpful bacteria directly to the gut, while prebiotics (found in foods like garlic, onions, and bananas) serve as nourishment for these beneficial bacteria.

By prioritizing whole, unprocessed foods, we support the balance and diversity of our microbiome, reducing systemic inflammation and fostering a more resilient gut-brain axis. In this way, dietary choices become a form of preventive medicine, offering protection not only against digestive issues but also against cognitive decline and mood disturbances. The gut-brain connection reveals an essential truth: what we eat doesn't just shape our body; it shapes our mind, emotions, and even our long-term mental resilience.

. . .

## Nutritional Strategies for Brain Health

Understanding the impact of diet on our brain empowers us to make choices that promote cognitive health and longevity. Rather than focusing on strict rules or restrictions, a brain-supportive diet encourages mindful selections that nurture brain function, protect memory, and reduce the risk of age-related cognitive decline. By emphasizing nutrient-rich, whole foods, we can create an environment where the brain thrives, adapting and regenerating throughout our lives.

## Reducing Sugar and Refined Carbohydrates

One of the most effective ways to support brain health is by moderating sugar intake and opting for complex carbohydrates instead of refined ones. Unlike refined sugars that cause rapid spikes and crashes in blood glucose, complex carbohydrates—found in foods like whole grains, legumes, and fiber-rich vegetables—offer a steady, slow-release energy source. This stable blood glucose helps maintain cognitive functions like memory and focus, while reducing the risk of insulin resistance, which is increasingly recognized as a factor in cognitive decline.

Switching to complex carbs also helps protect the hippocampus, a brain region essential for memory and learning. High-sugar diets have been shown to create inflammatory stress in this region, impairing its ability to form new memories. By choosing **low-glycemic foods** (foods that cause a slow, steady rise in blood sugar levels after eating), such as oats, sweet potatoes, and green leafy vegetables, we reduce this inflammation and support the brain's structural integrity.

## Incorporating Healthy Fats

Healthy fats are a cornerstone of a brain-supportive diet, particularly omega-3 fatty acids, which are known to combat inflammation and promote cellular health. Omega-3s, found in foods like fatty fish, flaxseeds, chia seeds, and walnuts, contribute to the flexibility of cell membranes, allowing neurons to communicate efficiently. This flexibility is crucial for neuroplasticity, the brain's ability to learn, adapt, and recover.

Omega-3s also stimulate the production of BDNF (brain-derived neurotrophic factor), the protein that promotes synaptic growth and repair. Higher levels of BDNF are associated with better learning capacity, improved memory, and enhanced mood regulation. By incorporating omega-3s into our diet, we're not only protecting our brain's physical structure but also improving its functional abilities.

In addition to omega-3s, monounsaturated fats—found in olive oil, avocados, and nuts—also offer brain benefits by reducing oxidative stress and supporting cardiovascular health. Since the brain relies on a consistent blood supply for oxygen and nutrients, keeping blood vessels healthy is essential. These healthy fats can reduce blood pressure, lower cholesterol, and improve blood flow to the brain, enhancing mental clarity and cognitive resilience.

**Fostering a Balanced Gut Microbiome**

The gut-brain connection underscores the importance of a balanced microbiome for mental and emotional health. Supporting gut health through a diet rich in prebiotics, probiotics, and fiber can reduce systemic inflammation, boost neurotransmitter production, and improve brain function.

- Prebiotic foods, like garlic, onions, bananas, and asparagus, feed the beneficial bacteria in the gut, promoting microbial diversity.
- Probiotic-rich foods, such as yogurt, kefir, sauerkraut, and kimchi, directly introduce helpful bacteria, balancing the gut's ecosystem.

- Fiber-rich foods, found in fruits, vegetables, and legumes, support digestion and reduce the risk of gut dysbiosis—a condition that can lead to neuroinflammation and cognitive issues.

Studies show that a healthy gut microbiome reduces the risk of anxiety, depression, and cognitive decline, linking gut health directly to brain function. By fostering a robust microbiome, we protect the brain's neurochemical environment, supporting clear thinking, stable moods, and healthy stress responses.

## Emphasizing Antioxidant-Rich Foods

Antioxidants are powerful defenders against oxidative stress, a process that accelerates brain aging and weakens cognitive function. Foods rich in antioxidants, such as berries, dark chocolate, nuts, and green leafy vegetables, help neutralize free radicals, protecting brain cells from damage. Research has shown that people who consume antioxidant-rich diets perform better in memory tasks and experience less cognitive decline as they age.

Polyphenols, a specific type of antioxidant found in foods like blueberries, green tea, and dark chocolate, have shown particular promise in brain health. They cross the blood-brain barrier and protect neurons from damage, support synaptic plasticity, and enhance learning and memory. Incorporating a variety of colorful fruits and vegetables can ensure a steady supply of these vital antioxidants, helping to safeguard our cognitive health over time.

## Staying Hydrated

Though often overlooked, hydration is essential for cognitive function. Our brain cells depend on a balanced supply of water to carry out their tasks effectively. Even mild dehydration can impair concentration, memory, and mood. Drinking water consistently throughout the day supports brain function, preventing the sluggishness and brain fog that can arise from dehydration. Herbal teas, infusions, and water-rich fruits like cucumber and watermelon are excellent sources for staying hydrated and alert.

## Eating for a Sharper Mind

Our dietary choices are not just about nutrition; they are an investment in cognitive health and emotional well-being. As we've seen, foods high in sugar, trans fats, and processed ingredients can quietly chip away at our brain's structure and function, leading to inflammation, oxidative stress, and neurodegeneration. But the story doesn't end there. By consciously choosing nutrient-rich, brain-supportive foods, we can foster a mind that remains sharp, resilient, and adaptable.

Dietary changes don't need to be drastic to be effective. Small, consistent shifts—like choosing whole grains over refined carbohydrates, healthy fats over trans fats, and colorful fruits and vegetables over processed snacks—can accumulate to create profound benefits. In embracing a balanced, whole-foods approach, we not only protect our cognitive abilities but also lay a foundation for lifelong mental wellness.

Each meal is an opportunity to feed not only our body but also our mind. By prioritizing foods that nourish the brain, we give ourselves the best chance to maintain cognitive clarity, emotional stability, and a sharp memory throughout the years. The path to cognitive longevity is, in many ways, laid out on our plates, inviting us to eat with intention and embrace a diet that sustains the brain and nurtures the mind.

# chapter 4 summary: diet, the brain and cognitive health

**How Diet Shapes Cognitive Health and Longevity**

- Our brains are highly sensitive to dietary choices, which affect memory, learning, and aging.
- A balanced diet with controlled glucose levels, healthy fats, and antioxidants supports brain function and protects against neurodegeneration.

**Glucose: Brain Fuel and Sugar's Hidden Risks**

- The brain depends on glucose but can suffer from excess refined sugars, leading to blood sugar spikes, "brain fog," and long-term cognitive decline.
- High-sugar diets also cause glycation, damaging proteins in the brain and increasing risk of memory issues and shrinkage in critical areas like the hippocampus.

**Fats for Brain Health: Omega-3s vs. Trans Fats**

- **Omega-3s** (found in fish, flaxseeds) support neuron structure and reduce inflammation, promoting learning and memory.

- **Trans fats** (in processed foods) harm neuron flexibility, lower BDNF (a protein crucial for neuroplasticity), and lead to cognitive rigidity and accelerated aging.

## Antioxidants: Brain Protectors

- Antioxidants from foods like berries and leafy greens counteract oxidative stress, preserving brain cells and cognitive functions.
- Diets rich in antioxidants support memory and reduce age-related brain decline.

## The Gut-Brain Connection and Processed Foods

- The gut microbiome affects cognitive and emotional health through the gut-brain axis.
- Processed foods disrupt gut balance, leading to systemic inflammation that can damage the brain and impact mood, memory, and learning.

## Nutritional Strategies for Brain Health

- **Reduce refined sugars**: Choose complex carbs like whole grains for stable energy and cognitive support.
- **Incorporate healthy fats**: Emphasize omega-3s and monounsaturated fats to enhance neuron flexibility and reduce inflammation.
- **Foster gut health**: Include fiber, prebiotics, and probiotics to support beneficial gut bacteria and reduce inflammation.
- **Increase antioxidants**: A variety of colorful fruits and vegetables can shield the brain from oxidative damage.
- **Stay hydrated**: Proper hydration supports concentration, memory, and mood stability.

**Eating for Cognitive Longevity**

- Nutrient-rich, whole foods create a resilient, adaptable brain.
- Small, consistent dietary shifts toward whole grains, healthy fats, and colorful produce can protect cognitive health and emotional well-being, sustaining the brain's peak performance over time.

# afterword

Diet plays a pivotal role in shaping cognitive health and promoting longevity. Our brains are deeply influenced by the foods we consume, with the right dietary choices supporting memory, learning, and protection against neurodegeneration. By maintaining balanced glucose levels, incorporating healthy fats like omega-3s, and consuming antioxidants, we can enhance brain function and reduce the risk of cognitive decline. Additionally, a healthy gut-brain connection is crucial for emotional and cognitive well-being, making it essential to nourish the gut with fiber, prebiotics, and probiotics. Small, consistent changes towards a nutrient-rich, whole-food diet can lead to lasting benefits, ensuring that our brains remain resilient, adaptable, and capable of peak performance for years to come.

# neuro-insights

"Neuroscience is clear: a healthy brain equals a healthier, longer life. Cognitive decline is not inevitable—our brain's health is within our control." – Dr. Michael Merzenich, Neuroscientist

"A healthy brain is the foundation of everything we do—without it, we cannot achieve longevity or sustain a high quality of life." – Dr. Deepak Chopra, Physician and Wellness Advocate

five
# sleep and brain health

IN THE QUIET, seemingly inactive hours of sleep, the brain is actually buzzing with essential tasks that go unnoticed by our conscious minds. Sleep is far from a simple "shut down" period; rather, it's a time when the brain performs critical housekeeping and maintenance functions that keep us mentally sharp, emotionally balanced, and physically healthy. Every night, as we drift through different stages of sleep, our brains are busy strengthening memories, processing emotions, and even clearing away toxic waste products that could otherwise accumulate and lead to neurological issues over time.

The sleep cycle itself is a finely tuned system comprising two primary types of sleep: **Non-Rapid Eye Movement (NREM)** sleep and **Rapid Eye Movement (REM)** sleep. NREM is subdivided into stages, progressing from *light sleep* (stages 1 and 2) to *deep, slow-wave sleep* (SWS, or stage 3), where the most restorative processes occur. Meanwhile, REM sleep, often referred to as "paradoxical sleep" because of its active brainwave patterns, is the stage most associated with vivid dreaming and significant cognitive processing. Each stage contributes in a unique way, allowing the brain to heal, grow, and prepare for the day ahead.

. . .

One of the most exciting revelations in modern sleep science is understanding the glymphatic system, a waste-clearing pathway that activates primarily during deep sleep. This system operates as the brain's detox center, flushing out metabolic waste products like beta-amyloid and tau proteins, which have been implicated in Alzheimer's disease. Without this nightly cleansing, harmful proteins could build up, increasing the risk of neurodegeneration over time. Thus, quality sleep isn't just beneficial; it's essential for maintaining a healthy brain, slowing the aging process, and reducing the risk of cognitive decline.

Moreover, sleep helps regulate the brain's emotional circuits, particularly through REM sleep, when the brain processes emotional experiences and fine-tunes its responses to stress. By recalibrating the brain's emotional centers, sleep fosters resilience, equipping us to face life's challenges with steadier moods and improved stress management.

In this chapter, we'll explore how each sleep stage contributes to different facets of brain health. From consolidating memories to detoxifying the brain and fostering emotional stability, we'll examine the fascinating science behind sleep and its irreplaceable role in cognitive and emotional wellness.

For a deeper understanding of sleep and its profound impact on brain health, I highly recommend exploring Book #2 in the 100+Living Series, *The Restorative Sleep Blueprint*. This book offers a comprehensive breakdown of the science behind sleep, along with actionable strategies to improve your sleep quality. By implementing these techniques, you can ensure that you wake up feeling refreshed, energized, and ready to tackle the day. Whether you're struggling with insomnia or simply looking to optimize your sleep for better brain function and overall well-being, *The Restorative Sleep Blueprint* provides the tools you need to achieve restorative rest and enhance your cognitive health.

• • •

**The Brain's Nightly Organizer: Sleep and Memory**

When it comes to memory, sleep is like the ultimate filing system. During the day, our brains are bombarded with information: facts, experiences, skills, and emotions. This constant influx of stimuli is processed initially in the hippocampus, a region responsible for short-term memory. However, to convert these fleeting moments into stable, long-term memories, the brain relies on a complex process known as **memory consolidation**—one of sleep's most critical functions.

Sleep stages, especially slow-wave sleep (SWS) and REM sleep, play specialized roles in this consolidation process. Early in the night, slow-wave sleep takes the lead. During SWS, the brain replays events from the day in a process called "replay" or "rehearsal." This replay primarily strengthens declarative memories—the kind of information-based memories you might use when recalling a conversation or memorizing facts for a test. At the same time, SWS reduces activity in the emotional centers of the brain, creating a more neutral context that facilitates the long-term storage of factual memories without the emotional interference that might cloud them during the day.

Later in the night, REM sleep steps in to work on procedural and emotional memories. Unlike the stable, synchronized waves of SWS, REM sleep is marked by erratic, high-frequency brain activity that looks surprisingly similar to wakefulness. This phase is associated with creative thinking, problem-solving, and emotional memory processing. REM sleep enables the brain to integrate new experiences with existing knowledge, fostering insights and innovation.

For instance, REM sleep has been shown to aid in the acquisition of motor skills, like learning to play an instrument or mastering a new physical activity. REM sleep's role in emotional memory processing is equally crucial, as it allows the brain to file away emotional experiences, helping us better manage stress and emotional responses over time. In fact, REM sleep may "soften" traumatic or highly charged memories, allowing us to retain essential details without the emotional weight that might otherwise hinder our well-being. This fine-tuned balance between slow-wave and REM sleep is what makes memory consolidation possible, strengthening the brain's ability to learn, retain, and adapt.

When sleep is disrupted, these processes are interrupted, resulting in fragmented memory storage and difficulties in learning. Without adequate slow-wave sleep, factual memories don't settle into long-term storage, making recall more challenging. Likewise, without sufficient REM sleep, emotional memories are left unprocessed, often leading to heightened stress or even emotional disturbances.

## Emotional Resilience: How Sleep is Our Stress Shield

Sleep is more than a time for physical rest; it's a crucial phase for emotional recalibration. Every night, as we sleep, our brains undergo essential processes that help us manage emotions, build resilience to stress, and maintain overall mental well-being. One of the most important phases for emotional processing is REM sleep. During this stage, the brain replays emotionally charged experiences, fine-tuning our responses to these memories and reducing their intensity. Think of it as an emotional editing process—REM sleep "softens" the emotional impact of stressful or troubling memories, helping us wake up with a clearer, more balanced perspective.

REM sleep's influence on emotional health centers on its effect on the limbic system, particularly the **amygdala**, which acts as the brain's alarm center for processing fear, anxiety, and stress. When REM sleep is disrupted, studies show that the amygdala becomes hyperactive, causing heightened emotional responses and reducing the brain's ability to regulate stress. This overactivation can lead to increased feelings of anxiety, irritability, and even depression. In contrast, after a night of undisturbed

REM sleep, the amygdala's activity levels normalize, allowing us to approach challenges with a sense of calm and emotional resilience.

Beyond REM, slow-wave sleep (SWS) also plays a significant role in reducing emotional reactivity. By activating the parasympathetic nervous system, SWS lowers heart rate and blood pressure, promoting a sense of calm and relaxation that aids the brain in handling stress. This deep sleep stage helps reset the brain's emotional circuits, essentially preparing us to face daily challenges with a steadier, more balanced mindset.

Interestingly, sleep loss impacts emotional resilience even more drastically than it does cognitive performance. While a single night of poor sleep can make us feel foggy or unfocused, it's prolonged sleep deprivation that often leads to pronounced mood changes, heightened stress responses, and even mental health disorders. Chronic REM sleep deprivation has been linked to an increased risk of mood disorders, including anxiety and depression, underscoring just how vital quality sleep is for emotional stability.

Ultimately, regular, high-quality sleep is essential for maintaining mental health. By allowing the brain to process emotions, reduce stress responses, and regulate mood, sleep strengthens our capacity to handle life's challenges, enhancing both our resilience and our overall sense of well-being.

**Detox Time: Sleep and Brain Health in Aging**

During the day, the brain works tirelessly, processing countless sensory inputs, forming thoughts, and making decisions. Like any hard-working system, this process creates waste—metabolic byproducts that, if left unchecked, can accumulate and harm brain cells over time. Fortunately, sleep provides an opportunity for the brain to clean up, particularly during deep, slow-wave sleep (SWS). In this stage, the brain's **glymphatic system** kicks into high gear, acting as a specialized detox system that flushes out toxins and waste products, including beta-amyloid and tau proteins, which are closely associated with Alzheimer's disease.

The glymphatic system, discovered relatively recently, relies on the movement of **cerebrospinal fluid (CSF)** through the brain's network of glial cells, which act as scaffolding and support for neurons. During SWS, the space between brain cells expands, allowing CSF to flow more freely through these channels, essentially "washing" the brain and removing potentially damaging proteins and waste products. This process reduces the risk of buildup and provides a nightly deep clean, essential for long-term brain health.

As we age, however, the quality of our sleep naturally declines, with less time spent in deep, restorative slow-wave sleep. This reduction in SWS means the glymphatic system becomes less efficient, allowing neuro-toxins to accumulate over time. Research shows that adults over 60 spend far less time in deep sleep compared to younger individuals, which could explain one of the many reasons why age-related cognitive decline and neurodegenerative diseases like Alzheimer's are more preva-lent among older adults.

Chronic sleep deprivation or poor sleep quality can further accelerate this buildup of toxic proteins, as the brain lacks the necessary time to effectively cleanse itself. In fact, studies suggest that even a single night of sleep deprivation can lead to a temporary increase in beta-amyloid levels, underscoring just how crucial consistent sleep is for brain health. Maintaining good sleep hygiene—regular sleep schedules, a comfortable sleep environment, and minimal light exposure at night—becomes espe-cially important as we age, as these habits can help preserve both sleep quality and the brain's detoxifying power.

. . .

In essence, deep sleep not only restores cognitive function but also protects the brain from aging-related diseases by removing harmful proteins. This "brain wash" is a fundamental mechanism in sleep's role as a guardian of neurological health, making quality sleep essential for preserving memory, cognitive clarity, and long-term mental wellness.

**Cognitive Clarity: Sleep's Impact on Attention and Decision-Making**

Sleep doesn't just affect how well we remember or how calm we feel; it also directly influences our daily cognitive functions like attention, decision-making, and processing speed. When we sleep, the brain has a chance to recalibrate, maintaining the sharpness and flexibility needed for the challenges of the day ahead. In fact, studies show that people who get adequate, high-quality sleep tend to make better decisions, respond more quickly to complex tasks, and are more creative and productive.

The effects of sleep on attention and decision-making are especially tied to REM sleep, the stage characterized by high brain activity and vivid dreams. During REM, the brain consolidates information and organizes it in ways that enhance our problem-solving skills and creativity. This process helps with cognitive flexibility—the ability to adapt to new information or circumstances—a key skill for complex decision-making. After a good night's sleep, our minds are better at synthesizing new ideas, recognizing patterns, and thinking critically.

On the other hand, when sleep is insufficient, our cognitive abilities quickly deteriorate. Sleep deprivation affects the **prefrontal cortex**, the area responsible for higher-order functions such as reasoning, impulse control, and emotional regulation. A sleep-deprived brain finds it harder to focus, often "filling in" details inaccurately due to poor attention and short-term memory function. This is why people often find themselves making more impulsive or risky decisions after a night of poor sleep—without enough rest, the prefrontal cortex isn't able to curb impulsive reactions as effectively.

A consistent lack of sleep also impairs processing speed, meaning that tasks requiring quick thinking, like responding to fast-changing situations or managing high-pressure decision-making, suffer. Even simple reaction times become slower when sleep is reduced. For instance, studies on medical professionals and first responders—who often endure long hours and disrupted sleep—have shown that sleep-deprived individuals are more likely to make errors, underscoring the essential role sleep plays in maintaining accuracy and reliability in decision-making.

Sleep further bolsters attention by allowing the brain's attentional networks to "reset" each night. Inadequate sleep disrupts this resetting process, leading to lapses in focus and a greater tendency for the mind to wander. When we sleep well, our attention span is longer, our focus sharper, and our ability to juggle multiple pieces of information stronger. This is particularly important in today's multitasking environments, where divided attention is often the norm. A good night's rest enables us to move through our day with clarity, maintaining mental sharpness and effectively managing cognitive demands.

In short, sleep isn't just restful; it's a performance enhancer for the brain, fueling the attention, decision-making, and creativity we need to thrive. Without it, we're left cognitively hampered, navigating our day in a fog. With it, we're sharper, quicker, and better equipped to handle life's complexities.

· · ·

**Brain Adaptability and Recovery: Sleep's Role in Plasticity and Neural Restoration**

Sleep is fundamental to the brain's adaptability—a phenomenon known as neuroplasticity, which is the brain's ability to reorganize itself, form new connections, and strengthen or weaken neural pathways based on experiences. Each day, as we learn, adapt, and respond to new situations, our brains undergo subtle yet essential structural changes, making room for new information while fine-tuning existing knowledge. Sleep, particularly the REM and slow-wave sleep (SWS) stages, supports these neural adjustments, allowing the brain to reinforce learning, recover from mental strain, and prepare for future growth.

Throughout the day, as we experience, learn, and interact, neural connections in the brain grow stronger and, in some cases, multiply—a process essential for memory formation and skill acquisition. However, without sleep, these newly formed connections become vulnerable to "overload," a state where too many active neural pathways make it harder for the brain to function efficiently. During sleep, especially in SWS, the brain "resets" this overload through a mechanism called synaptic homeostasis. Essentially, synaptic homeostasis involves scaling back or pruning some of the day's accumulated neural connections, helping neurons return to a baseline that enables new learning and efficient functioning the next day.

REM sleep also plays a distinct role in fostering brain plasticity. While SWS is mainly involved in pruning and resetting, REM sleep allows for further consolidation and integration of memories across different brain regions, aiding creative problem-solving and emotional processing. During REM sleep, the brain becomes highly active, replaying experiences and exploring different neural pathways, which can lead to insights, solutions, and new ways of thinking. This creative boost helps us make connections between seemingly unrelated concepts, reinforcing flexible, adaptive thinking.

. . .

**Sleeping into Better Neurodevelopment**

For children and young adults, whose brains are still developing, the neuroplastic benefits of sleep are even more critical. During childhood and adolescence, sleep not only supports learning but also influences the physical structure of the brain, guiding its maturation and preparing it for complex cognitive and social functions. Research shows that children who get enough sleep display better attention, learning capacity, and emotional regulation, highlighting sleep's role in neurodevelopment. Inadequate sleep in these formative years can lead to developmental challenges that may persist into adulthood, affecting cognitive and emotional resilience.

In adults, sleep continues to support plasticity by refining neural circuits and allowing the brain to adapt to new experiences and knowledge. This ongoing adaptability is vital as we learn new skills, adapt to life changes, and maintain cognitive health throughout our lives. For older adults, regular, quality sleep can help slow age-related cognitive decline, supporting memory, processing speed, and problem-solving abilities.

By fostering neuroplasticity, sleep keeps the brain agile and prepared for new learning, helping us adapt and thrive in an ever-changing world. Without it, the brain's networks become strained, less capable of handling new information, and more susceptible to cognitive decline. In this way, sleep isn't just restorative; it's fundamentally regenerative, allowing the brain to grow, adapt, and continually fine-tune itself.

**Sleep Across the Lifespan: Developmental Benefits**

Sleep is essential at every stage of life, but its role shifts in focus as the brain grows, develops, and ages. From infancy to old age, sleep is the underlying rhythm that guides cognitive growth, emotional regulation, and physical health. Each phase of life brings unique sleep needs, reflecting the brain's developmental milestones and the demands of different life stages.

. . .

**Early Life and Adolescence: The Building Blocks of Brain Development**

In infancy and early childhood, sleep is perhaps the most critical for brain development. Babies and young children spend a large portion of their time asleep, with newborns needing up to 16 hours a day. This intense sleep schedule isn't just about physical growth; it's during these hours of sleep that the brain undergoes rapid neurodevelopment. New neural connections form at an astonishing rate as infants and young children learn about their environment, developing foundational skills for language, movement, and social interaction.

Slow-wave sleep (SWS) and REM sleep are both crucial at this stage, as they contribute to the creation and strengthening of neural pathways. SWS supports memory formation and helps cement new knowledge, while REM sleep is tied to the processing of sensory information and the development of visual and motor skills. For instance, babies' rapid eye movement during REM sleep has been linked to visual system development, helping them understand shapes, colors, and facial expressions as they grow. Additionally, studies suggest that REM sleep is essential for developing emotional and social understanding, as the brain works on early emotional processing.

As children transition to adolescence, sleep continues to play a vital role in brain maturation. Teenagers still need between 8 to 10 hours of sleep each night, yet many do not get enough due to early school start times, social commitments, and the natural shift in their biological clocks that makes them "night owls." Inadequate sleep in these years can have lasting consequences, as the teenage brain is still highly plastic, undergoing significant changes in areas responsible for decision-making, impulse control, and emotional regulation. In fact, during adolescence, the prefrontal cortex—responsible for complex thinking and self-control—matures, and sleep is essential in supporting this development.

. . .

Research has shown that sleep-deprived teenagers are at a higher risk for mood disorders, impulsive behaviors, and cognitive impairments, as insufficient sleep disrupts the refinement of neural networks and emotional processing. In contrast, adequate sleep during these critical years strengthens the brain's cognitive and emotional foundation, setting up young adults for more effective learning, decision-making, and emotional resilience.

**Adulthood: Sustaining Cognitive Health and Emotional Balance**

In adulthood, sleep's role shifts toward maintaining the cognitive, emotional, and physical gains established in earlier years. While adults generally need between 7 and 9 hours of sleep, many often fall short due to work, family responsibilities, or lifestyle factors, like increased screen time or irregular schedules. But sleep isn't a luxury; it's a necessity for sustaining mental clarity, emotional stability, and physical health.

Adults rely on a balanced sleep cycle to manage the daily stresses of work and personal life. SWS helps adults consolidate knowledge and recover from mental fatigue, while REM sleep continues to support creativity, emotional resilience, and adaptive thinking. This restorative function of sleep in adulthood is critical, as it allows the brain to "reset," maintaining a healthy balance between work, family, and personal life. Lack of sleep, on the other hand, can increase susceptibility to stress, impair cognitive performance, and heighten emotional reactivity, affecting both personal and professional relationships.

Furthermore, sleep continues to play a protective role against cognitive decline, which often begins subtly in mid-life. Adults who prioritize sleep have been shown to have better memory retention and sharper cognitive abilities, as sleep allows for the removal of toxins and the maintenance of neural connections, which help preserve cognitive health.

. . .

## Older Adults: Protecting Against Cognitive Decline

As we age, changes in sleep patterns are common, often resulting in lighter and shorter sleep. Older adults spend less time in deep, slow-wave sleep and experience more fragmented sleep, often waking up frequently throughout the night. This decrease in slow-wave and REM sleep can impact memory consolidation and the brain's ability to detoxify through the glymphatic system. These age-related sleep changes have been linked to an increased risk of cognitive decline and neurodegenerative diseases, including Alzheimer's and other forms of dementia.

For older adults, regular, quality sleep becomes a crucial factor in maintaining cognitive health. Good sleep hygiene—such as keeping a consistent sleep schedule, avoiding caffeine and heavy meals before bed, and creating a calm sleep environment—can help counterbalance these natural age-related changes. Studies suggest that older adults who maintain consistent, restorative sleep are better able to preserve memory, attention, and executive functioning, helping to delay cognitive decline.

In addition to preserving cognitive function, sleep in older adults also supports immune health and physical recovery. With age, the body's ability to repair itself becomes slower, and good sleep can aid in reducing inflammation and promoting physical resilience, which is essential for overall quality of life in later years.

Sleep, therefore, is not only a pillar of health throughout the lifespan but also an evolving process that adapts to the brain's needs at different stages. By understanding the specific sleep requirements of each life phase, we can make informed choices to protect and enhance brain health, setting a strong foundation for mental agility, emotional resilience, and overall well-being as we age.

. . .

**The Essential Role of NREM and REM Sleep Stages**

Each night, our brains progress through a structured sleep cycle comprising several stages, each with its unique contributions to brain health and cognitive function. The cycle begins with Non-Rapid Eye Movement (NREM) sleep, which includes the light sleep of stages 1 and 2, followed by the deep, restorative slow-wave sleep (SWS) of stage 3. Finally, the brain shifts into Rapid Eye Movement (REM) sleep, often referred to as "dream sleep." These stages repeat cyclically throughout the night, with each cycle lasting about 90 minutes. By morning, the brain will have navigated through four to six of these cycles, with each one placing a different emphasis on NREM or REM sleep.

Understanding the unique functions of NREM and REM sleep gives us a clearer picture of why a full night of sleep is so essential for maintaining mental, emotional, and physical health.

**Non-REM (NREM) Sleep: The Foundation of Restoration**

NREM sleep begins with stages 1 and 2, known as light sleep, which help transition the brain into deeper rest and stabilize the sleep cycle. In these initial stages, the body and mind begin to relax, with heart rate, breathing, and brain activity gradually slowing. This phase acts as a bridge, moving us from the wakeful state into deeper restorative sleep. While the benefits of light sleep are often overshadowed by the more profound impact of deep sleep, these stages help prepare the brain for the maintenance and recovery functions that occur later in the cycle.

The real work of NREM sleep, however, happens in stage 3, the deep, slow-wave sleep (SWS) phase. During SWS, the brain experiences large, synchronized waves of electrical activity, creating an ideal environment for restoration. This stage is where the body performs much of its physical repair work, releasing growth hormones that help tissues heal and muscles recover. In the brain, SWS is when **synaptic homeostasis**—the pruning and fine-tuning of neural connections—takes place. By scaling back the connections formed during the day, SWS clears space for new learning and prevents cognitive overload.

SWS is also essential for memory consolidation, particularly for declarative or fact-based memories. Throughout SWS, the hippocampus, which holds short-term memories, replays information and transfers it to the neocortex, where it becomes part of long-term memory. This neural "rehearsal" is critical for integrating new information and for tasks that require recalling factual knowledge, like learning a language or studying for an exam. Additionally, SWS activates the glymphatic system, the brain's waste-clearing mechanism, which flushes out harmful proteins and toxins that can accumulate throughout the day. By maintaining a clean, balanced brain environment, SWS provides the foundation for cognitive resilience and longevity.

**REM Sleep: The Brain's Playground for Emotion and Creativity**
After NREM sleep, the brain enters REM sleep, a phase marked by rapid, low-amplitude brain waves and, as the name suggests, rapid eye movements. Although the body remains immobilized during this stage, the brain is extraordinarily active, processing emotions, consolidating memories, and stimulating neural pathways. REM sleep is often called the brain's "playground" due to the vivid dreams that commonly occur in this phase, which can range from mundane recollections to complex, surreal narratives.

REM sleep plays a crucial role in emotional health by recalibrating the brain's emotional circuits, particularly those associated with the limbic system, such as the amygdala. By replaying and integrating emotional experiences, REM sleep reduces the intensity of negative emotions linked to specific memories, helping us process difficult experiences without becoming overwhelmed. This process allows for better emotional regulation during waking hours, fostering resilience against stress, anxiety, and depression.

. . .

Creativity and problem-solving also flourish during REM sleep. Studies suggest that during REM, the brain revisits and reorganizes information in novel ways, allowing us to make connections between unrelated ideas and generate innovative solutions. In fact, many people report having "aha" moments after a good night's sleep, as REM enables the brain to integrate learned material in a way that sparks insight and creativity.

REM sleep is equally vital for procedural memory, which involves the retention of skills and learned tasks. For example, if you're learning to play the piano or practice a new sport, REM sleep helps the brain consolidate motor skills and refine techniques, allowing for steady improvement over time. This stage ensures that we not only retain information but also develop the muscle memory needed to perform complex tasks seamlessly.

## The Delicate Balance: Why We Need Both NREM and REM Sleep

NREM and REM sleep stages work together in a balanced cycle, each contributing to different aspects of mental and physical health. While NREM sleep provides a restorative foundation, focusing on physical repair, memory consolidation, and toxin clearance, REM sleep enhances emotional processing, creative thinking, and skill refinement. A full night's sleep is essential to experience these benefits, as the time spent in REM sleep typically increases in the later cycles, near morning.

When sleep is fragmented or cut short, the balance between these stages is disrupted, compromising brain function and resilience. For example, if you only sleep for five or six hours, you may miss out on the critical REM stages that occur in the early morning, affecting your emotional processing and creativity. Similarly, fragmented or shallow sleep can reduce time in SWS, undermining memory consolidation and toxin clearance, which are essential for long-term brain health.

By embracing the full sleep cycle, we allow both NREM and REM sleep to perform their unique, complementary roles. Each stage works like a chapter in the brain's nightly manual, tackling the body's and mind's diverse needs so that we wake up refreshed, resilient, and ready for the day.

**Wrapping It Up**

Sleep is a complex, dynamic process that does far more than recharge the body; it fortifies and revitalizes the brain. Each stage—whether the restorative depths of NREM slow-wave sleep or the creative, emotionally regulating REM sleep—provides unique benefits that are essential for mental clarity, emotional stability, and long-term brain health. By understanding the intricate roles of NREM and REM sleep, we gain insight into why a full night's rest is not merely helpful but vital for our cognitive and emotional resilience.

Prioritizing good sleep isn't just a commitment to better mornings; it's an investment in a sharper, more adaptable brain that's equipped to thrive through every stage of life. By embracing quality sleep, we can ensure our minds are not only capable of managing today's challenges but prepared for whatever tomorrow may bring.

# chapter 5 summary: sleep and brain health

**The Essential Role of Sleep in Brain Health**

- Sleep is not a passive "shut down" but an active time for brain maintenance and restoration, supporting cognitive, emotional, and physical health.
- Sleep cycles include Non-Rapid Eye Movement (NREM) sleep and Rapid Eye Movement (REM) sleep, each offering distinct benefits for brain function.

**Memory and Learning: The Brain's Nightly Organizer**

- **Slow-wave sleep (SWS)** in NREM stages consolidates factual and declarative memories, while **REM sleep** strengthens procedural and emotional memories.
- SWS allows the hippocampus to transfer information to long-term memory, while REM enhances problem-solving and creativity by integrating new experiences with existing knowledge.

### Emotional Resilience: Sleep as a Stress Shield

- REM sleep processes emotionally charged experiences, reducing their intensity and recalibrating emotional circuits, especially in the amygdala (the brain's fear center).
- Lack of REM sleep heightens emotional reactivity and stress, while quality sleep strengthens resilience against mood disorders.

### Brain Detoxification: The Glymphatic System

- SWS activates the glymphatic system, the brain's waste-clearance pathway, flushing out harmful proteins like beta-amyloid, which are linked to Alzheimer's.
- As we age, SWS decreases, reducing the glymphatic system's efficiency, emphasizing the importance of consistent, quality sleep for lifelong brain health.

### Cognitive Clarity: Focus, Decision-Making, and Creativity

- REM sleep enhances cognitive flexibility, decision-making, and attention by organizing information, fostering creative thinking, and supporting complex problem-solving.
- Sleep deprivation impairs the prefrontal cortex, leading to poor attention, impulsive decisions, and slower reaction times.

### Neuroplasticity and Adaptability: Sleep's Role in Brain Recovery

- Sleep supports **neuroplasticity**, enabling the brain to adapt and form new connections, which aids in learning and recovery.
- SWS helps reset neural connections through synaptic pruning, while REM sleep strengthens and integrates new neural pathways, aiding cognitive flexibility.

## Sleep Across the Lifespan

- In childhood and adolescence, sleep is vital for brain development, supporting neuroplasticity, emotional regulation, and learning.
- For adults, sleep sustains cognitive and emotional health, while in older adults, quality sleep helps prevent cognitive decline by supporting memory and attention.

## The Balance of NREM and REM Sleep Stages

- **NREM sleep** focuses on physical repair, memory consolidation, and waste clearance, while **REM sleep** supports emotional processing, creativity, and skill refinement.
- Both stages are essential, working in cycles to meet the brain's various needs for restoration, emotional stability, and cognitive performance.

# afterword

Sleep is a fundamental process that supports memory, emotional health, cognitive function, and neuroplasticity, crucially impacting brain health across all life stages. By prioritizing quality sleep, we invest in mental resilience, cognitive sharpness, and overall well-being, preparing the brain to handle today's challenges and thrive tomorrow.

# neuro-insights

**"The brain's power to adapt and change through neuroplasticity gives us hope. It's never too late to protect your brain and optimize your cognitive health."** – Dr. Richard Davidson, Neuroscientist

**"Chronic stress and poor diet are killing our brains and ultimately shorten our lives. Protecting the brain is paramount to ensuring a long, disease-free life."** – Dr. Robert Sapolsky, Neuroendocrinologist

six
# the dopamine-serotonin symphony and the modern mind

OUR BRAINS ARE marvels of chemistry and connectivity, a vast network of neurons sending and receiving signals that shape our thoughts, emotions, and behaviors. At the core of this complex system are two essential neurotransmitters: dopamine and serotonin. While both play distinct roles, together they form a delicate and dynamic duo that profoundly influences how we experience pleasure, manage stress, form habits, and stay motivated.

In today's fast-paced, high-stimulation world, understanding how dopamine and serotonin function can offer powerful insights into brain health and mental well-being. This chapter delves into the roles these neurotransmitters play in shaping our habits, moods, and focus, and explores how modern life challenges our ability to maintain balance. By understanding the chemistry behind dopamine and serotonin, we can gain tools to improve our mental resilience, manage habits, and protect our cognitive health.

**The Role of Dopamine and Serotonin in Brain Health**
Dopamine and serotonin are essential for maintaining a stable

mental environment, each contributing in unique yet complementary ways.

**Dopamine**, often called the "reward neurotransmitter," drives us to seek pleasure, accomplish goals, and push through challenges. It plays a critical role in reinforcing behaviors by producing satisfaction and reward, helping us to learn and remember actions that yield positive outcomes. This is why dopamine is crucial for motivation—it's what gives us the drive to get things done, whether it's a simple task or a major milestone.

**Serotonin**, meanwhile, acts as a mood stabilizer, bringing calm and balance. It's often thought of as the brain's natural mood regulator, helping us feel content and resilient. Higher serotonin levels are associated with feelings of well-being, emotional stability, and a sense of inner peace, while low serotonin can contribute to mood disorders like anxiety and depression. Together, dopamine and serotonin create a balance that enables us to respond appropriately to life's many demands, ensuring we stay motivated while also maintaining emotional equilibrium.

When these two neurotransmitters are in balance, we experience a stable sense of well-being where positive habits can flourish, emotions remain manageable, and resilience against stress is strong. However, disruptions to this balance—often triggered by lifestyle, environment, or stress—can lead to various mental health challenges. When dopamine levels are too high or serotonin is out of sync, impulsive behaviors, mood swings, or a persistent sense of dissatisfaction can arise.

## Dopamine, Motivation, and Reward: The Habit-Building Mechanism

Dopamine is deeply tied to how we form and maintain habits. Every time we experience a reward or achieve something meaningful, dopamine is released, marking the behavior as one worth repeating. This reinforcement process lies at the heart of habit-building, as dopamine essentially "stamps in" rewarding actions, encouraging us to seek out similar experiences in the future.

Dopamine isn't just about rewards; it also works on a prediction model, adjusting its release based on how expected or unexpected a reward is. If a reward surpasses our expectations, dopamine spikes even more, strongly reinforcing the behavior that led to it. However, if the reward is as expected or less than anticipated, dopamine release is more moderate. This nuanced response is why novelty can feel so rewarding—new experiences often surprise us, resulting in an extra boost of dopamine that drives us to explore and learn.

This cycle of reward and reinforcement plays a central role in forming lasting habits, helping the brain efficiently store behaviors that enhance survival or well-being. But this reward system can be easily hijacked. Activities that offer intense, immediate dopamine rewards—such as unhealthy food, social media, or addictive substances—can override more beneficial but less intense activities.

These "quick rewards" make it easier to form habits around instant gratification, which may feel good in the short term but often detract from long-term well-being.

**Overstimulation in the Modern World: The Risks of Dopamine Overload**

Our brains evolved in environments where dopamine rewards were few and far between, released primarily during survival activities like hunting, socializing, or securing shelter. In such settings, dopamine helped humans stay motivated and adaptable by reinforcing behaviors essential for survival. Today, however, we live in a world that's a constant source of high-stimulation triggers—social media notifications, streaming platforms, processed foods, and even online shopping. These modern dopamine triggers are designed to capture our attention, giving us frequent, often immediate dopamine hits that keep us coming back for more.

This constant stimulation can lead to what's known as **dopamine overload**. When we're exposed to an unending stream of rewards, the brain adapts by adjusting its dopamine receptors, reducing both their number and sensitivity in a process known as **downregulation**. This adjustment helps protect the brain from overstimulation, but it also reduces our ability to feel pleasure from smaller, more natural and less stimulating rewards. As a result, activities that were once enjoyable— like reading, spending time outdoors, or chatting with a friend—can feel less satisfying. This creates a cycle where the brain increasingly seeks out stronger stimuli to achieve the same level of pleasure, sometimes resulting in compulsive behaviors that are hard to break.

Dopamine overload has significant implications for mental health. As the brain's reward pathways become overstimulated, it becomes harder to maintain balance in mood, motivation, and impulse control. People may find it challenging to experience joy in simple pleasures, a condition called **anhedonia**, often linked to depressive states. Additionally, this constant engagement in high-stimulation activities can increase irritability and impatience, as the brain becomes accustomed to frequent gratification.

This effect is particularly concerning for children and adolescents, whose brains are still developing. Studies have shown that heavy exposure to social media and digital platforms during adolescence can lead to mental health issues, including anxiety, lower self-esteem, and even symptoms of depression. The developing brain is highly sensitive to dopamine and learns quickly from repetitive behavior, meaning these early dopamine-heavy experiences can shape patterns of reward and motivation well into adulthood.

**Impact of Dopamine Regulation on Focus and Cognitive Health**

Balanced dopamine levels are crucial not only for experiencing pleasure but also for maintaining focus and cognitive stability. When dopamine levels are well-regulated, the brain can prioritize tasks, sustain attention, and make effective decisions. The prefrontal cortex, the brain region associated with planning, decision-making, and impulse control, relies on a steady flow of dopamine for optimal functioning.

In a world full of quick-fix dopamine sources, however, this balance can be easily disrupted, leading to what some call "dopamine-driven distraction." The brain's natural tendency to seek novelty and reward can make it difficult to concentrate on tasks that don't offer immediate gratification, like reading, studying, or working on a long-term project. As the brain adapts to frequent dopamine spikes from activities like social media or gaming, it becomes increasingly challenging to focus on less stimulating but important tasks.

Children and adolescents are particularly vulnerable to this phenomenon, as their prefrontal cortex is still developing and more susceptible to dopamine's influence. Without proper regulation, high-dopamine activities can condition the brain to expect constant stimulation, making it difficult to sit through classes, focus on homework, or engage in activities that require sustained attention. Over time, this pattern can contribute to a reduced attention span and even symptoms similar to ADHD, making it harder to manage daily responsibilities and engage in meaningful activities.

. . .

## Dopamine Control: Building Resilience Against Destructive Habits

Recognizing dopamine's role in forming habits and behaviors gives us the power to reshape how we interact with dopamine triggers. By learning to manage dopamine levels, we can protect ourselves from impulsive behaviors and form healthier habits. This concept of "dopamine control" involves regulating our exposure to high-stimulation activities, allowing the brain to recalibrate and restore sensitivity to natural, sustainable sources of pleasure.

One popular approach for dopamine control is called **dopamine fasting**. This practice involves stepping back from activities that provide instant, high-intensity dopamine spikes—such as social media scrolling, streaming services, processed foods, and other instant rewards. The goal is to give the brain a break from constant stimulation, allowing dopamine receptors to "reset" and increasing sensitivity to more subtle, natural rewards. Dopamine fasting isn't about cutting out enjoyment but about reestablishing a balance where simple activities can once again bring satisfaction.

During dopamine fasting, people typically engage in low-stimulation activities that don't overload the brain with dopamine. These can include meditation, journaling, reading, or spending time outdoors. These activities allow the brain's reward system to rest and reset, encouraging a shift away from quick fixes toward experiences that promote long-term well-being. Over time, dopamine fasting can make us more attuned to simpler rewards, helping to reduce the pull of impulsive or compulsive behaviors and re-establishing a healthier baseline for satisfaction.

Another critical aspect of dopamine control is the practice of **delayed gratification**. Delayed gratification is the ability to resist the temptation of an immediate reward in favor of a more meaningful, long-term goal.

This skill directly impacts dopamine's role in motivation by stabilizing dopamine levels and training the brain to seek rewards from activities that require patience and persistence.

When we resist quick dopamine hits—like avoiding that impulse snack or limiting social media time—dopamine levels gradually balance out. Studies show that those who practice delayed gratification tend to have stronger self-control, better stress management, and a greater ability to pursue long-term goals. This process strengthens the prefrontal cortex, the area of the brain responsible for decision-making, impulse control, and focus, all of which are vital for building mental resilience and achieving long-term satisfaction.

By practicing delayed gratification, we train our brains to prioritize meaningful, enduring rewards over fleeting dopamine spikes, which can help diminish the allure of high-stimulation activities and create pathways for healthier habits.

**Finding Balance: Integrating Low- and High-Dopamine Activities**

Achieving dopamine balance doesn't mean eliminating high-reward activities altogether. Rather, it's about finding a sustainable rhythm between high- and low-stimulation activities that nurtures our well-being. Integrating low-dopamine activities—like exercise, creative hobbies, spending time outdoors, and connecting with loved ones—can help reset the brain's reward system while still offering pleasure and fulfillment. These activities produce dopamine in a more gradual, controlled manner, allowing us to enjoy the benefits without overwhelming the brain.

For example, physical exercise is an effective way to boost dopamine sustainably. Aerobic exercises like jogging, cycling, or swimming encourage steady dopamine production over time, which enhances mood, motivation, and resilience without creating intense spikes.

Creative pursuits, like painting or writing, can also offer slow-release rewards, encouraging dopamine flow in a way that supports focus and engagement. Mindfulness activities, including meditation or simply spending quiet time in nature, can further promote dopamine balance, encouraging calm and clarity.

Balancing these low-stimulation activities with mindful limits on high-dopamine triggers is key to building a lifestyle that supports brain health. This might mean setting boundaries on screen time, scheduling specific times for social media, or even creating "dopamine-free" blocks during the day. By establishing these routines, we make room for the slower but more satisfying rewards that come from creative and meaningful pursuits.

Incorporating these activities not only improves our brain's ability to handle stress but also provides a buffer against impulsivity. For instance, reading or creative arts release dopamine gradually, which helps keep the brain engaged without the intense peaks and troughs that quick-reward activities produce. By weaving in regular low-dopamine activities, we build resilience and train our brain to appreciate deeper, more lasting sources of fulfillment.

**Practical Strategies for Dopamine Management**

Adopting a balanced approach to dopamine management can be woven seamlessly into daily life through mindful routines and intentional choices. Small, consistent practices help cultivate dopamine control while promoting mental clarity, emotional stability, and overall well-being.

One effective strategy is to **set clear boundaries for high-stimulation activities**. Designating specific times for social media, streaming, or other dopamine-heavy activities reduces the risk of compulsive use and prevents dopamine desensitization. Taking "dopamine breaks" periodically, even for just a few hours, allows the brain to recalibrate and increases our sensitivity to natural, subtle rewards.

**Celebrate small accomplishments** throughout the day to create "micro-wins" that provide a gentle dopamine boost. These achievements, no matter how minor, help maintain motivation without relying on artificial dopamine spikes. Recognizing small wins also reinforces progress on long-term goals, keeping us engaged and positive.

**Physical activity** plays a powerful role in dopamine management. Exercise, especially aerobic activity, is one of the most reliable ways to boost dopamine gradually, supporting brain health and increasing overall mental resilience. Regular physical activity encourages the brain to produce dopamine at a sustainable rate, improving focus, mood, and motivation.

Practicing **mindfulness and meditation** can also enhance dopamine control by cultivating self-awareness and increasing our ability to manage dopamine-driven impulses. By focusing on the present moment, mindfulness teaches us to observe our thoughts and reactions without acting on them impulsively, helping us to make more deliberate choices.

Finally, focusing on **long-term goals** provides a steady, ongoing source of dopamine, helping us stay motivated without needing instant rewards. Setting goals and breaking them into smaller milestones offers a series of achievable steps, keeping the brain engaged in meaningful progress and providing a sense of purpose.

**Long-Term Benefits of Dopamine Management**
Practicing dopamine control offers profound benefits that go far

beyond immediate mental clarity and focus. Over time, a balanced approach to dopamine can enhance emotional resilience, improve cognitive function, and support overall brain health. Individuals who manage dopamine exposure effectively tend to experience improved concentration, heightened self-control, and a greater sense of purpose, as they are no longer driven by the impulsive need for quick rewards.

By avoiding overstimulation, we give the brain space to build mental resilience, enabling it to prioritize long-term goals over fleeting temptations. This skill is foundational to living a more intentional life. The ability to delay gratification allows us to pursue what truly matters—whether that's personal development, deep relationships, or meaningful accomplishments. When dopamine is regulated, the brain's executive functions are strengthened, including decision-making, problem-solving, and impulse control, all of which are essential for handling life's challenges with patience and purpose.

From a cognitive perspective, balanced dopamine levels support brain flexibility, making it easier to adapt to new situations and tackle complex tasks. This adaptability is especially important in maintaining cognitive health as we age, helping to protect memory and other critical brain functions. For individuals prone to impulsive behaviors or addiction, dopamine control provides a tool to reduce dependency on high-stimulation triggers, fostering healthier, more fulfilling habits.

Overall, regulating dopamine isn't about giving up pleasure—it's about cultivating a balanced relationship with rewards. By understanding how dopamine impacts behavior and implementing strategies to manage it, we can build a foundation of mental clarity and resilience. This balance empowers us to engage with life more fully, choosing purpose-driven actions over impulsive responses, and creating a life that is both deeply satisfying and mentally sustainable.

•  •  •

**Putting It Together**

In a world of endless distractions and quick dopamine fixes, understanding the roles of dopamine and serotonin in brain health offers a powerful framework for maintaining well-being. By learning to manage our exposure to high-dopamine activities and balancing these with meaningful, slower-reward experiences, we can protect our brain's natural reward system and strengthen our mental resilience. This knowledge enables us to navigate the challenges of modern life with a focus on what truly brings fulfillment, helping us to create a life rich with purpose, satisfaction, and lasting well-being.

# chapter 6
# summary: dopamine
# and serotonin

**Dopamine and Serotonin: The Brain's Balance of Motivation and Mood**

- **Dopamine** drives motivation, reward-seeking, and habit formation by reinforcing actions with pleasure, essential for goal achievement and resilience.
- **Serotonin** acts as the brain's mood stabilizer, creating calm, contentment, and emotional balance. Low serotonin can lead to mood disorders, while balanced levels support well-being.
- Together, they enable us to stay motivated and emotionally stable, but imbalances—often from lifestyle and stress—can lead to impulsivity, mood swings, or dissatisfaction.

**Dopamine's Role in Habit-Building**

- Dopamine release strengthens rewarding behaviors, reinforcing habits by marking behaviors as "worth repeating."
- This reward cycle adapts based on reward predictability: unexpected rewards spike dopamine, driving novelty-seeking and learning.

- Modern life's instant dopamine sources (e.g., social media, processed foods) can hijack this system, leading to a preference for quick rewards over long-term benefits.

## Dopamine Overload in the Modern World

- High-stimulation environments create **dopamine overload**, causing the brain to downregulate dopamine receptors, making everyday activities feel less satisfying.
- This cycle pushes the brain to seek more intense stimuli, potentially leading to compulsive behaviors and mental health issues like anxiety, impatience, and anhedonia.
- Children and adolescents are especially vulnerable, as their brains adapt quickly, shaping future patterns in reward and motivation.

## Dopamine and Focus: The Challenge of Distraction

- Balanced dopamine is key for sustained attention, impulse control, and effective decision-making, primarily within the prefrontal cortex.
- Overexposure to quick dopamine sources can reduce attention spans and increase "dopamine-driven distraction," making it harder to focus on low-stimulation tasks.
- For young people, this can contribute to reduced attention and even mimic ADHD symptoms, affecting learning and daily functioning.

## Dopamine Control: Building Resilience

- **Dopamine fasting** limits high-dopamine activities (e.g., social media) to recalibrate the brain, restoring sensitivity to natural, low-stimulation rewards.
- **Delayed gratification** helps stabilize dopamine, training the brain to seek satisfaction from meaningful, long-term

goals rather than quick fixes, strengthening impulse control and decision-making.

## Achieving Dopamine Balance: High- and Low-Stimulation Activities

- Balance involves incorporating low-dopamine activities (e.g., exercise, creative hobbies, nature time) to foster sustained satisfaction without overwhelming dopamine spikes.
- Exercise, especially aerobic activity, boosts dopamine sustainably, enhancing motivation and resilience.
- By establishing routines with limited high-stimulation exposure, we train the brain to find joy in simple, long-term rewards.

## Strategies for Dopamine Management

- Set clear boundaries for high-stimulation activities, taking regular "dopamine breaks" to prevent desensitization.
- Celebrate small achievements ("micro-wins") for consistent dopamine boosts without relying on intense rewards.
- Engage in physical activity and mindfulness practices to build self-awareness, improving dopamine regulation and fostering mental clarity.

## Long-Term Benefits of Dopamine Control

- Balanced dopamine levels enhance focus, impulse control, and resilience, providing a foundation for meaningful goals and personal growth.
- Effective dopamine management supports adaptability, cognitive health, and long-term satisfaction, especially crucial as we age.
- Regulating dopamine helps curb impulsive behaviors, fostering habits aligned with purpose, self-discipline, and sustained mental well-being.

# afterword

By understanding dopamine and serotonin's roles in motivation, mood, and habit formation, we can better navigate modern life's challenges. Practicing dopamine control allows us to protect our brain's reward system, prioritize meaningful experiences, and cultivate resilience. This balance leads to a life rich in purpose, satisfaction, and sustainable mental health, empowering us to make deliberate choices in a world of constant stimulation.

# neuro-insights

"The spine and the brain are intricately connected. When the spine is healthy, the brain is healthier, and when the brain is healthy, the whole body thrives." – Dr. Donald Epstein, Chiropractor

"The most important system in the body is the brain, as it controls and coordinates all other systems. Without brain health, we lose the ability to function at our best." – Dr. John E. Sarno, Medical Doctor

# brain health in the context of stress, anxiety, depression, and the gut-brain axis

INTRODUCTION: **Navigating the Inner Terrain of Brain Health**

In today's hyper-connected world, the human brain is continually adapting to more than it ever has in history. With every buzz of our phones, each deadline met, and every stressful headline, our mental landscape is tested, molded, and reshaped. It's no wonder, then, that stress, anxiety, and depression are not merely temporary states; they've become prevalent aspects of modern life. To truly grasp what's happening in our minds, it's essential to look at what these experiences do to the brain and how they relate to a surprising new player in mental health: our gut.

The brain, far from being a static, unchangeable structure, is a dynamic organ—constantly evolving, rewiring, and adapting. When exposed to chronic stress, anxiety, and depression, however, this adaptability can become a double-edged sword. These states are more than feelings; they are powerful forces that reshape the very architecture of our minds. When left unchecked, chronic mental health struggles can weaken the brain's resilience, making it harder to bounce back from emotional difficulties. This leads to changes not only in how we think and feel but in the structure and function of critical brain areas involved in memory, decision-making, and emotional control.

. . .

But there's another dimension to mental health—one that starts not in the mind but in the body. Recent science has unveiled a bi-directional communication pathway between our brain and our gut, known as the **gut-brain axis**. This axis is a kind of "dialogue" that bridges the brain and the gut's microbial environment, which consists of trillions of bacteria and other microorganisms collectively known as the microbiome. These microbes, once thought to be confined to digestion, influence everything from our immune response to neurotransmitter production and even our resilience to stress. As such, they play a significant role in our mental health and can either strengthen or weaken our ability to withstand stress, anxiety, and depression.

In this chapter, we're peeling back the layers on these complex interactions, examining how chronic stress, anxiety, and depression alter brain health. We'll also explore how the gut-brain axis intertwines with these mental states, revealing that brain health isn't confined to the head but is part of a larger, interconnected system within our bodies. By understanding these connections, we can unlock insights into building emotional resilience, promoting mental clarity, and ultimately nurturing the health of our minds from a holistic standpoint.

**The Impact of Stress, Anxiety, and Depression on Brain Health**
 **Chronic Stress and Its Neurological Effects**

Stress in moderation is like a shot of adrenaline—it sharpens focus, quickens reactions, and boosts survival instincts. In evolutionary terms, stress was a lifesaving response, an efficient way for early humans to navigate immediate dangers, like the presence of a predator or environmental hazards.

However, our modern-day stressors are not as clear-cut or short-lived. They linger, sometimes for days, months, or even years, turning what was once a life-saving mechanism into a chronic and pervasive influence. This sustained stress fundamentally alters the way our brain functions and even its physical structure.

At the heart of our stress response is the **hypothalamic-pituitary-adrenal (HPA) axis**, a central neuroendocrine system that controls the release of cortisol, often called the "stress hormone." The HPA axis begins its cascade when the **hypothalamus** (the part of the brain that regulates essential bodily functions, including temperature, hunger, thirst, sleep, and emotional responses, by linking the nervous system to the endocrine system) detects stress and signals the **pituitary gland** (known as the "master gland" which controls the endocrine system, regulating growth, metabolism, and reproductive functions through hormone secretion). In response, the pituitary prompts the **adrenal glands** (which regulate metabolism, immune response, and the body's response to stress), sitting atop the kidneys, to release cortisol into the bloodstream. This hormone initiates a range of physiological changes: heightening alertness, increasing heart rate, and diverting energy to muscles over other bodily processes, which helps us respond to immediate threats.

However, when the brain perceives ongoing, chronic stress, it keeps the HPA axis engaged, maintaining a steady flow of cortisol in the system. This continuous activation doesn't just prepare the body for a single emergency; it alters brain function over time. High cortisol levels are especially damaging to two critical areas: the hippocampus and the prefrontal cortex.

The **hippocampus**, which plays a central role in learning and memory, is particularly sensitive to cortisol. Chronic exposure to this hormone disrupts neurogenesis—the formation of new neurons—in the hippocampus, making it harder for the brain to process new information and store memories. Over time, this can lead to noticeable cognitive decline. Additionally, the hippocampus helps regulate the HPA axis itself, meaning that damage to this region can create a feedback loop where the brain becomes less able to shut off its stress response, leading to even higher cortisol levels and further damage.

The **prefrontal cortex**, our center for reasoning, decision-making, and impulse control, is also deeply affected by chronic stress. Prolonged cortisol exposure can weaken the connections within this region, leading to difficulties in regulating emotions and a decreased capacity to focus or make balanced decisions. It's no surprise, then, that people experiencing chronic stress often report feeling "foggy" or emotionally volatile. Brain imaging studies have shown that individuals exposed to long-term stress have visibly diminished prefrontal cortex function, which contributes to behaviors associated with mental health disorders like depression and anxiety.

**The Long-Term Impact of Chronic Stress on Mental Health**
As stress wears away at the brain, it doesn't simply change how we respond to challenging situations; it impacts mental health on a broader scale. Chronic stress is a well-known risk factor for both anxiety and depression, conditions marked by changes not just in mood but in the very chemistry and structure of the brain. As stress damages the prefrontal cortex and hippocampus, it can reduce our ability to cope with stressors, increasing our susceptibility to anxious and depressive thinking patterns. This cyclical relationship—where stress damages the brain, which in turn makes us more sensitive to future stress—can create a self-sustaining loop of emotional and cognitive vulnerability.

What's more, chronic stress alters the levels of certain key neurotransmitters, particularly serotonin, dopamine, and norepinephrine, each of which plays a significant role in mood regulation. Lowered serotonin is commonly associated with depressive symptoms, while dopamine deficiency often manifests in reduced motivation and pleasure, further exacerbating the toll that stress takes on our emotional well-being.

For a more in-depth exploration of stress and its impact on brain health, I encourage you to read Book #6 in the 100+Living Series, *Stress Less, Live More*. This book provides a complete breakdown of stress, its effects on both the brain and body, and proven strategies to manage it effectively. You'll find guidance on how to develop your own personalized stress management plan, helping you not only reduce stress but also build resilience. By applying these strategies, you can regain control over your mental and emotional well-being, improve cognitive function, and create a balanced, healthier life. *Stress Less, Live More* is an essential resource for anyone looking to thrive in today's fast-paced world while protecting their brain health.

**Anxiety and Structural Changes in Brain Pathways**

Anxiety is a universal feeling, a sense of unease or worry that most of us have experienced. In many ways, it's the brain's "early warning system," an alert that heightens our awareness of potential threats. However, when anxiety is constant and pervasive, it moves from being protective to becoming a form of chronic stress in itself, impacting the brain in profound ways. Pathological anxiety, as seen in anxiety disorders, transforms how the brain operates, particularly in its fear circuitry.

In the brain, the **amygdala** is the center of our emotional response system, especially fear. The amygdala receives sensory information from our environment and determines whether a situation requires a fear response. Under conditions of chronic anxiety, the amygdala becomes hyperactive, meaning it starts to perceive threats even in benign situations. Studies reveal that this overactivity in the amygdala leads to structural changes within its pathways, making it more sensitive to potential threats and sending the body into a near-constant state of alert.

· · ·

Meanwhile, the prefrontal cortex—normally responsible for regulating emotions and keeping the amygdala's reactivity in check—loses some of its control under chronic anxiety. As a result, the brain's fear circuitry becomes imbalanced: the amygdala fires frequently and intensely, while the prefrontal cortex struggles to mitigate these reactions. Over time, this dynamic creates a feedback loop where heightened amygdala activity reinforces feelings of anxiety, and the prefrontal cortex's diminishing role in emotional regulation further fuels those fears. This combination of a hyper-responsive amygdala and a compromised prefrontal cortex is why people with chronic anxiety often find themselves unable to "turn off" their worries, even in situations where there's no actual danger.

This imbalance extends beyond emotional regulation and into cognitive functioning. Studies indicate that chronic anxiety impacts memory, attention, and learning. Because the amygdala is continually signaling "threat," the brain prioritizes immediate survival-focused responses over the processing and retention of new information. Thus, individuals with chronic anxiety may find it challenging to focus, make decisions, or retain details.

Ready for the next section on depression's impact on brain health? Let me know, and I'll continue.

## Depression's Lasting Impact on Brain Health

While we often think of depression as a matter of feeling low or losing interest in life, its effects run deeper, penetrating into the very architecture of the brain. Depression alters how different regions of the brain communicate and even affects their physical structure. This condition is far more than a temporary mood shift; for many, it is a persistent neurological state that reshapes their mental and emotional landscape.

One of the hallmarks of depression is reduced activity in the brain's prefrontal cortex, hippocampus, and amygdala—regions critical for mood regulation, memory, and emotional processing. When a person is chronically depressed, these areas begin to operate differently. Imaging studies reveal decreased prefrontal cortex activity, which compromises our ability to make decisions, regulate emotions, and even interact with others. This diminished activity translates into what many people with depression experience as a sense of mental "numbness" or an inability to feel fully engaged with the world around them.

The hippocampus, responsible for memory and learning, is another major area affected by depression. Research has consistently shown that individuals with chronic depression often experience reduced hippocampal volume, which correlates with memory difficulties and an increased vulnerability to emotional dysregulation. Neuroimaging studies reveal that prolonged depression leads to a loss of volume in the hippocampus, sometimes by as much as 10-20% in severe cases. This structural change makes it harder to form and retain new memories, contributing to the cognitive fog that many people with depression describe.

## The Neurological Toll of Depression: How Inflammation and Neuroplasticity Impact Recovery

One of the most challenging aspects of depression's impact on the brain is its connection to neuroinflammation. Depression is now widely recognized as not only a psychological but also a physiological condition, involving inflammation at a cellular level. Chronic inflammation in the brain disrupts neurotransmitter pathways, particularly those involving serotonin and dopamine, which are essential for mood stability, motivation, and feelings of pleasure. When inflammation interferes with these pathways, it reduces the brain's neuroplasticity—its ability to adapt and form new connections—making recovery more challenging and relapse more likely. This inflammatory response is also associated with increased levels of cytokines, proteins that play a role in immune signaling, which can create a cascade of cellular stress, further exacerbating symptoms of depression.

. . .

The damage from depression can also extend to the amygdala, the part of the brain responsible for processing emotions. In individuals with depression, the amygdala often becomes overactive, leading to heightened sensitivity to negative stimuli. This can make everyday experiences feel overwhelming, fueling a cycle where negative emotions become more intense and prolonged. As the amygdala over-responds to negative stimuli, the brain becomes more prone to anxiety and rumination, trapping the person in a loop of negativity and fear. This overactive amygdala essentially trains the brain to focus on negative experiences and perceive them as more emotionally charged than they may objectively be, reinforcing a depressive outlook.

Compounding these neurological changes is the loss of neurogenesis, particularly in the hippocampus. Neurogenesis, the process of creating new neurons, is crucial for learning and adapting to new experiences. In a depressed brain, neurogenesis slows significantly, meaning that the brain's capacity to adapt and "reset" is impaired. As new neurons fail to replace old ones, cognitive flexibility decreases, and individuals with depression may find themselves struggling to shift their mindset, feel hope, or engage with life in meaningful ways.

The long-term effects of depression on brain health are profound. These structural and functional changes create a feedback loop where the brain's diminished capacity for emotional and cognitive regulation increases susceptibility to further episodes of depression. For this reason, early and consistent intervention is crucial. Strategies that support neurogenesis, reduce neuroinflammation, and promote neuroplasticity, such as certain types of therapy, medication, and lifestyle changes, can help the brain recover from depression. However, the challenge lies in addressing both the psychological and physiological roots of depression to break the cycle and restore brain health.

. . .

**Early Life Stress and Long-Term Brain Health**

The experiences we have in childhood do more than shape our memories and personalities—they can fundamentally mold our brain's structure and influence our mental health for a lifetime. Early life stress, including prenatal stress and childhood adversity, has profound effects on brain development that can persist well into adulthood. When the brain is still in its formative stages, it is particularly sensitive to environmental influences, both positive and negative. Stress during these early stages doesn't just affect how we feel in the moment; it changes how the brain grows, learns to regulate itself, and responds to future challenges.

In cases of early life stress, such as neglect, abuse, or even prolonged exposure to stressful environments, the brain's stress-response system, including the HPA axis, is frequently activated. As the young brain endures repeated bouts of stress, it becomes "wired" to anticipate and respond to threats. This repeated activation of the HPA axis results in chronic elevation of cortisol, which, as in adult brains, can be toxic over time. In a child's developing brain, chronic cortisol exposure can disrupt the growth and function of the hippocampus and prefrontal cortex, two regions critical for emotional regulation, memory, and cognitive control.

The **hippocampus**, which plays a central role in learning and memory, is especially vulnerable during early life. Chronic exposure to high cortisol levels disrupts neurogenesis and leads to a reduction in hippocampal volume. Research indicates that children who experience high levels of early stress often show deficits in memory and learning abilities that can persist into adulthood. These deficits are not just a matter of retaining information but extend to emotional memory as well, meaning that individuals who have experienced early life stress may be more likely to hold onto negative memories and experiences.

Similarly, the **prefrontal cortex**, which is involved in decision-making, impulse control, and future planning, is affected by early life stress.

Chronic stress during childhood can hinder the prefrontal cortex's growth, resulting in a reduced ability to regulate emotions and behavior. This impaired emotional regulation is why people who experience early life stress often struggle with impulse control, exhibit riskier behaviors, and may find it challenging to break free from cycles of anxiety or depression. When the brain learns from a young age that the world is unpredictable or unsafe, it wires itself to respond accordingly, sometimes at the expense of emotional resilience.

The **amygdala**, the brain's fear center, is another region impacted by early life stress. While the prefrontal cortex and hippocampus typically grow more slowly and gradually, the amygdala develops relatively quickly, making it particularly sensitive to early experiences. Repeated exposure to stress in childhood can make the amygdala hypersensitive to threats, increasing the likelihood of an exaggerated fear response. This heightened sensitivity to potential threats means that individuals with early life stress may perceive even benign situations as stressful or fear-inducing, setting a foundation for anxiety that persists into adulthood.

Perhaps one of the most significant findings in this area is the link between early life stress and adult mental health conditions, including anxiety disorders, depression, and even post-traumatic stress disorder (PTSD). Longitudinal studies following children exposed to high levels of stress have shown that these individuals are at a higher risk of developing mental health challenges later in life. The physical changes that stress imprints on the brain do not simply disappear; they linger, creating an underlying vulnerability to stress that can manifest in various ways as the individual encounters life's inevitable ups and downs.

On a molecular level, early life stress has been shown to influence gene expression in ways that increase susceptibility to mental health disorders. The phenomenon, known as epigenetic modification, means that experiences in childhood can "turn on" or "turn off" specific genes that regulate the stress response, immune function, and even neuroplasticity. For example, certain genes associated with resilience may be downregulated in response to chronic stress, making the individual more prone to anxiety and depression in adulthood. This genetic programming can persist for years, creating a biological memory of stress that shapes the brain's development and functioning.

While these changes paint a stark picture, they also underscore the importance of early intervention. Supporting children who experience early life stress with therapies, safe environments, and stability can mitigate some of these long-term effects. Additionally, understanding the mechanisms behind early life stress helps researchers develop targeted treatments that can promote resilience and potentially reverse some of the structural and functional changes induced by stress. The young brain, after all, is still remarkably plastic, capable of remarkable healing and adaptation when given the right tools and support.

**The Gut-Brain Axis and Its Role in Emotional Well-Being**

As scientists uncover the intricate connections within our bodies, few discoveries have been as surprising—or as game-changing—as the gut-brain axis. Once considered separate realms, the brain and the gut are now understood to engage in constant, dynamic communication, affecting not only our physical health but also our mental and emotional states. At the center of this connection lies the microbiome, a complex ecosystem of trillions of bacteria, viruses, and other microorganisms residing in the gut. These microscopic residents do far more than aid in digestion; they play a profound role in shaping our brain function, mood, and resilience.

The gut-brain axis operates as a bi-directional pathway, meaning the brain communicates with the gut and vice versa. This conversation occurs through neural, hormonal, and immune pathways, creating a system where our emotional and cognitive states can be influenced by what happens in the gut and, conversely, where our mental health can impact gut health. This axis involves several communication routes, including the vagus nerve—a major cranial nerve that links the brain directly to the gastrointestinal tract. The vagus nerve serves as a super-highway for gut-brain messages, transmitting sensory information about gut health, nutrient levels, and even microbial activity to the brain.

One of the most fascinating aspects of the gut-brain axis is the influence of the microbiome on mental health. The gut microbiota produce numerous bioactive compounds, such as **short-chain fatty acids (SCFAs)** and neurotransmitter-like substances, that directly affect brain function. SCFAs, for example, are metabolic byproducts produced by certain gut bacteria during the digestion of fiber. These molecules can cross the blood-brain barrier and influence the brain's immune response, mood regulation, and even neuroplasticity—the brain's ability to form new neural connections. Research shows that a balanced production of SCFAs is associated with improved emotional well-being and resilience, while disruptions in SCFA levels are linked to increased anxiety and depression.

The microbiome also plays a significant role in regulating the HPA axis, the same stress-response system involved in chronic stress. When the microbiome is healthy and balanced, it produces metabolites that keep the HPA axis in check, moderating cortisol release and helping the body respond appropriately to stress. However, when the microbiome falls into dysbiosis—an imbalance where harmful bacteria outnumber beneficial ones—the signals it sends to the brain can shift dramatically. Dysbiosis has been linked to exaggerated HPA axis activity, leading to heightened cortisol release, increased stress sensitivity, and inflammation. This cascade creates a feedback loop in which an imbalanced gut drives the brain toward states of anxiety or depression, which in turn can further disrupt gut health.

. . .

## The Gut-Immune-Brain Connection

The immune system plays a crucial intermediary role in this gut-brain communication. Around 70% of the body's immune cells reside in the gut, constantly interacting with the microbiome. When the gut is healthy, it maintains a balanced immune response, supporting both physical and mental health. But in cases of dysbiosis, gut bacteria can provoke an inflammatory response that doesn't just stay in the gut; it travels through the bloodstream, reaching the brain. This neuroinflammation is associated with disrupted neurotransmitter activity, particularly in pathways involving serotonin and dopamine, two chemicals integral to mood regulation. Research has shown that people with depression often have higher levels of systemic inflammation, a response that may very well begin in the gut.

Interestingly, certain strains of bacteria in the gut produce neurotransmitters, including serotonin, dopamine, and gamma-aminobutyric acid (GABA), all of which play direct roles in mental health. Approximately 90% of the body's serotonin, often called the "feel-good hormone," is produced in the gut. Gut bacteria can stimulate serotonin production, which can influence mood and mental clarity. When the gut microbiome is balanced, serotonin levels are maintained at healthy levels, supporting emotional resilience and stability. However, when the microbiome is disrupted, serotonin production in the gut can decline, contributing to mood swings, irritability, and symptoms of depression.

## How Gut Dysbiosis Affects Mood and Mental Health

**Gut dysbiosis**—a condition where the gut microbial community becomes imbalanced—can set the stage for a wide array of mental health challenges. Dysbiosis often results from factors like poor diet, prolonged stress, antibiotic use, and even lack of sleep, all of which disturb the natural equilibrium of gut bacteria. When dysbiosis occurs, harmful bacteria can release endotoxins, triggering an inflammatory response in the gut that reaches the brain and promotes neuroinflammation. This inflammatory response can interfere with neurotransmitter production, alter mood, and contribute to conditions like anxiety and depression.

Studies show that people with depression or anxiety often exhibit signs of gut dysbiosis, with reduced diversity in their microbiome and an increase in inflammatory bacterial strains. This imbalance can trigger not only physical symptoms, such as digestive issues, but also significant emotional distress. Interventions that restore microbial balance, such as dietary changes and probiotic supplementation, have shown promise in alleviating some symptoms of depression and anxiety by reducing inflammation, enhancing neuroplasticity, and stabilizing neurotransmitter levels.

## Psychobiotics: A New Frontier for Emotional Health

The term "psychobiotics" refers to probiotics with potential mental health benefits—a concept that is transforming our approach to treating mood disorders. Unlike traditional probiotics that mainly target digestive health, psychobiotics are strains specifically studied for their impact on the gut-brain axis. Research suggests that certain strains, such as *Lactobacillus* and *Bifidobacterium*, can modulate brain function, improve mood, and even reduce stress.

These strains work by influencing several gut-brain pathways. For example, certain psychobiotic strains can stimulate the production of GABA, a neurotransmitter that helps reduce anxiety and promote relaxation. Others boost serotonin production, supporting a stable mood. Psychobiotics also seem to lower the body's inflammatory response, promoting a balanced immune system and reducing the risk of neuroinflammation. Early trials have shown that supplementing with these specific strains can lead to improved emotional regulation, reduced stress responses, and even enhanced resilience in the face of mental health challenges.

As our understanding of the gut-brain axis expands, psychobiotics represent an exciting, non-invasive tool in the fight against mental health disorders. Rather than relying solely on pharmaceutical treatments, which often come with side effects, psychobiotics provide a gentler, holistic approach, addressing the underlying biological factors that contribute to anxiety, depression, and other mood disorders. While more research is needed to identify the most effective strains and dosages, psychobiotics offer a promising new pathway toward achieving mental wellness.

Let me know if you'd like to proceed to the next section on integrating brain and gut health for emotional resilience.

**Integrating Brain and Gut Health for Emotional Resilience**
The emerging science behind brain health and the gut-brain axis paints a clear picture: mental health is not confined to the brain but is part of a broader, interconnected system that includes our gut, our immune system, and our overall physiological balance. With this understanding, a holistic approach to mental health—one that integrates brain and gut health—offers promising potential for building resilience against stress, anxiety, and depression. Rather than addressing symptoms in isolation, this integrated approach considers the body's complex internal ecosystem, recognizing that mental wellness requires nurturing both the mind and the microbiome.

Research has demonstrated that traditional mental health treatments like cognitive-behavioral therapy (CBT) or medications can be significantly enhanced by integrating dietary changes, gut-supportive therapies, and lifestyle interventions. For example, CBT helps people reframe their thought patterns and develop emotional coping skills. When combined with dietary adjustments and probiotics, the brain may become more responsive to CBT, as the gut-brain axis influences mood and mental resilience. This is because a healthier gut can lead to reduced inflammation, balanced neurotransmitter production, and improved cognitive function, creating a "brain environment" that is more receptive to change and healing.

Diet is a key component of this holistic approach. Numerous studies highlight the impact of diet on mental health, particularly diets rich in fiber, omega-3 fatty acids, vitamins, and antioxidants. Fiber, for instance, supports the growth of beneficial gut bacteria, which in turn produce SCFAs that promote brain health and emotional balance. Omega-3 fatty acids, commonly found in fish, walnuts, and flaxseeds, are essential for brain cell membrane integrity and neurotransmitter function. These nutrients have anti-inflammatory properties that protect brain cells from stress-induced damage and help stabilize mood.

**Beyond Diet**

Incorporating physical activity and mindfulness practices can support both brain and gut health. Exercise is known to promote neurogenesis, particularly in the hippocampus, which improves memory and cognitive flexibility. Physical activity also boosts beneficial gut bacteria, supporting microbial diversity and enhancing the production of SCFAs. Mindfulness practices, such as meditation and deep-breathing exercises, have been shown to reduce cortisol levels, dampen the body's stress response, and improve emotional regulation. By calming the HPA axis and decreasing inflammation, mindfulness can benefit both brain and gut health, providing a powerful buffer against stress and anxiety.

The role of probiotics and psychobiotics in this integrated approach cannot be overlooked. Regular use of probiotics, especially strains like *Lactobacillus* and *Bifidobacterium*, can help restore microbial balance in the gut, reduce systemic inflammation, and support immune function. In doing so, they can positively influence mood and emotional resilience, allowing the brain to better cope with stress and depressive symptoms. While probiotics alone may not cure mood disorders, they can complement psychological therapies and create a more favorable internal environment for healing.

Integrating gut and brain health isn't about finding a one-size-fits-all solution; rather, it's about tailoring a combination of practices that work in harmony to support the body's natural resilience. For some, this might mean combining psychotherapy with dietary shifts, regular exercise, and probiotic supplementation. For others, it could involve mindful eating, managing sleep patterns, and using psychobiotics to alleviate anxiety and depression symptoms. As research grows, clinicians are increasingly recognizing that mental health treatment can be enhanced by viewing the body as a holistic system, where brain health and gut health work together to build emotional resilience.

This integrated approach may offer more lasting effects than isolated treatments by targeting the root causes of mental health issues and addressing them at multiple levels—cognitive, physiological, and microbial. The goal isn't just to alleviate symptoms temporarily but to create a foundation for sustained mental wellness by nurturing the brain-gut connection. In the long term, this holistic strategy allows individuals to cultivate emotional resilience, improve their cognitive health, and enjoy a greater sense of well-being by supporting the mind and body in unison.

**A Holistic Approach to Mental Wellness**

As we've explored throughout this chapter, brain health is deeply interconnected with every aspect of our physiology, extending far beyond the confines of the skull. Our mental and emotional well-being is influenced not only by what we experience and think but also by what we eat, how we move, and even by the microorganisms living within us. Stress, anxiety, and depression are not simply psychological conditions;

they involve biological and physiological changes that reshape the brain and impact every aspect of our lives. Understanding and addressing these factors through an integrated approach that considers both brain and gut health offers a pathway to greater resilience and more sustainable mental wellness.

# chapter 7 summary: stress, depression and the gut brain axis

**Navigating Modern Mental Health: A Holistic Perspective**

In today's overstimulated world, stress, anxiety, and depression have become daily companions for many, reshaping the brain and impacting mental health. Recent research shows that understanding these mental states goes beyond the brain alone; it involves our whole physiology, especially the gut-brain axis—a critical communication link between the brain and gut microbiome. This connection reveals that brain health is part of an interconnected system within the body, influencing everything from resilience to emotional well-being.

**Chronic Stress and Brain Health**

- The **hypothalamic-pituitary-adrenal (HPA) axis** regulates stress responses, releasing cortisol for short-term survival, but chronic stress keeps cortisol levels high, damaging critical brain areas over time.
- **Hippocampus**: Chronic stress disrupts neurogenesis here, impairing learning and memory. Damage to the hippocampus also weakens its ability to regulate stress, creating a cycle of elevated cortisol.

- **Prefrontal Cortex**: Prolonged cortisol weakens this area, reducing emotional control, focus, and decision-making, often leading to cognitive "fog."
- Chronic stress fuels **anxiety and depression** by altering neurotransmitter levels, including serotonin and dopamine, affecting mood regulation and further weakening the brain's resilience.

## Anxiety's Structural and Functional Effect

- While occasional anxiety serves as an alert system, chronic anxiety overstimulates the **amygdala** (the brain's fear center), making it hypersensitive to threats.
- The **prefrontal cortex** loses control over emotional regulation, leading to constant feelings of unease. Anxiety prioritizes survival responses, impacting focus, memory, and decision-making.

## Depression's Lasting Neurological Impact

- Depression diminishes activity in the **prefrontal cortex, hippocampus,** and **amygdala,** affecting mood regulation, memory, and emotional processing.
- **Neuroinflammation** disrupts serotonin and dopamine pathways and reduces neuroplasticity, making recovery challenging.
- Depression's effects extend to neurogenesis, slowing the brain's ability to adapt, leading to a loss of cognitive flexibility and reinforcing cycles of negative thinking.

## Early Life Stress and Long-Term Mental Health

- Early life stress primes the brain to expect and respond to threats, with lasting changes in the **HPA axis** and chronic cortisol levels affecting brain development.

- Early stress reduces the **hippocampus** (memory) and **prefrontal cortex** (emotional regulation) capacities, heightening vulnerability to stress in adulthood.
- The **amygdala** becomes hypersensitive, creating a foundation for lifelong anxiety, risk-taking, and emotional challenges.

## The Gut-Brain Axis: A New Frontier in Mental Health

- The **gut-brain axis** allows bi-directional communication, with the gut microbiome playing a significant role in neurotransmitter production, immune response, and resilience to stress.
- **Short-chain fatty acids (SCFAs)** produced by gut bacteria can cross the blood-brain barrier, influencing mood, neuroplasticity, and inflammation.
- Gut dysbiosis (imbalance) disrupts neurotransmitters like serotonin and dopamine and can lead to **neuroinflammation,** impacting mental health and heightening stress, anxiety, and depression.

## Gut Dysbiosis and Mood Disorders

- Gut dysbiosis often results from poor diet, stress, antibiotics, or lack of sleep, leading to inflammation and a disruption of the gut-brain axis.
- Imbalance in the gut microbiome is linked to depression and anxiety, often presenting alongside physical digestive issues.
- **Psychobiotics** (probiotics specifically supporting mental health) like Lactobacillus and Bifidobacterium show promise in reducing stress, enhancing resilience, and lowering neuroinflammation.

**Integrating Brain and Gut Health for Resilience**

- Mental health treatments, including **cognitive-behavioral therapy (CBT),** are more effective when combined with a healthy diet, gut-supportive therapies, and regular exercise.
- **Diet:** A fiber-rich, omega-3, and antioxidant diet supports brain and gut health, promoting mental clarity and stability.
- **Exercise:** Regular activity boosts neurogenesis and benefits the gut, enhancing emotional resilience.
- **Probiotics and psychobiotics** help restore microbial balance, reduce inflammation, and stabilize neurotransmitter production, complementing mental health therapies.

# afterword

Modern mental health challenges are deeply interconnected with both our brain and body, requiring a holistic approach to achieve lasting wellness. Chronic stress, anxiety, and depression not only impact brain function but also influence the gut-brain axis, highlighting the importance of addressing both mental and physical health in tandem. By understanding the profound effects of stress on brain structures, the role of gut health in mental clarity, and the potential of lifestyle changes like diet, exercise, and probiotics, we can foster resilience and break free from the cycles of mental health struggles. Integrating these practices into our daily lives offers a powerful path to healing, mental clarity, and emotional well-being, paving the way for a more balanced and fulfilling life.

# neuro-insights

"The brain needs nourishment and protection as much as the heart and lungs. Cognitive decline is preventable if we take the right steps to care for our brain early on." – Dr. Mehmet Oz, Cardiothoracic Surgeon

"The aging brain does not need to mean cognitive decline. Through proactive care of your brain and spinal health, you can extend not just your years, but your years of vitality." – Dr. Lisa Mosconi, Neuroscientist

eight
# the spine's influence on brain health

SPINAL ALIGNMENT AND BRAIN HEALTH: **How the Posture Supports Cognitive and Emotional Well-being**

The human body is a web of interconnected systems, each part influencing the others in ways that modern science is still uncovering. While the brain is often held up as the primary control center, orchestrating everything from breathing to emotion, it relies heavily on the structure and alignment of the body around it. The spine, the main axis of our skeleton, supports this delicate organ with both physical stability and a protective pathway for the nervous system that connects the brain to the rest of the body.

For most of us, the spine is simply the "backbone," a pillar of bones that supports our posture and keeps us upright. But new findings indicate that it's far more than just a structural component. Each segment of the spine houses and protects spinal nerves that extend from the brain, forming a lifeline of communication. This network allows the brain to monitor and adjust bodily functions in real time.

Every movement, sensation, and reflex is a result of the seamless flow of information between the brain and the body through the spinal cord and neural network. But what happens when this flow is disrupted? The answer is that even a subtle misalignment or unnatural curvature in the spine can set off a cascade of effects, impacting not just physical health but mental and emotional well-being as well.

From slight curvatures like forward head posture to more pronounced conditions such as scoliosis, spinal misalignments can influence neurological pathways, alter blood flow, and restrict cerebrospinal fluid circulation. These issues may sound technical, but their effects are tangible: reduced cognitive clarity, increased stress responses, and even challenges in maintaining balance or recovering from injuries. When spinal alignment falters, the brain may begin to struggle, compensating for impaired communication and blood flow that hinder its optimal functioning.

This chapter explores the profound relationship between spinal alignment and brain health, using scientific research and clinical insights to illustrate how misalignments can affect the nervous system and overall well-being. By examining the science behind **Chiropractic BioPhysics (CBP)**—an approach specifically designed to restore spinal alignment—we gain a clearer understanding of how supporting the spine can also support the brain, enhancing not only physical wellness but also cognitive and emotional resilience.

For readers looking to take a deeper dive into the importance of spinal health and its direct impact on brain health, I encourage you to explore Book #1 in the 100+Living Series, *Your Complete Posture Guide* by my co-author Dr. Graham Jenkins. This comprehensive guide provides practical exercises and expert tips to help you improve your posture, which in turn supports your brain health and overall nervous system function. By focusing on posture restoration, you can enhance cognitive clarity, emotional resilience, and physical vitality—essential components of lasting brain health.

. . .

## The Spine and the Nervous System

Our spine's significance extends well beyond mere support; it's the primary conduit for the central nervous system, the superhighway for signals traveling between the brain and the body. Imagine the central nervous system as a sprawling network of highways, with the spine housing the main roads that connect every organ, muscle, and tissue to the brain's command center. This structure is remarkably effective—until it's disrupted. Spinal misalignments, whether due to injury, posture, or congenital conditions, have the potential to obstruct or distort this flow of information, creating what could be considered a series of traffic jams within the nervous system.

The spine's curves are intentional and fundamental to its function. Normally, it features four gentle curves—**cervical** (neck), **thoracic** (upper back), **lumbar** (lower back), and **sacral** (pelvic region)—designed to balance the body's weight, distribute impact, and absorb the forces of movement. These curves are carefully crafted by nature to maintain an even distribution of force across the vertebrae and allow the spinal cord and nerves to flow with minimal restriction.

When the spine deviates from this balanced curvature, as in cases of **scoliosis** (side-to-side curvature) or **kyphosis** (an excessive forward curve), the tension on the spinal cord and nerves increases. This can lead to functional disturbances, affecting how signals are relayed between the brain and body. Studies indicate that spinal misalignments can contribute to conditions like **autonomic dysfunction**, where the body struggles to maintain basic functions such as heart rate, digestion, and respiration. This happens because an imbalanced spine exerts tensile or compressive forces on specific nerves that control these involuntary processes, disrupting the **autonomic nervous system's (ANS)** ability to regulate them.

. . .

More subtle misalignments, like those resulting from prolonged poor posture, may lead to milder but still impactful disruptions. Over time, misalignments can cause sensory distortions—where the brain's interpretation of sensory input is altered—and motor deficits, such as reduced control over movement. Even emotions can be impacted by these physical constraints on the nervous system. The spine is, therefore, not just the back support but a dynamic component of our mental and physical equilibrium.

Research into this area continues to uncover just how crucial spinal alignment is to maintaining clear lines of communication within the nervous system. The spine's alignment is like tuning an instrument; a finely tuned spinal column allows for a harmonious flow of information, while a misaligned spine disrupts this delicate balance, often with consequences for mental clarity, physical performance, and overall health. As we continue to understand the spine's role in health, it becomes clear that correcting spinal alignment is not only a matter of physical posture but a way to ensure the brain's messages are received accurately throughout the body.

### Impact on Cerebrospinal Fluid (CSF) Flow

**Cerebrospinal fluid (CSF)** is an essential component of brain health, flowing continuously between the brain and spinal cord to nourish, protect, and cleanse the central nervous system. This clear, nutrient-rich fluid provides a kind of cushion for the brain, protecting it from impacts while also assisting in waste removal and delivering vital substances needed for brain function. Think of CSF as a river that not only quenches the brain's metabolic thirst but also carries away waste products. The movement of this fluid is crucial—if it slows down or becomes restricted, brain function can suffer.

CSF flow is highly dependent on the spine's alignment. When the spine is in its natural, curved state, the fluid flows easily through the narrow passageways that run along the spinal cord, providing the brain with the nutrients it needs and removing metabolic byproducts. But conditions like scoliosis or hyperkyphosis disrupt this flow. Misalignments, even subtle ones, can press on the CSF channels, creating areas of stagnant flow or even blockages that hinder circulation.

A study involving zebrafish models of scoliosis provided a revealing insight into how spinal curvature affects CSF dynamics. Researchers observed that as the spine's curvature increased, the **ability of the motile cilia**—tiny, hair-like structures that help propel CSF along its path—to move the fluid was reduced. This disruption in CSF circulation led to nutrient deficiencies within the central nervous system and an accumulation of waste products that couldn't be flushed out as efficiently. This seemingly minor disturbance in zebrafish mirrored issues seen in human patients with scoliosis or other spinal deformities, where poor CSF flow is often linked to cognitive difficulties and emotional imbalances.

In humans, restricted CSF flow due to spinal misalignment has been associated with symptoms ranging from headaches and dizziness to cognitive fog and mood disturbances. Limited CSF flow can also mean less efficient removal of neurotoxic waste, which, if allowed to build up, may contribute to neurodegenerative processes over time. Researchers believe that conditions such as **idiopathic intracranial hypertension**, characterized by increased CSF pressure and severe headaches, may in some cases be connected to issues in spinal alignment affecting CSF dynamics.

Through therapies that correct spinal alignment, there's potential to restore smoother CSF flow, offering relief from pressure buildup and enhancing nutrient delivery to the brain. Chiropractic adjustments, for example, aim to relieve compression on spinal joints and allow the CSF to flow more naturally. When alignment is restored, this crucial fluid can once again flow uninhibited, supporting the brain's health by delivering essential nutrients and removing metabolic waste, which is essential for maintaining optimal neurological function.

These insights reveal just how intertwined our spinal health is with the very fluid that sustains our brain. Spinal alignment may seem, at first glance, like an issue limited to physical posture, but its influence reaches the brain's doorstep, impacting mental clarity, mood stability, and cognitive resilience.

## Autonomic Nervous System Regulation

The **autonomic nervous system (ANS)** is one of the body's most intricate control systems, operating largely outside our conscious awareness. It governs essential, automatic functions like heart rate, digestion, respiration, and even immune responses. Essentially, the ANS keeps us alive and balanced without requiring conscious effort. However, it operates in two modes: the **sympathetic "fight-or-flight"** response and the **parasympathetic "rest-and-digest"** response.

These two branches work in harmony, ensuring the body reacts to stress appropriately and returns to a state of calm afterward. Yet, when this balance is disrupted, especially by structural issues like spinal misalignment, the ANS can be pushed into a state of chronic imbalance, with significant consequences for overall health.

One of the surprising discoveries in recent years is how closely spinal alignment is tied to the ANS. The spine's alignment impacts the nerve roots that exit from each vertebra and reach out to the body's organs, influencing the ANS's control over involuntary functions. Misalignments in the spine, especially in the cervical (neck) and thoracic (upper back) regions, can irritate or compress these nerve roots, potentially causing overstimulation of the sympathetic nervous system. This imbalance triggers the "fight-or-flight" response more frequently than necessary, leaving the body in a constant state of stress. Over time, this heightened stress response can strain the body, leading to a cascade of symptoms, from anxiety and insomnia to increased heart rate and digestive disturbances.

When the **sympathetic nervous system** remains activated, stress hormones like cortisol are released continuously, impacting not only the body but also the brain. Chronic stress has been shown to shrink areas in the brain associated with memory and emotional regulation, particularly the hippocampus. Additionally, persistent sympathetic dominance increases inflammation in the body, which can harm brain tissues over time and contribute to neurodegenerative diseases.

The **parasympathetic nervous system**, on the other hand, is our body's brake pedal, slowing things down and allowing for recovery and restoration. But with an imbalanced spine, it's often under-activated, unable to counterbalance the high-alert state of the sympathetic system. Restoring spinal alignment through chiropractic care can relieve pressure on autonomic nerves and help reestablish balance between these two systems. By doing so, the body is better able to "switch off" the fight-or-flight response, reducing stress-related inflammation, allowing the brain to rest and recover, and lowering the risk of long-term health consequences related to chronic stress.

**Better Stress Coordination**

Research demonstrates that adjustments targeting the cervical and thoracic spine can improve heart rate variability (HRV), a measure of autonomic balance and resilience to stress. HRV is an indicator of how well the body transitions between the sympathetic and parasympathetic states. Studies show that patients receiving spinal adjustments often experience increased HRV, reflecting a healthier, more flexible ANS capable of adapting to stress without getting "stuck" in fight-or-flight mode. This balance between stress and calm is not only essential for physical health but also supports mental clarity, emotional stability, and cognitive resilience.

In a way, the spine serves as a regulator for how well we handle life's stressors. An aligned spine promotes a well-functioning ANS, allowing for a natural ebb and flow between activity and relaxation, which is critical for both brain and body health. Spinal health is, therefore, more than just physical—it's integral to maintaining the mental and emotional equilibrium necessary for a healthy, fulfilling life.

## Spinal Curvature and Brain Metabolism

Brain metabolism is the process through which the brain converts nutrients into energy, a task essential for everything from thought processing and memory retention to managing emotions and responding to physical sensations. Unlike other organs, the brain is energy-intensive, using about 20% of the body's energy despite making up only 2% of its weight. This high demand means that the brain requires a constant, uninterrupted supply of oxygen and glucose to function optimally. Surprisingly, research now shows that spinal alignment plays a significant role in this metabolic process, affecting how well the brain receives and utilizes these vital resources.

One fascinating finding involves the influence of chiropractic adjustments on brain metabolism, especially in areas related to emotional regulation and pain processing, such as the prefrontal cortex. Neuroimaging studies using tools like MRI and PET scans reveal that specific chiropractic adjustments can stimulate metabolic activity in the prefrontal cortex, where many of our higher cognitive functions—such as decision-making, social interactions, and emotional regulation—take place. Misalignments, particularly in the cervical (neck) region, can lead to restrictions that alter blood flow and nutrient delivery to these brain areas, reducing their metabolic efficiency. Correcting these misalignments allows the brain to receive an unimpeded supply of glucose and oxygen, improving cognitive clarity, emotional stability, and even pain tolerance.

For example, a study found that when patients underwent spinal adjustments, there was a measurable increase in glucose metabolism in the prefrontal cortex. This suggests that correcting spinal issues can enhance not only physical well-being but also brain function, potentially making the brain more resilient to stress and supporting better cognitive performance. In some cases, patients reported feeling less stressed, more focused, and emotionally balanced after consistent adjustments, indicating that the spine-brain relationship influences the very way we experience and interpret the world around us.

**Spinal    Alignment    Influences    Pain    Sensitivity    and Neuroinflammation**

The spine also affects areas of the brain that process pain, like the somatosensory cortex and anterior cingulate cortex. Chronic misalignments can lead to persistent low-level pain signals, constantly stimulating these brain regions. Over time, this can create a state of "central sensitization," where the brain becomes overly responsive to pain signals, making a person more sensitive to both physical and emotional stress. By addressing spinal misalignment, chiropractic adjustments may reduce this excessive pain signaling, helping the brain to regulate pain more effectively, lowering perceived pain levels, and reducing stress-related fatigue.

Furthermore, the spine's alignment plays a role in how efficiently the brain can manage inflammation. Misalignments can lead to localized inflammation around spinal joints, which, if persistent, can release inflammatory markers that enter the bloodstream. Chronic inflammation in the body can influence brain function by crossing the blood-brain barrier and triggering neuroinflammation, which has been linked to mood disorders, cognitive decline, and neurodegenerative diseases. Restoring alignment reduces inflammatory stress on spinal structures, thereby decreasing the release of these harmful markers and supporting a healthier brain environment.

In this light, spinal alignment emerges as a surprisingly powerful contributor to brain metabolism. It's a dynamic relationship where even slight improvements in alignment can enhance blood flow, optimize glucose metabolism, and reduce inflammation. By maintaining proper spinal health, we not only support our posture and relieve back pain but also help our brains operate at peak efficiency. This connection suggests that regular attention to spinal alignment may be a practical, proactive step in preserving mental acuity, emotional resilience, and overall brain health throughout life.

**The Influence of Spinal Curvature Disorders on Injury Risk**

When we think of spinal curvature disorders—conditions like scoliosis, hyperkyphosis, and even hyperlordosis—we often focus on their visible effects: postural deviations, uneven shoulders, or a rounded back. But these structural imbalances have far-reaching implications, affecting not only physical appearance but also the body's susceptibility to injury and the brain's ability to function optimally. Research has shown that abnormal spinal curvatures increase the risk of physical injuries, which, in turn, places added strain on the brain and nervous system.

Imagine the spine as the core of our body's framework, responsible for distributing weight and absorbing impact. When its natural alignment is altered, the spine becomes less efficient at bearing weight, placing unevenstress on certain regions. For example, individuals with scoliosis experience an uneven distribution of force across the vertebrae and spinal joints. This added pressure doesn't just increase wear and tear on the bones and ligaments; it also heightens the risk of nerve compression and injury. In fact, studies confirm that those with significant spinal curvature disorders are twice as likely to suffer from injuries involving nerve trauma, including fractures, nerve compression, and spinal cord irritation.

The nervous system is deeply intertwined with spinal structure, as each spinal segment houses nerves that extend out to various parts of the body. Any injury or compression along this pathway has the potential to affect not only the local area but also the communication between the brain and body. For instance, nerve injuries stemming from scoliosis or kyphosis can alter the brain's interpretation of sensory input, impacting everything from pain perception to motor control. In other words, when the spine is misaligned and susceptible to injury, the brain's normal functions can be disrupted, leading to issues like chronic pain, reduced muscle coordination, and heightened stress responses.

## Neuroplasticity and Postural Stability

The human brain has an extraordinary ability to adapt and reorganize itself, a property known as **neuroplasticity**. This capacity allows the brain to form new neural connections in response to learning, experience, and even injury, helping us adapt to changing environments, recover from trauma, and acquire new skills. While we often think of neuroplasticity in the context of brain functions like memory or learning, emerging research reveals that it also plays a significant role in physical stability and posture—two aspects heavily influenced by spinal alignment.

**Postural stability** is our body's ability to maintain an upright position against gravity, an essential function for movement, balance, and orientation in space. The brain depends on a constant stream of sensory information from the body, especially from the spine, to gauge spatial orientation and adjust posture. Spinal misalignments, however, can disrupt this stream, leading to altered or confusing sensory input. For example, conditions like scoliosis or kyphosis send skewed proprioceptive signals to the brain, challenging its ability to maintain accurate balance and posture.

This altered feedback requires the brain to exert more effort to achieve stability, engaging neuroplastic processes to compensate for the spine's structural deviations.

The concept of neuroplasticity in relation to posture becomes even more relevant when we consider the role of spinal alignment in **proprioception**—the body's awareness of its position in space. Spinal misalignments can distort proprioceptive feedback, leading the brain to work harder to interpret spatial cues, which in turn can create a chronic low-level stress on the nervous system. Over time, this additional cognitive load can impact mental clarity and contribute to feelings of fatigue.

Neuroplasticity allows the brain to adapt to these altered signals, but the adaptations can also reinforce poor postural patterns and imbalances, creating a cycle of compensation that is difficult to break.

**Spinal Health Enhances Brain Adaptability and Recovery**

Interestingly, chiropractic adjustments targeting spinal misalignments have been shown to influence neuroplasticity in a positive way, especially in areas of the brain associated with motor control and proprioception. Studies suggest that spinal adjustments may stimulate changes in these brain regions, improving proprioceptive accuracy and postural stability. By restoring alignment, chiropractic care (following the Chiropractic BioPhysics protocols) provides the brain with clearer, more accurate sensory input, reducing the strain on neural pathways involved in maintaining balance. The result is often an improvement in stability, movement coordination, and even cognitive focus, as the brain is freed from the constant effort of compensating for poor spinal alignment.

Neuroplasticity's involvement doesn't stop at posture—it also extends to recovery from injuries that affect balance and stability, such as strokes or **traumatic brain injuries (TBIs)**. Research indicates that spinal alignment adjustments can facilitate neuroplastic responses, helping the brain rewire and rebuild pathways damaged by injury. For patients with conditions affecting their nervous system, such as stroke survivors, these adjustments may support the brain's natural recovery processes, enhancing physical rehabilitation efforts. Proper spinal alignment aids in distributing the body's weight more evenly, reducing stress on the nervous system and allowing the brain to focus on healing rather than compensating for misalignment.

Spinal alignment, therefore, plays a critical role not only in physical stability but also in supporting the brain's capacity to adapt and heal. By ensuring accurate posture and alignment, we provide the brain with a more stable foundation for engaging its neuroplastic potential. Chiropractic adjustments and therapies focused on spinal alignment can help the brain's plasticity work for us rather than against us, allowing for improvements in postural stability, balance, and even mental focus. When spinal alignment is corrected, the brain can operate with greater efficiency, redirecting energy toward growth, learning, and adaptation, rather than compensating for physical imbalances.

Through this lens, it becomes clear that spinal health is fundamental to the brain's adaptability and resilience. By aligning the spine, we support the body's natural mechanisms for stability and neuroplasticity, creating the physical and mental conditions needed for the brain to thrive.

**Improving Blood Flow to the Brain with Curve Correction**

The brain's need for a steady, rich supply of blood cannot be overstated. Blood flow provides essential oxygen and nutrients, while also removing metabolic waste, ensuring the brain has the energy it needs for everything from basic functioning to complex cognitive tasks. Any disruption to this critical circulation can impair brain health, leading to symptoms ranging from mental fatigue and brain fog to increased vulnerability to neurodegenerative conditions. Recent research underscores how spinal alignment, especially in the cervical spine (neck area), directly influences blood flow to the brain, adding yet another layer to the spine-brain connection.

The cervical spine is unique in its role in facilitating blood flow. It houses and protects two vertebral arteries that run along each side of the neck vertebrae, carrying blood from the heart to key areas of the brain. These arteries are particularly sensitive to alignment because even small shifts or misalignments in the cervical vertebrae can cause compression or kinking of these arteries, restricting blood flow. Conditions like forward head posture, cervical kyphosis (where the natural neck curve reverses), and "military neck" (a straightened neck alignment) can all place tension on the vertebral arteries, limiting circulation and potentially compromising the brain's access to oxygen and nutrients.

Dr. Evan Katz's research has highlighted how restoring normal cervical curvature improves blood flow to the brain, suggesting that chiropractic corrections done through CBP which focus on the cervical spine may help relieve vascular strain. By restoring the cervical curve, CBP practitioners can alleviate pressure on the vertebral arteries, enhancing blood flow to critical brain regions and supporting cerebral health. Dr. Katz's studies demonstrated that patients with corrected cervical alignment showed improved blood flow and reported fewer symptoms related to poor circulation, such as dizziness, headaches, and cognitive fog.

**Enhancing Neurovascular Health through Spinal Care**

Imaging techniques like Doppler ultrasound have corroborated these findings, showing that cervical misalignment reduces blood perfusion to the brain. When postural deviations in the neck are corrected, perfusion improves, ensuring that the brain receives a steady supply of oxygenated blood. This circulation is not only crucial for immediate cognitive performance but also plays a protective role, as restricted blood flow has been linked to conditions such as chronic migraines, dizziness, and even the risk of transient ischemic attacks (mini-strokes).

Furthermore, the influence of spinal alignment on blood flow impacts neurovascular health, which is central to preventing and managing neurodegenerative diseases like Alzheimer's. Restricted blood flow can lead to hypoxia (oxygen deficiency) in brain tissues, contributing to cellular damage and accelerating cognitive decline over time. By supporting healthy circulation, particularly in the cervical spine, chiropractic care helps ensure that the brain's energy needs are met, reducing the risk of vascular-related cognitive impairments.

Patients who undergo CBP treatments often report an increase in mental clarity, a reduction in neurological symptoms like vertigo, and even relief from chronic headaches and migraines. This improvement in brain function and reduction in neurological distress highlights the spine's impact on vascular health and the brain's broader health landscape.

In understanding the profound relationship between cervical alignment and brain blood flow, we see yet another reason why spinal health is essential to overall brain function. By ensuring that the vertebral arteries remain unobstructed, CBP provides a vital pathway for supporting cerebral blood flow, enriching cognitive performance, and fortifying the brain against vascular-related challenges. The process of aligning the spine, especially the cervical region, creates a foundation for improved neurovascular health and long-term brain vitality.

**Chiropractic BioPhysics (CBP): Beyond Recovery – Preventing Future Neurological Health Issues**

As we've explored, Chiropractic BioPhysics (CBP) is a powerful tool for supporting recovery after a concussion or spinal injury. But its benefits don't stop at recovery; CBP also offers preventive health benefits, making it a valuable approach for maintaining long-term neurological and overall wellness. By addressing spinal alignment and promoting optimal nerve function, CBP can reduce the risk of developing neurological and systemic health issues that arise from chronic misalignment.

Many health challenges, such as tension headaches, migraines, chronic neck and back pain, and even cognitive conditions, can be traced back to poor spinal health and misalignment. These issues often stem from prolonged stress on nerves, reduced blood flow, and impaired communication between the brain and body. Chronic spinal misalignments can act as a constant source of low-level stress on the nervous system, affecting how the body and brain function daily. Over time, this stress can contribute to systemic inflammation, hormonal imbalances, and heightened stress responses, all of which can accelerate aging and increase susceptibility to neurological conditions.

CBP's approach to maintaining optimal spinal health involves more than just symptom relief; it emphasizes the prevention of long-term structural and neurological issues. By ensuring that the spine maintains its ideal curvature and alignment, CBP practitioners help protect the spinal cord and nervous system from unnecessary strain and compression. This ongoing alignment allows nerves to operate freely without interference, supports a steady flow of blood and cerebrospinal fluid, and promotes a balanced autonomic nervous system (ANS). These factors play a significant role in reducing risks of neurodegenerative conditions like Alzheimer's, Parkinson's, and other cognitive disorders linked to inflammation and poor circulation.

**Strengthening Stress Resilience and Neurovascular Health Through CBP**

In fact, studies indicate that when spinal alignment is maintained, individuals are better equipped to manage both physical and emotional stress. Chronic stress impacts brain health by releasing stress hormones like cortisol, which, over time, can damage brain cells, particularly in areas associated with memory and emotional regulation, such as the hippocampus and amygdala. Proper spinal alignment reduces the chronic activation of the sympathetic "fight-or-flight" response, helping to calm the nervous system, lower cortisol levels, and prevent the adverse effects of prolonged stress on the brain. In doing so, CBP not only protects physical health but also strengthens mental resilience.

One of the most remarkable benefits of CBP as a preventive practice is its potential to preserve neurovascular health. With age, the vertebral arteries, which travel alongside the cervical spine and supply blood to the brain, become more susceptible to compression. This risk is heightened when the natural cervical curve is lost due to postural issues like forward head posture or conditions like "military neck," where the neck becomes straightened. By maintaining the cervical curve through CBP protocols, patients can reduce stress on these arteries, ensuring that blood flow to the brain remains steady and robust throughout life. This circulation is essential for cognitive function and helps guard against vascular-related conditions, such as **ischemic strokes** and **vascular dementia**, which are linked to restricted blood flow in the brain.

The preventive aspects of CBP extend beyond brain health, as spinal alignment also supports immunity and the body's ability to fight off infections and heal efficiently. The nervous system has a profound influence on immune function, with the spine acting as a critical interface. Misalignments in the spine, particularly around the thoracic and cervical regions, can disrupt nerve signals that help regulate immune responses. CBP adjustments ensure these signals reach the immune system unimpeded, bolstering the body's defense mechanisms and making it more resilient to infections and inflammatory conditions that can exacerbate neurological health.

. . .

Moreover, CBP helps individuals maintain balance and coordination as they age by providing the brain with clear, accurate proprioceptive input. Our sense of balance relies on signals from the spine and joints that inform the brain about body position. Chronic spinal misalignments can distort this feedback, making it harder for the brain to maintain balance and coordination, leading to an increased risk of falls and injuries, particularly in older adults. By keeping the spine aligned, CBP helps preserve postural stability, supporting a confident, active lifestyle and reducing the risk of accidents that can lead to further spinal or neurological damage.

## CBP as a Lifelong Health Strategy: Aligning Spine and Lifestyle for Holistic Wellness

For those seeking a holistic approach to health, CBP offers a comprehensive pathway to prevent future neurological and physical health challenges by addressing the spine's alignment in a way that harmonizes the entire body. CBP practitioners also educate patients on lifestyle choices, ergonomics, and posture-strengthening exercises to help maintain alignment outside the clinic. This education, coupled with regular assessments, empowers patients to take proactive steps toward preserving their health, giving them the tools to prevent common issues associated with aging and poor posture.

In this way, CBP becomes not just a treatment but a lifelong strategy for health, supporting mental clarity, reducing stress, and maintaining physical vitality. By focusing on spinal alignment, CBP practitioners provide a foundation for wellness that strengthens the body's defenses, enhances cognitive performance, and guards against the degenerative effects of aging. Chiropractic BioPhysics thus bridges the gap between short-term relief and long-term health, empowering individuals to thrive physically and mentally well into their later years. Through CBP's preventive approach, spinal health becomes a vital element of whole-body wellness, ensuring that the brain and body remain connected, resilient, and balanced for life.

. . .

**Final Thoughts on CBP and Todays Evidence Based Chiropractic**

Our spine is far more than a structural pillar; it is a dynamic system that profoundly impacts every part of our body, from basic movements to complex brain functions. Each curve, each vertebra, and each nerve that runs through it contributes to a symphony of communication between the brain and the body. Through the emerging research and insights explored in this chapter, it's clear that the health of our spine is directly linked to the health of our brain. Spinal misalignments, whether caused by injury, postural habits, or curvature disorders, can disrupt this connection, impairing blood flow, cerebrospinal fluid circulation, and nerve function, all of which play a role in cognitive clarity, emotional resilience, and overall neurological health.

Chiropractic BioPhysics (CBP) stands as a groundbreaking approach to spinal care, going beyond symptomatic relief to address the foundational alignment of the spine. By restoring natural curvature, CBP facilitates better circulation, clearer nerve signaling, and a balanced autonomic nervous system, supporting both physical and mental well-being. For those recovering from conditions like concussion, CBP provides a structured, evidence-based approach to restore alignment, reduce stress on the nervous system, and create an optimal environment for brain healing. For others seeking long-term health, CBP offers preventive strategies to maintain alignment, preserve neurovascular health, and protect against the degenerative effects of aging on the spine and brain.

The spine is not just a "backbone" but a lifeline—one that influences everything from cognitive function and stress response to immune health and balance. Through Chiropractic BioPhysics, we have the tools to align, support, and strengthen this lifeline, empowering us to live with greater mental clarity, physical resilience, and overall vitality. In nurturing spinal health, we give the brain the freedom to operate at its highest potential, unencumbered by the silent strains of misalignment, and enable ourselves to move through life with both strength and stability. The journey to optimal health is complex, but by embracing the foundational role of spinal alignment, we take a powerful step toward achieving lasting wellness for both body and mind.

# chapter 8 summary:
# the spine's influence
# on brain health

**Introduction: Beyond Structure**

- The spine is more than a structural support; it's essential for brain health and cognitive function.
- Proper spinal alignment ensures seamless communication between the brain and body.
- Misalignments disrupt blood flow, cerebrospinal fluid (CSF) circulation, and nerve signals, impacting mental and physical wellness.

**The Spine and the Nervous System**

- The spine houses the central nervous system (CNS), enabling communication between brain and body.
- Four natural curves distribute weight, absorb impact, and maintain even nerve flow.
- Misalignments lead to "traffic jams" in the CNS, causing: Sensory disturbances, motor deficits and autonomic imbalances (heart rate, digestion)
- Disrupted alignment affects mental clarity, physical performance, and emotional regulation.

## Impact on Cerebrospinal Fluid (CSF) Flow

- CSF cushions, nourishes, and cleanses the brain.
- Proper spinal alignment supports smooth CSF flow along the spinal cord.
- Misalignments restrict CSF movement, leading to: Reduced nutrient delivery, waste buildup in brain tissue and symptoms like headaches, cognitive fog and mood issues.
- Realignment therapies (e.g., CBP) restore CSF flow, supporting cognitive and emotional health.

## Autonomic Nervous System (ANS) Regulation

- The ANS controls essential bodily functions (heart rate, digestion).
- Misalignments, especially in the neck and upper back, overactivate the sympathetic "fight-or-flight" response.
- Chronic sympathetic dominance leads to: Anxiety, insomnia, high cortisol levels and inflammation that can damage brain cells (hippocampus)
- Spinal alignment helps balance ANS, lowering stress, improving heart rate variability (HRV), and supporting mental clarity and emotional stability.

## Brain Metabolism and Blood Flow

- Cervical spine alignment influences blood flow to the brain.
- Misalignments compress vertebral arteries, limiting oxygen and nutrient delivery.
- Effects of reduced blood flow: Mental fatigue, brain fog, increased neurodegenerative risks
- Chiropractic adjustments improve circulation, enhancing cognitive clarity and reducing neurological symptoms (e.g., migraines, dizziness).

## Neuroplasticity and Postural Stability

- Neuroplasticity (brain's adaptability) is linked to posture and alignment.
- Misalignments disrupt proprioceptive signals (body's spatial awareness), affecting balance.
- Chronic misalignment creates "low-level stress" on the nervous system, impacting mental clarity.
- Correcting alignment improves neuroplasticity, reducing cognitive strain and enhancing physical coordination.

## Preventive Health and Chiropractic BioPhysics (CBP)

- CBP offers preventive care, supporting long-term wellness and neurological health.
- Benefits of CBP: Reduced tension headaches, chronic pain, cognitive decline risks, lower stress and cortisol levels, supporting brain health, improved neurovascular health, reducing vascular-related cognitive decline and better postural stability, balance, and fall risk reduction in older adults
- CBP aligns spine and lifestyle, helping maintain neurovascular health, stress resilience, and cognitive performance into later life.

# afterword

The health of the spine is fundamental to brain health, as it supports cognitive clarity, emotional resilience, and physical vitality. Through Chiropractic BioPhysics (CBP), spinal alignment plays a critical role in maintaining proper blood flow, nerve signaling, and cerebrospinal fluid circulation, all of which contribute to overall mental and physical wellness. By prioritizing spinal alignment, we can enhance brain function and unlock the full potential of both body and mind, fostering lasting wellness.

# a request for your
# honest feedback

Now that you are part way through my book I'd like to invite you to share your thoughts and experiences by leaving an honest review on Amazon. Your feedback is not only important to me but also instrumental in enhancing the overall quality of this book. I am committed to delivering content that goes above and beyond your expectations, and your insights play a crucial role in achieving this.

Reviews not only help prospective readers make informed decisions but also provide me with an opportunity to address any areas that may need further clarification or expansion. Your observations and suggestions are immensely valuable as I strive to create a resource that truly empowers and supports you on your health journey.

Your reviews enable me to refine the content, fill any gaps that may exist, and ensure that the information presented is accessible and applicable to a wide audience.

My commitment to you is to deliver more value than you expect from this book. Your feedback will not only help shape the future editions but also contribute to the creation of a community dedicated to positive change and holistic well-being.

Thank you again for investing your time with my book, I look forward to hearing your thoughts and insights. Together, we can make a difference in the lives of many.

Wishing you health and happiness,

Dr. Heinrich

# neuro-insights

"Understanding the importance of the brain and spine in our overall health is the first step to living a long and successful life. Protecting them is key to longevity." – Dr. John L. D. Williams, Neurologist

"The brain is the key to our physical, mental, and emotional well-being. By ensuring it functions at its peak, we create the foundation for a healthy, vibrant life." – Dr. Tieraona Low Dog, Integrative Medicine Expert

# the science of brain health; exploring the role of supplements, nutrients, and gut-brain connections

**INTRODUCTION: The Brain-Body Connection in Wellness**

Our brains are as complex as they are miraculous. They govern our thoughts, emotions, memories, and essentially everything that makes us who we are. For centuries, humanity has searched for ways to enhance cognitive ability, improve memory, and delay mental decline. But in recent decades, the scientific quest to protect and enhance our minds has intensified, driven by the knowledge that our mental health is influenced by more than just genes or brain exercises. What we consume—from our diets to specific supplements—plays a vital role in shaping our cognitive resilience and capacity.

At first, it may seem odd to think that a fish oil capsule or a cup of green tea could impact our mood, memory, or mental clarity. But advances in neurobiology and nutrition science have revealed that the brain is highly sensitive to the chemical compounds circulating through our body. Our neurons, or brain cells, rely on a continuous supply of specific nutrients to build and repair themselves, communicate effectively, and manage the inevitable stresses they face daily.

This connection between what we eat and our brain health is known as *nutritional neuroscience*, an emerging field dedicated to understanding how dietary patterns, individual nutrients, and supplements influence the brain's structure and function. For instance, a lack of essential fatty acids can lead to impaired cell membrane function, affecting how neurons transmit signals. A deficit in vitamins like B12 and folate could result in cognitive decline due to rising homocysteine levels, a compound known to damage brain cells. In contrast, antioxidants like those in vitamin E can neutralize free radicals—unstable molecules that contribute to aging and neurodegeneration.

But the science of brain health extends beyond individual nutrients. Recent research has uncovered a fascinating link between our gut health and brain function, a connection known as the **gut-brain axis**. This bidirectional pathway enables the gut microbiota—trillions of microorganisms living in our intestines—to communicate with the brain, influencing mood, stress levels, and even cognitive function. Through intricate neural, hormonal, and immune mechanisms, our gut bacteria send signals that can either support or compromise our mental wellbeing.

In this chapter, we'll dive deep into these components of brain health: natural supplements, the gut-brain axis, essential vitamins, and how they all work together. Through exploring these elements, we'll see how each contributes to a holistic approach to cognitive vitality. This isn't just about adding years to life; it's about adding life to years, keeping our minds sharp, resilient, and prepared for the challenges and pleasures that lie ahead.

Each section will bring a sharper focus to the science behind these compounds and mechanisms. We'll explore which nutrients have been shown to protect the brain, enhance focus, and reduce the risk of neurodegenerative diseases—and perhaps most importantly, how these tools can be used synergistically to build a stronger, healthier brain.

## Natural Supplements for Cognitive Enhancement

### Omega-3 Fatty Acids

Let's start with the remarkable ***omega-3 fatty acids***, a group of polyunsaturated fats that our brains depend on, particularly the types called **DHA** (docosahexaenoic acid) and **EPA** (eicosapentaenoic acid). Think of these as the "good fats" that help to construct and maintain the integrity of our brain cells. About 60% of the human brain is made up of fat, and DHA is a major structural component of the cell membranes that enclose our neurons. These membranes are essential for brain cell communication, affecting everything from memory to mood.

Research into omega-3 fatty acids has shown their ability to reduce inflammation, one of the biggest contributors to age-related neurodegeneration. Inflammation, although a natural response to injury or infection, can become chronic due to factors like poor diet, stress, or environmental toxins. When that happens, the brain's cells become stressed, their function impaired, and they're more prone to damage. Studies show that higher levels of omega-3s can reduce these inflammatory markers, protecting neurons from the wear and tear that accumulates over time. In older adults, omega-3 supplementation has been linked to improved memory, attention, and processing speed, essentially slowing down the cognitive aging process.

Dr. Graham Jenkins, my co-author, explores this science in depth in *The Omega Solution: Fix Your Fats, Fuel Your Future*, the fifth book in the *100+ Living* series. Dr. Jenkins' analysis delves into the mechanisms by which omega-3s interact with cellular structures to support not only brain health but overall longevity. His work highlights the critical role these fatty acids play in both preventing and mitigating chronic inflammation, offering practical insights for incorporating them effectively into a daily regimen.

### Ginkgo Biloba

Moving on to another staple of brain supplements, ***Ginkgo Biloba*** is an ancient plant that has long been revered in traditional medicine, especially in Eastern cultures, for enhancing memory and mental clarity. The unique properties of Ginkgo come largely from its ability to enhance cerebral blood flow, providing neurons with a steady supply of oxygen and nutrients. This is especially relevant for aging populations, as blood flow to the brain naturally declines with age. Moreover, Ginkgo has antioxidant properties that protect brain cells from oxidative stress, a process in which free radicals damage cell membranes and DNA.

Ginkgo also influences neurotransmitters, the chemical messengers that relay signals between neurons. It's particularly beneficial for supporting dopamine and acetylcholine, two neurotransmitters that play essential roles in memory, learning, and attention. Additionally, Ginkgo has shown potential in reducing beta-amyloid accumulation—a hallmark of Alzheimer's disease—offering a degree of neuroprotection that makes it a valuable component in cognitive health supplements.

### L-Theanine and Caffeine

Next, consider the pair of *L-theanine and caffeine*, often consumed together in a simple cup of tea. Caffeine, a stimulant that most of us know well, can temporarily increase alertness and mental energy, but it often comes with a downside: jitteriness or a crash in energy later. Enter **L-theanine**, an amino acid found in tea leaves that provides a unique balancing effect. When paired with **caffeine**, L-theanine modulates brain waves, promoting a calm yet focused mental state without the overstimulation associated with caffeine alone.

Research has shown that this duo can improve focus and attention by increasing alpha brain waves, which are associated with relaxed alertness. This means L-theanine and caffeine allow us to concentrate more effectively while minimizing distractions and mental fatigue. It's a pairing that's increasingly used in cognitive supplements, offering an immediate boost in mental clarity and focus without the usual pitfalls of stimulants.

### Curcumin

Then there's *curcumin*, the active component of turmeric, a bright-yellow spice that has been used for centuries in Ayurveda and traditional medicine. Curcumin's benefits stem from its potent anti-inflammatory and antioxidant properties, which support the brain's natural defense against oxidative stress. It helps by reducing levels of inflammatory molecules like cytokines and promoting the production of neuroprotective proteins.

Curcumin also promotes neurogenesis—the creation of new neurons—a process critical for memory and learning. This is achieved through curcumin's ability to boost brain-derived neurotrophic factor (BDNF), a protein essential for the growth and survival of neurons. In this way, curcumin acts not just as a protector but as a promoter of new neural connections, helping to maintain cognitive function as we age.

Each of these natural supplements—omega-3s, Ginkgo Biloba, L-theanine with caffeine, and curcumin—offers unique benefits to brain health. But what's even more intriguing is how they can complement each other. When taken together, their individual mechanisms can amplify overall cognitive benefits, creating a multi-layered approach to brain health that supports everything from memory retention to focus and mood stability.

Before starting any supplementation, it's essential to consult your primary healthcare provider to ensure it's safe and appropriate for your individual needs.

## Gut-Brain Axis – The Role of Probiotics and Prebiotics

A fascinating area of modern science has uncovered that our gut health is far more than just a digestive concern; it's deeply intertwined with brain health, forming what scientists call the **gut-brain axis**. This is a network that allows our gut to communicate with our brain, with each influencing the other through a series of neural, hormonal, and immune pathways.

One of the primary ways the gut and brain communicate is through the **vagus nerve**, a long cranial nerve that acts like a superhighway for signals. In the gut, trillions of microorganisms—our gut microbiota—break down food, produce essential vitamins, and help maintain immune health. These microbes also produce neurotransmitters, like serotonin and dopamine, which play roles in mood regulation and cognitive function. About 90% of serotonin, often called the "happiness neurotransmitter," is actually produced in the gut. This intricate connection is why an imbalance in gut bacteria, or dysbiosis, can lead not only to digestive problems but also to anxiety, depression, and even cognitive issues.

**Probiotics**, the beneficial bacteria we can consume through foods like yogurt, kefir, or supplements, have been shown to influence mental health. When they reach the gut, probiotics can strengthen the gut lining, enhance the immune response, and promote the release of brain-supportive compounds like BDNF. By increasing the production of BDNF, probiotics directly support neuroplasticity, or the brain's ability to adapt and grow new connections. Studies have linked certain strains of probiotics to reduced symptoms of anxiety and depression, as well as improved mental flexibility and memory in older adults.

**Prebiotics**, the non-digestible fibers that feed probiotics, play a critical supporting role in this gut-brain connection. Prebiotics are found in foods like garlic, onions, and bananas and serve as fuel for the beneficial bacteria in our gut. When these bacteria consume prebiotics, they produce short-chain fatty acids like butyrate, which have anti-inflammatory properties. Butyrate and other short-chain fatty acids can cross the blood-brain barrier, reaching the brain and exerting anti-inflammatory and neuroprotective effects.

In aging populations, where cognitive decline can be exacerbated by inflammation and poor gut health, prebiotics provide a way to support a healthier microbiome, thereby indirectly supporting brain health. In fact, recent studies have suggested that both probiotics and prebiotics may play roles in reducing symptoms of Alzheimer's disease, likely by modulating inflammation and supporting the gut-brain axis in ways that positively impact cognitive function.

Together, probiotics and prebiotics form a foundational support system for the gut-brain axis. When used in tandem, they create an environment in the gut that fosters communication and balance with the brain, aiding in mood regulation, stress resilience, and cognitive clarity.

Dr. Graham Jenkins, my co-author, explores this relationship extensively in his book *Gut Mastery: Transform Your Health with Probiotics*, the third book in the *100+ Living* series. In it, he discusses how probiotics impact not only digestion but also mental wellness by balancing the microbiome and promoting the gut-brain connection. Jenkins' insights offer a comprehensive guide on how to harness probiotics for both physical and cognitive health, underscoring their importance in a holistic approach to well-being.

### Essential Vitamins for Brain Health

Vitamins are well known for supporting bodily health, but they play an equally crucial role in brain function, with certain vitamins directly affecting memory, mood, and cognitive resilience. Our focus here is on three vitamins that have shown powerful effects on the brain: Vitamin E, B-Vitamins, and Vitamin D.

### Vitamin E

Let's begin with *Vitamin E*, a fat-soluble antioxidant that is often praised for its protective effects on cells. The brain, rich in fatty tissue, is especially vulnerable to oxidative stress, which occurs when harmful free radicals build up and start damaging cells. This oxidative stress accelerates aging and has been linked to neurodegenerative diseases, including Alzheimer's. Vitamin E's ability to neutralize free radicals makes it an essential guard against this form of cellular decay.

Vitamin E doesn't just prevent damage; it also helps stabilize cell membranes, which are essential for the proper functioning of neurons. When cell membranes are healthy, neurons can efficiently transmit electrical signals, supporting both short-term and long-term memory. Studies have shown that individuals with higher levels of vitamin E have a slower rate of cognitive decline, suggesting that regular vitamin E intake may help preserve memory and cognitive function as we age. In particular, a form of Vitamin E known as alpha-tocopherol has demonstrated neuroprotective properties, specifically benefiting older adults who may be more susceptible to cognitive decline.

### B-Vitamins

Next are the *B-Vitamins*, which play multiple roles in brain health, particularly in energy metabolism, neurotransmitter synthesis, and DNA repair. Three B-vitamins—B6, B12, and folate—are especially critical for cognitive function. One of their main functions is to help regulate levels of homocysteine, an amino acid that, when elevated, has been associated with increased risks of Alzheimer's disease and other forms of cognitive decline. High homocysteine levels can lead to vascular issues and inflammation, which compromise blood flow to the brain, leading to potential neuron damage.

B12 and folate, in particular, are vital for DNA synthesis and cell repair, processes essential for maintaining a healthy brain. These vitamins also assist in producing neurotransmitters such as serotonin, dopamine, and GABA, which are closely linked to mood regulation and cognitive function. Studies have shown that B-vitamin supplementation can improve memory, reduce depressive symptoms, and slow cognitive decline in older adults. B6, B12, and folate together offer a targeted approach to protecting mental clarity and supporting overall brain health, particularly as we age.

### Vitamin D

Finally, there's *Vitamin D*, a vitamin that has recently gained attention for its wide-ranging effects on both physical and mental health. Known as the "sunshine vitamin" due to the body's ability to synthesize it when exposed to sunlight, Vitamin D plays a vital role in neuroprotection and immune modulation. The brain contains many vitamin D receptors, suggesting that this vitamin is deeply integrated into cognitive processes. Low levels of Vitamin D have been linked to a greater risk of mood disorders like depression, as well as to increased symptoms of anxiety and cognitive impairment.

One of the ways Vitamin D supports brain health is by reducing inflammation. In the brain, inflammation can disrupt the connections between neurons, impairing both memory and mood regulation. Vitamin D also influences the production of neurotrophic factors, which help neurons grow, survive, and form connections. This process, called neurogenesis, is crucial for learning and memory. For these reasons, maintaining adequate Vitamin D levels has been shown to support memory retention, mood stability, and general mental wellness. Given that many people are deficient in Vitamin D due to limited sun exposure or dietary intake, supplementation may offer a straightforward yet powerful way to bolster cognitive resilience.

Together, Vitamin E, B-Vitamins, and Vitamin D create a nutrient framework for brain health. Each of these vitamins plays a unique role, from protecting cells against oxidative damage to supporting neuro-transmitter production and promoting neurogenesis. By ensuring adequate levels of these essential vitamins, individuals can build a foundation for mental clarity, mood stability, and long-term cognitive function.

### Synergistic Effects and Practical Applications

One of the most exciting findings in the study of brain health is the realization that nutrients don't act in isolation. Many of the supplements, vitamins, and nutrients discussed so far can work together, amplifying their effects when combined. This concept of synergy, where the combined effect is greater than the sum of individual effects, is especially powerful in the context of cognitive health.

Consider, for example, the pairing of *L-theanine and caffeine*, as discussed earlier. L-theanine tempers the stimulating effects of caffeine, allowing for improved focus and mental clarity without the overstimulation that caffeine alone often causes. This makes the combination ideal for people who need sustained attention for extended periods, such as during study sessions or intense work tasks.

Another synergistic combination is *probiotics and prebiotics*, which

work together to support the gut-brain axis. Probiotics introduce beneficial bacteria into the gut, while prebiotics provide the necessary fuel for
these bacteria to thrive. Together, they create a healthy gut environment,
facilitating communication between the gut and brain. This combination can result in improved mood, reduced stress, and enhanced cognitive flexibility, all outcomes that are increasingly linked to a healthy
microbiome.

The synergy between *omega-3 fatty acids and B-vitamins* is also
noteworthy. Omega-3s provide the structural support for brain cells,
ensuring that cell membranes remain flexible and capable of efficient
communication. B-vitamins, on the other hand, support the brain's
energy metabolism and neurotransmitter synthesis, essential processes
for optimal cognitive performance. When combined, these nutrients
can enhance mental clarity, focus, and memory retention, offering
comprehensive support for cognitive health.

Then, there's the combination of *curcumin and vitamin D*, both of
which possess anti-inflammatory properties but through different
mechanisms. Curcumin reduces inflammatory cytokines, molecules that
trigger inflammation in the brain, while vitamin D modulates the
immune system and reduces chronic inflammation. Together, they
provide a robust defense against inflammation, which is a significant
contributor to cognitive decline. Regular supplementation with
curcumin and vitamin D may help prevent the onset of neurodegenerative diseases, supporting cognitive health well into later life.

### Building a Strong Foundation for Lifelong Brain Health

The path to cognitive wellness is multifaceted, encompassing diet,
lifestyle, and the targeted use of supplements. The science behind
omega-3 fatty acids, Ginkgo Biloba, curcumin, vitamins, and the gut-
brain connection reveals how much influence we can have over our
mental resilience. By thoughtfully incorporating these nutrients into
daily life, we can build a stronger, more adaptable brain capable of
facing the demands of modern life.

Each nutrient discussed in this chapter plays a part in the broader puzzle of brain health, whether by protecting neurons from damage, enhancing focus, or supporting the mood. Taken together, these supplements and vitamins offer a comprehensive strategy for maintaining cognitive vitality, not just in the immediate sense but as a long-term investment in mental well-being. With an understanding of how these compounds work and how they complement one another, anyone can take steps toward a future filled with mental clarity, emotional balance, and lifelong cognitive health.

# chapter 9 summary: nutrients and supplements for brain health and longevity

**Introduction: The Brain-Body Connection**

- The brain relies on nutrients and supplements to build, repair, and optimize neuron function.
- **Nutritional neuroscience** studies the impact of diet and nutrients on brain health, revealing links to memory, mood, and neurodegeneration.
- The **gut-brain axis** connects the gut microbiota with brain function, influencing mood, stress, and cognition.
- The chapter explores natural supplements, essential vitamins, and the gut-brain connection for cognitive vitality.

**Natural Supplements for Cognitive Enhancement**

1. **Omega-3 Fatty Acids**
2. DHA and EPA are essential for neuron cell membrane structure and communication.
3. Reduce inflammation and protect against neurodegeneration.
4. Linked to improved memory, attention, and slower cognitive decline
5. **Ginkgo Biloba**

6. Improves cerebral blood flow, enhancing oxygen and nutrient delivery to neurons.
7. Offers antioxidant protection and supports neurotransmitters like dopamine and acetylcholine.
8. May reduce beta-amyloid accumulation linked to Alzheimer's.
9. **L-Theanine and Caffeine**
10. Pairing promotes focused alertness without overstimulation.
11. Increases alpha brain waves for calm concentration.
12. Enhances mental clarity and reduces distractions.
13. **Curcumin**
14. Active compound in turmeric with potent anti-inflammatory and antioxidant properties.
15. Promotes neurogenesis by increasing brain-derived neurotrophic factor (BDNF).
16. Protects against oxidative stress and supports cognitive function as we age.

## Gut-Brain Axis: Role of Probiotics and Prebiotics

- **Gut-brain axis**: Bi-directional communication system linking the gut and brain through neural, hormonal, and immune pathways.
- **Microbiota's Role**: Produces neurotransmitters (e.g., serotonin, dopamine) and impacts mood and cognition.
- **Probiotics**:
- Beneficial bacteria found in yogurt, kefir, and supplements.
- Enhance gut lining, immune response, and BDNF production.
- Linked to reduced anxiety, depression, and improved memory.
- **Prebiotics**:
- Non-digestible fibers in garlic, onions, and bananas.
- Feed gut bacteria, producing anti-inflammatory short-chain fatty acids like butyrate.
- Support cognitive health and reduce Alzheimer's risk.

**Essential Vitamins for Brain Health**

1. **Vitamin E**

- Fat-soluble antioxidant protecting brain cells from oxidative stress.
- Slows cognitive decline and preserves neuron membrane health.

1. **B-Vitamins** (B6, B12, Folate)

- Regulate homocysteine levels, reducing risks of cognitive decline.
- Essential for DNA repair and neurotransmitter production (serotonin, dopamine).
- Improve memory, mood, and mental clarity.

1. **Vitamin D**

- Reduces inflammation and promotes neurogenesis (new neuron growth).
- Low levels linked to depression and cognitive impairment.
- Supports memory retention and mood stability.

**Synergistic Effects of Nutrients**

- **L-Theanine + Caffeine**: Boosts focus while reducing overstimulation.
- **Probiotics + Prebiotics**: Strengthens the gut-brain axis, supporting mood and cognition.
- **Omega-3s + B-Vitamins**: Enhances neuron function and energy metabolism.
- **Curcumin + Vitamin D**: Dual anti-inflammatory effects protect against cognitive decline.

**Building a Foundation for Brain Health**

- A holistic approach includes diet, lifestyle, and targeted supplementation.
- Combining nutrients amplifies their effects, supporting long-term mental resilience.
- Strategic use of supplements (omega-3s, Ginkgo, curcumin, vitamins) builds a healthier, sharper brain.
- A well-rounded plan nurtures cognitive vitality, emotional balance, and lifelong mental clarity.

# afterword

The nutrients and supplements we choose play a crucial role in maintaining brain health and promoting longevity. By incorporating essential vitamins, natural supplements like omega-3 fatty acids, ginkgo biloba, curcumin, and the powerful effects of the gut-brain axis, we can optimize cognitive function, reduce the risk of neurodegeneration, and support emotional well-being. A holistic approach that includes a balanced diet, targeted supplementation, and healthy lifestyle choices not only nurtures the brain but also enhances its resilience over time. By strategically combining these nutrients, we can build a stronger, sharper brain and foster lifelong mental clarity and vitality.

# neuro-insights

"We must keep our brain in mind as we age. A healthy brain can preserve the quality of life, prevent mental decline, and promote overall vitality as we grow older." – Dr. Sandra Bond Chapman, Cognitive Neuroscientist

"The best way to avoid neurodegeneration is to nurture the brain early and consistently—through good nutrition, physical activity, and mental stimulation." – Dr. Steven Gundry, Cardiologist

# environmental toxins and everyday chemicals: hidden threats to brain health

**INTRODUCTION: The Brain and Environmental Toxins**

In this chapter, we're going to dive into a world of scientific names and terms that may feel a bit like reading the back of a chemistry textbook. You'll encounter words like "polybrominated diphenyl ethers" and "methylmercury," and you might be tempted to skip over them, thinking they're too complex or irrelevant. But here's why it's worth paying attention: recognizing these names and understanding where they come from is the first step in protecting yourself and your loved ones from their potential harm.

These compounds aren't just technical jargon—they represent real, everyday threats to our brain health, and they're all around us. The list of neurotoxic chemicals we'll cover in this chapter is by no means exhaustive; our world contains far more than we could fit on a page. But by familiarizing yourself with some of the main offenders and how they impact the brain, you'll gain the knowledge to make informed, healthier choices in a world filled with hidden neurotoxins.

So, why does this all matter? The human brain is an astonishingly complex organ. It's the command center for everything we think, feel, remember, and experience. With its intricate network of neurons, the brain manages countless processes, from regulating our mood and emotions to solving problems and creating memories. But this powerful organ is also incredibly sensitive to outside influences, especially during early developmental stages and as we age. From the air we breathe to the products we bring into our homes, our environment can impact our cognitive health in profound ways.

Some of the chemicals and pollutants that we'll discuss may already sound familiar, like lead and mercury. Others, like polybrominated diphenyl ethers (PBDEs) and chlorpyrifos, might be less known but are just as concerning. These substances can accumulate in our bodies, interfere with the brain's communication pathways, and even cause lasting damage that's difficult to reverse. Understanding how they impact the brain helps us to better protect it, especially for those more vulnerable, like children and older adults.

One of the primary ways environmental toxins harm the brain is through oxidative stress—a process that damages brain cells by increasing free radicals, unstable molecules that wreak havoc on cell structures. When these free radicals overpower our body's natural defenses, they cause inflammation, cellular damage, and ultimately disrupt brain function. Over time, this can lead to cognitive issues, mood disorders, and even neurodegenerative diseases like Alzheimer's. For children, whose brains are still developing, the consequences can be even more significant, affecting IQ, memory, and behavior.

The brain's blood-brain barrier, a selective filter that prevents many harmful substances from reaching delicate neural tissue, is designed to protect us from these dangers. Yet, certain pollutants, especially tiny particles in air pollution and fat-soluble chemicals, can cross this barrier, embedding themselves in brain tissues where they continue to do damage. Understanding how these neurotoxins evade our body's defenses sheds light on why seemingly minor exposures can build up to pose serious threats over time.

In this chapter, we'll cover some of the main neurotoxins you're likely to encounter in daily life, where they come from, how they affect the brain, and what you can do to reduce exposure. We'll explore:

•**Heavy metals** like lead and mercury, which can impair cognitive function and are especially harmful to children's developing brains.

•**Air pollutants** that enter our systems through the very air we breathe, triggering inflammation and oxidative stress.

•**Household chemicals** hidden in everyday products, from cleaners to scented sprays, that disrupt brain function and mood.

•**Medications** like acetaminophen, commonly used but with emerging research suggesting caution during pregnancy and childhood.

•**Persistent organic pollutants** like PBDEs and pesticides, which linger in our environment and enter our bodies through food, water, and household items.

As we go through each of these, remember that knowledge is power. These substances may be invisible, but learning how to recognize and reduce exposure to them gives us a powerful tool to protect brain health. While it might feel overwhelming, know that even small, mindful changes can make a difference. Whether it's choosing a safer cleaning product or advocating for cleaner air, every step counts toward a healthier future for yourself and those you care about.

Let's begin our exploration of these hidden but manageable threats to brain health, one complex name at a time.

## Heavy Metals: Silent Saboteurs of Cognitive Health

Heavy metals—such as lead, mercury, cadmium, and arsenic—are naturally occurring elements that, in trace amounts, are present in various parts of our environment. However, human industrial activity has dramatically elevated our exposure to these metals, and they now present a significant risk to brain health. Unlike some toxins that the body can metabolize and eliminate relatively quickly, heavy metals tend to accumulate within the body, embedding themselves in tissues, including the brain, where they can disrupt cellular processes essential for cognitive function and neurodevelopment.

This section delves into the unique risks posed by each metal, explaining how these "silent saboteurs" infiltrate our lives and the physiological toll they take on the brain.

**Lead: The Hidden Neurotoxin in Everyday Life**

Lead is one of the most studied and well-known neurotoxic heavy metals, and for good reason. Despite widespread efforts to remove it from household paints, gasoline, and other consumer products, it persists in our environment, especially in older buildings, industrial areas, and contaminated soil. Once lead enters the body, it disrupts the balance of essential neurotransmitters—chemicals that transmit signals between nerve cells—by competing with calcium. Since calcium plays a crucial role in synaptic function and neurotransmitter release, lead can interfere with learning, memory, and attention processes by effectively hijacking the communication network within the brain.

The impacts of lead are particularly concerning in young children. Studies show that even low levels of lead exposure during critical periods of brain development can lead to irreversible reductions in IQ, as well as behavioral issues such as hyperactivity and aggression. One key reason for children's increased vulnerability is that their blood-brain barriers are still developing, making it easier for lead to penetrate and accumulate in brain tissues. Lead exposure has also been linked to reduced gray matter in the prefrontal cortex, the part of the brain responsible for decision-making, self-regulation, and complex problem-solving. This anatomical change corresponds to deficits in executive function, illustrating how lead can cause lasting cognitive impairments.

**Methylmercury: The Neurotoxin in Our Oceans**

Methylmercury, an organic form of mercury, is primarily found in certain types of fish and seafood. When mercury from industrial emissions enters the ocean, it is converted by aquatic microorganisms into methylmercury, which then accumulates in the food chain, particularly in predatory fish like tuna, swordfish, and king mackerel. Methylmercury is highly lipophilic, meaning it binds to fats, which allows it to pass through the blood-brain barrier and accumulate in brain tissues.

For the developing brain, methylmercury poses particularly grave risks. Prenatal exposure occurs when a pregnant individual consumes contaminated seafood, with the toxin crossing the placental barrier to the fetus. Studies on methylmercury exposure during pregnancy reveal that it can disrupt neural migration, a crucial process during which neurons travel to their designated locations in the brain. Disruptions in this process have been linked to cognitive and motor skill deficits in children, including lower IQ, language delays, and impaired fine motor skills.

In adults, chronic exposure to methylmercury can affect brain regions responsible for motor control, attention, and memory, leading to symptoms that range from tremors to difficulties with concentration and recall. Given these risks, health guidelines recommend that vulnerable populations, especially pregnant individuals and young children, limit their intake of high-mercury fish to reduce the potential neurotoxic impact.

**Cadmium and Arsenic: Toxic Elements with Lasting Consequences**

Cadmium and arsenic are lesser-known neurotoxins but pose equally significant risks to brain health. Cadmium exposure commonly occurs through contaminated air (due to industrial emissions), cigarette smoke, and certain foods, such as rice and leafy vegetables that absorb it from the soil.

. . .

Cadmium interferes with calcium channels in neurons, much like lead, and disrupts dopamine and serotonin regulation, neurotransmitters essential for mood and cognitive processing. Studies have linked chronic cadmium exposure to impairments in learning, memory, and emotional regulation.

Arsenic, often found in contaminated groundwater and certain foods like rice, disrupts cellular respiration, impairing the brain's energy production. The result is neurotoxic effects that manifest in various ways, from cognitive inflexibility to difficulties in processing new information. Research has shown that chronic arsenic exposure in children can result in long-lasting developmental issues, affecting language, spatial abilities, and overall intelligence.

**How Heavy Metals Impact the Brain at a Cellular Level**

What makes heavy metals particularly insidious is their ability to generate oxidative stress within the brain. As they accumulate in neural tissues, they promote the production of **reactive oxygen species (ROS)**, a type of free radical. These free radicals can damage proteins, lipids, and DNA within brain cells, disrupting cellular processes and potentially leading to neuron death. Over time, this oxidative damage can alter the structure of brain cells, disrupt neurotransmitter function, and impair synaptic plasticity—the brain's ability to form and reorganize synaptic connections in response to new information, a foundation for learning and memory.

Heavy metals are also known to disrupt the homeostasis of essential minerals in the brain, such as calcium, iron, and zinc, all of which are crucial for healthy brain function. For instance, lead and cadmium interfere with calcium signaling pathways, which are fundamental to neurotransmitter release, synaptic plasticity, and neuronal excitability.

Disruptions in these pathways can compromise the brain's ability to process information and respond to stimuli, leading to cognitive impairments and mood disorders.

**Reducing Exposure: Practical Steps for Everyday Protection**

Given the profound and potentially irreversible impact of heavy metals on the brain, reducing exposure is essential. While some sources of heavy metals may be unavoidable, several steps can help minimize contact:

- **Use Water Filters**: Invest in a high-quality water filter that can remove heavy metals, particularly if you live in an area with known water contamination issues. Look for filters certified to remove lead, mercury, and arsenic, as these metals are commonly found in municipal water supplies due to outdated piping and environmental runoff.
- **Choose Low-Mercury Seafood**: While seafood is an excellent source of essential nutrients like omega-3 fatty acids, some species contain high levels of methylmercury. Opt for lower-mercury choices, such as salmon, shrimp, and sardines, especially if you are pregnant or feeding young children.
- **Avoid Exposure to Contaminated Soil**: If you live in an area with industrial pollution or older buildings with lead-based paint, be cautious about soil exposure, particularly for children. Contaminated soil can be inadvertently ingested through hand-to-mouth contact, so encourage children to wash their hands after playing outside, and consider planting gardens in raised beds with uncontaminated soil.
- **Select Household Products Wisely**: Many common household products, including certain paints, ceramics, and batteries, can contain heavy metals. When possible, choose items labeled as free of lead, cadmium, or mercury, and consider replacing older items that may contain these metals.

- **Regular Testing for Heavy Metals**: For individuals concerned about chronic exposure, particularly in high-risk environments, regular testing can help monitor levels of heavy metals in the body. Medical professionals can provide tests for lead, mercury, and other heavy metals, offering insights into potential exposure sources and guiding further preventive measures.

Heavy metals, though seemingly invisible in our daily lives, have a powerful impact on brain health, accumulating silently and steadily in our bodies. By understanding how these neurotoxins enter our environment and affect our physiology, we can take informed steps to reduce exposure and protect our brains, especially during the vulnerable stages of childhood and pregnancy.

## Neurotoxic Chemicals in Everyday Products

Our homes are our sanctuaries, places where we expect to feel safe and secure. Yet, an unsettling reality lies beneath the surface of our everyday products: many contain chemicals that are quietly harming our brain health. From household cleaners and personal care products to the fragrances we use to make our spaces smell pleasant, these products can contain neurotoxic compounds capable of affecting our cognitive function. While most people are unaware of these risks, emerging research is shedding light on the ways common chemicals disrupt the delicate balance of our brain chemistry, leading to memory problems, mood disturbances, and even neurological diseases over time.

## Household Cleaners: The Unseen Neurotoxins in Our Homes

Household cleaners are a staple in nearly every home, designed to sanitize, disinfect, and polish. However, many of these products contain **volatile organic compounds (VOCs)**, a class of chemicals that readily evaporate into the air we breathe. VOCs are often used as solvents and include substances such as toluene, xylene, and acetone. These compounds can cross the blood-brain barrier, causing neuroinflammation and disrupting neural processes crucial for memory, learning, and emotional regulation.

**Toluene,** for example, is a solvent commonly found in multipurpose cleaners, industrial degreasers, and even some paints. This chemical has been shown to impair brain function by reducing levels of glutamate—a neurotransmitter that plays a central role in learning and memory—in the hippocampus. Research on prolonged exposure to toluene reveals that it affects the brain's white matter, the "wiring" that connects different regions, leading to cognitive decline and memory deficits. In severe cases, chronic exposure can result in symptoms that mimic those of dementia, illustrating how potent this chemical can be over time.

Another common chemical, **tetrachloroethylene,** often called "PERC," is a solvent widely used in dry cleaning and some household products. Studies indicate that PERC exposure has long-term effects on memory and executive function, with workers in the dry-cleaning industry reporting higher incidences of memory deficits and cognitive impairment. Even short-term exposure can cause dizziness and disorientation, illustrating its immediate effects on brain function. While exposure levels in household environments are typically lower than in industrial settings, repeated, low-level exposure adds up, potentially affecting cognitive abilities in subtle but significant ways.

Reducing exposure to these neurotoxins is achievable with some simple adjustments. Switching to non-toxic cleaning alternatives like vinegar, baking soda, and essential oils can provide effective cleaning power without the harmful side effects. Additionally, ensuring good ventilation when using any cleaning products can help disperse harmful VOCs, minimizing inhalation of these neurotoxic compounds.

**Fragrances and the Brain: Scents with Consequences**

The scent of a fresh home is something many people strive for, with air fresheners, scented candles, and perfumes often used to enhance the ambiance. However, these fragrances frequently contain a cocktail of synthetic chemicals, including phthalates and VOCs, which have been linked to neurological disturbances. While these substances are added to enhance and prolong scents, they can alter brain wave activity, leading to disruptions in mood, memory, and overall cognitive function.

**Phthalates**, often used as "fixatives" to make scents last longer, are especially concerning. These chemicals are endocrine disruptors, meaning they interfere with hormone systems that regulate everything from metabolism to mood. Phthalates have been linked to increased oxidative stress in the brain, a process that damages cells and accelerates aging. Studies reveal that regular exposure to phthalates can lead to symptoms such as headaches, mood swings, and cognitive impairments. Additionally, phthalates can interfere with neurotransmitter levels, potentially triggering neurological symptoms such as anxiety, irritability, and even cognitive confusion.

Fragrance chemicals can also exacerbate neurological symptoms in individuals with chemical sensitivities, including those with autism or asthma. Many people report experiencing migraines, brain fog, and even short-term memory lapses when exposed to fragrances in everyday environments. This phenomenon, sometimes referred to as "fragrance sensitivity," affects a significant portion of the population, with studies showing that up to 30% of individuals experience adverse neurological reactions to fragranced products.

To reduce the impact of fragrance chemicals on brain health, consider switching to unscented or naturally scented products. Essential oils, for example, can offer a pleasant scent without the neurotoxic side effects. Advocating for fragrance-free policies in workplaces and public spaces can also help protect those with fragrance sensitivities, creating a healthier environment for everyone.

## Neurotoxic Ingredients in Personal Care Products

Personal care products, including lotions, shampoos, and cosmetics, are designed to be applied directly to the skin, which is our body's largest organ and an effective absorption pathway for chemicals. Many of these products contain neurotoxic chemicals, such as parabens, triclosan, and formaldehyde-releasing preservatives. While these compounds are often present in small amounts, frequent, cumulative exposure can lead to adverse neurological effects over time.

Take **triclosan**, for example. This antimicrobial agent was widely used in hand sanitizers, soaps, and toothpaste for its bacteria-fighting properties. However, recent research suggests that triclosan can disrupt hormonal balance and contribute to oxidative stress in the brain. Triclosan has been found to inhibit a specific enzyme crucial for brain cell energy production, which may affect cognitive function when exposure is chronic. Due to these risks, the FDA banned triclosan in hand soaps, but it still exists in various other products, including certain toothpastes and cosmetics.

**Parabens**, commonly used as preservatives, also pose neurotoxic risks. These chemicals mimic estrogen, a hormone that plays a vital role in brain health, particularly in areas related to mood regulation and cognitive processing. Parabens have been linked to oxidative stress and mitochondrial dysfunction in brain cells, processes that can accelerate aging and lead to cognitive decline. Research indicates that regular use of paraben-containing products can lead to accumulation in the body, with potential long-term impacts on cognitive and emotional health.

. . .

To reduce exposure to neurotoxic personal care ingredients, look for "paraben-free" or "formaldehyde-free" labels, and consider switching to natural personal care products. Checking ingredient lists and opting for brands that prioritize non-toxic formulations can go a long way in reducing cumulative neurotoxin intake.

## Practical Strategies for Reducing Neurotoxic Exposure from Everyday Products

Protecting yourself and your family from neurotoxic chemicals requires awareness and small but impactful changes. Here are some key strategies for reducing exposure:

1. **Choose Non-Toxic Cleaning Products**: Look for natural, non-toxic alternatives to conventional cleaners. Vinegar, baking soda, and essential oils are all effective and safe choices for various cleaning needs.
2. **Opt for Fragrance-Free or Naturally Scented Products**: If fragrance is essential, opt for products scented with pure essential oils instead of synthetic fragrances, which often contain neurotoxic compounds.
3. **Select Organic Produce When Possible**: Organic farming limits pesticide use, reducing the risk of pesticide residues on fruits and vegetables.
4. **Read Labels on Personal Care Products**: Choose products that are free from parabens, triclosan, formaldehyde, and other potentially neurotoxic ingredients.

Everyday products are meant to make life more convenient and enjoyable, but when they contain neurotoxic chemicals, they become hidden threats to brain health. By understanding these risks and making informed choices, we can create a safer environment at home, reducing exposure to neurotoxins and promoting lifelong cognitive wellness.

**Fluoride: Balancing Benefits and Neurotoxic Risks**

Fluoride, a mineral added to water supplies in many areas to reduce dental decay, has sparked considerable debate regarding its neurotoxic potential. While fluoride in small, controlled doses has clear dental benefits, recent studies suggest that high concentrations may carry neurodevelopmental risks. Research has associated excessive fluoride exposure with reduced IQ scores and cognitive issues, especially in children whose developing brains are more susceptible to environmental influences.

The proposed mechanism involves fluoride's potential to affect the pineal gland, which helps regulate melatonin production and circadian rhythms. Disruption in this gland's function may indirectly influence cognitive and behavioral outcomes. Additionally, some researchers propose that high fluoride levels contribute to oxidative stress in brain cells, although further studies are needed to confirm this effect in humans.

To balance the dental benefits with potential neurotoxic risks, consider the following strategies:

- **Filter Drinking Water**: For those concerned about fluoride exposure, a reverse osmosis filter can help reduce fluoride levels in drinking water.
- **Check Local Fluoride Levels**: Some areas have naturally high fluoride levels in groundwater, and many municipalities provide information on fluoride concentration. Knowing the fluoride levels in your local water supply can help you make informed choices.
- **Consider Fluoride-Free Dental Products for Children**: For very young children, whose developing brains are most vulnerable, some parents choose fluoride-free toothpaste until they are old enough to reliably avoid swallowing it.

## Folic Acid, Tylenol, and Brain Health: Potential Risks for Pregnant Mothers

Acetaminophen, better known by its popular brand name Tylenol, has long been a staple in medicine cabinets around the world. It's one of the most commonly used over-the-counter medications for relieving pain and reducing fever, praised for its effectiveness and availability. Pregnant individuals, in particular, are often encouraged to use Tylenol as a safer alternative to other pain relievers like ibuprofen, which is generally advised against during pregnancy. However, recent research is raising questions about whether this household go-to might carry hidden risks, particularly for the developing brain of a fetus or young child.

## The Role of Glutathione and the Brain's Defense Against Oxidative Stress

To understand why scientists are rethinking acetaminophen use during pregnancy and early childhood, it's important to look at a substance called glutathione. Glutathione is a powerful antioxidant that protects brain cells from oxidative stress, a type of cellular damage caused by free radicals—unstable molecules that can harm DNA, proteins, and cell membranes. Oxidative stress is a natural byproduct of many bodily processes, but when it becomes excessive, it can damage neurons, the specialized cells in the brain responsible for communication and memory.

In adults, oxidative stress is linked to various neurodegenerative diseases like Alzheimer's and Parkinson's, but in developing brains, the stakes are even higher. Babies and young children have limited reserves of antioxidants like glutathione, making them more vulnerable to oxidative damage.

For the fetal brain, which is rapidly developing new neurons and connections, protecting against oxidative stress is critical. Any reduction in glutathione can compromise this delicate balance, potentially leading to lasting effects on brain structure and function.

## How Acetaminophen Impacts Glutathione Levels

While acetaminophen is widely viewed as safe, it has a lesser-known side effect: it depletes glutathione levels. The mechanism is simple—acetaminophen is processed in the liver, where it undergoes a transformation that uses up glutathione as part of the detoxification process. In small doses, this depletion isn't necessarily dangerous, as the body can usually restore its glutathione levels after the medication is metabolized. However, when acetaminophen is taken frequently, as it often is by those managing chronic pain or frequent discomfort, glutathione depletion can become more significant, leaving the body with reduced defenses against oxidative stress.

For adults, occasional use may not lead to lasting issues, but in pregnant individuals and young children, who already have limited antioxidant defenses, this depletion poses a particular concern. Studies suggest that when glutathione levels are lowered, the fetal brain becomes more vulnerable to oxidative damage, potentially interfering with normal brain development and setting the stage for cognitive and behavioral challenges later in life.

## Acetaminophen, Brain Development, and Research Findings

In recent years, scientific interest in acetaminophen's impact on brain health has led to multiple studies exploring the drug's effects on neurodevelopment, particularly during pregnancy and infancy.

One key area of research has focused on how acetaminophen affects the formation of neural connections and neurotransmitter levels in developing brains. Neurotransmitters like dopamine and serotonin are crucial for mood regulation, learning, and memory, and even slight disruptions during brain development can lead to long-term effects.

. . .

Animal studies provide some compelling evidence about the potential risks. One study found that acetaminophen exposure in young mice was associated with memory deficits and altered brain chemistry, particularly in regions responsible for learning and spatial memory.

While animal models don't always translate directly to humans, these findings underscore the need for caution, as the mechanisms of brain development are often similar across species. The observed memory impairments and changes in neurotransmitter systems align with what researchers might expect to see in young children exposed to the same chemical stressors.

Further human studies offer additional insights. A large study published in 2021 examined acetaminophen use in pregnant individuals and linked frequent use to an increased risk of neurodevelopmental issues in children, such as attention-deficit hyperactivity disorder (ADHD) and autism spectrum disorder (ASD). While these findings don't conclusively prove a causal relationship, they do suggest that regular acetaminophen use during pregnancy could have subtle, long-lasting effects on the child's brain function. This data encourages pregnant individuals to approach acetaminophen with caution and to consult with healthcare providers before using it frequently.

**The Folate Connection: Protecting Fetal Development from the Start**

Alongside the acetaminophen conversation, another crucial factor in prenatal health is ensuring the right form of vitamin B9—folate—is part of the maternal diet. Folate supports DNA synthesis, cell division, and neural tube development, all essential for a healthy pregnancy.

Folic acid, the synthetic form of folate, is a common ingredient in prenatal vitamins and fortified foods. However, it requires enzymatic conversion by the body into its active form, 5-methyltetrahydrofolate (5-MTHF). For many, this process is seamless. But for roughly 60% of individuals, a genetic mutation in the *MTHFR* gene reduces their ability to convert folic acid effectively. This can lead to unmetabolized folic acid accumulating in the bloodstream, potentially elevating homocysteine levels, which are associated with pregnancy complications like preeclampsia and fetal growth restriction.

Unmetabolized folic acid may also impact mental health. Methylation, the biochemical process supported by active folate, is critical for neurotransmitter synthesis. Impaired folate metabolism can contribute to postpartum depression, as the body struggles to maintain the necessary processes for mood regulation.

For mothers with *MTHFR* mutations—or anyone looking to ensure optimal nutrient absorption—choosing supplements with 5-MTHF instead of folic acid is a smart alternative. Unlike folic acid, 5-MTHF is bioavailable immediately, bypassing the need for enzymatic conversion. This adjustment can lower the risk of neural tube defects, support maternal mental health, and promote healthier pregnancy outcomes overall.

**Practical Recommendations for Pregnant Individuals**

Given these findings, pregnant individuals should consider a holistic approach to their health:

- **Limit Acetaminophen Use**: Only take acetaminophen when absolutely necessary, and consult with a healthcare provider for alternative pain management strategies.
- **Prioritize Folate Sources**: Choose prenatal vitamins with 5-MTHF instead of folic acid to ensure better absorption and reduce potential risks associated with folic acid buildup.
- **Consult Your Provider**: Regularly discuss supplement choices, pain relief methods, and overall health strategies

with a healthcare professional to tailor recommendations to your specific needs.

By addressing both medication use and nutrient support, pregnant individuals can better navigate these critical months and prioritize both their health and their baby's development. Making informed choices—about what you put in your body and why—is one of the most empowering steps toward a healthy pregnancy and beyond.

**Creating a Safer Environment for Brain Health**

Our brains are remarkable, intricate organs that power everything we do, from thinking and feeling to learning and creating. They are also incredibly vulnerable to environmental toxins—substances that are often invisible, insidious, and intertwined with the conveniences of modern life. From the air we breathe to the products we use, these neurotoxic threats may seem overwhelming, but understanding them gives us a powerful tool: the ability to make informed choices.

In this chapter, we explored how heavy metals, air pollutants, household chemicals, and even certain medications can affect cognitive function, brain development, and mental health over time. By delving into the science of how these substances interact with our brain cells and impact neurodevelopment, we've uncovered the pathways through which these toxins create harm. While the risks are real, they are also manageable. Small but intentional steps can reduce our exposure, protecting both our health and that of future generations.

# chapter 10 summary: neurotoxins in our environment, homes, foods and medications

**Introduction: The Brain and Environmental Toxins**

- **Neurotoxic chemicals** from our environment can harm brain health through oxidative stress, inflammation, and direct disruption of neural processes.
- Key culprits include heavy metals, air pollutants, household chemicals, pesticides, and certain medications.
- The brain's **blood-brain barrier** filters toxins but is not impervious to all harmful substances.
- Vulnerable populations include children (developing brains) and older adults (aging neural systems).
- Understanding and reducing exposure to neurotoxins is critical for lifelong brain health.

**Heavy Metals: Silent Saboteurs of Cognitive Health**
**1. Lead**

- Found in old paints, contaminated soil, and industrial areas.
- Interferes with calcium, disrupting neurotransmitter function, memory, and attention.
- Particularly harmful to children, leading to reduced IQ, behavioral issues, and prefrontal cortex damage.

## 2. Methylmercury

- Present in seafood like tuna, swordfish, and king mackerel.
- Crosses the placental and blood-brain barriers, disrupting neural migration in fetuses.
- Impairs motor control, memory, and attention in adults.

## 3. Cadmium and Arsenic

- **Cadmium**: Found in cigarette smoke, contaminated air, and certain foods. Disrupts calcium channels and neurotransmitter regulation, impairing memory and mood.
- **Arsenic**: Found in groundwater and rice. Impairs brain energy production and cognitive flexibility, especially in children.

## 4. How Heavy Metals Affect the Brain

- Accumulate in brain tissues, causing **oxidative stress** and neuron damage.
- Disrupt essential mineral homeostasis (e.g., calcium, iron, zinc), impairing synaptic plasticity and cognition.

## 5. Reducing Exposure

- Use water filters to remove lead, mercury, and arsenic.
- Choose low-mercury seafood (e.g., salmon, shrimp, sardines).
- Avoid contaminated soil; wash hands after outdoor activities.
- Opt for household items labeled free of heavy metals.

**Neurotoxic Chemicals in Everyday Products**
### 1. Household Cleaners

- Contain **volatile organic compounds (VOCs)** like toluene and acetone, which cross the blood-brain barrier.
- Cause neuroinflammation, memory deficits, and cognitive decline.
- Reduce exposure by switching to non-toxic cleaners (e.g., vinegar, baking soda) and improving ventilation.

### 2. Fragrances

- Contain synthetic chemicals like **phthalates** that disrupt hormones and increase oxidative stress.
- Linked to headaches, mood swings, and cognitive impairments.
- Opt for unscented or naturally scented products (e.g., essential oils).

### 3. Personal Care Products

- Contain neurotoxic chemicals like **triclosan** and **parabens**, which disrupt brain energy production and neurotransmitter levels.
- Opt for products labeled "paraben-free" and "formaldehyde-free."

### 4. Fluoride

- Excessive exposure is linked to reduced IQ and cognitive issues.
- Use reverse osmosis filters and consider fluoride-free toothpaste for young children.

## Folic Acid, Tylenol, and Brain Health
### 1. Acetaminophen (Tylenol)

- Depletes **glutathione**, reducing antioxidant defenses against oxidative stress.
- Prenatal and early-life use linked to memory deficits, ADHD, and autism spectrum disorder (ASD).
- Limit acetaminophen use during pregnancy and consult healthcare providers for alternatives.

### 2. Folate (Vitamin B9)

- Critical for DNA synthesis, neural tube development, and neurotransmitter production.
- **5-MTHF** (active folate) is preferable to folic acid for individuals with MTHFR gene mutations.

# afterword

Environmental toxins represent a significant yet manageable threat to cognitive health. By raising awareness and making small, intentional changes, we can reduce exposure, particularly for vulnerable populations. Protecting brain health requires making informed choices regarding the products we use, the food we eat, and the lifestyle habits we adopt, all of which contribute to ensuring lifelong cognitive wellness.

# neuro-insights

"If we take care of our brain and nervous system, we will not only extend our lives but enhance the quality of those years, free from disease and mental decline." – Dr. Daniel G. Amen, Psychiatrist and Brain Health Expert

"Our brains are responsible for everything we do, think, and feel. Maintaining brain health is key to maintaining a long, successful life." – Dr. Richard Carmona, Former Surgeon General of the United States

eleven

## cultivating focus in the age of overstimulation: a path to brain health

IN THE MODERN WORLD, our attention is one of the most valuable commodities—targeted by companies, entertainment platforms, and social networks all designed to keep us engaged and coming back for more. The mechanisms behind these distractions are deliberate and precise, harnessing behavioral science to capture and hold our focus. Apps, games, and social media use notifications, endless scrolling, and personalized recommendations to deliver a constant stream of stimulation. This has transformed our environment into one of unending engagement, where even brief moments of silence or stillness can feel almost uncomfortable.

The result? A collective drop in our ability to focus. Studies are beginning to reveal the depth of this problem, highlighting how our interactions with technology are fundamentally changing our brains. Neuroplasticity, the brain's ability to reorganize itself by forming new neural connections, means that our daily habits can alter our cognitive architecture. When we frequently engage with fast, fragmented information online, our brains adapt to this environment, becoming more prone to distraction and craving the constant "hit" of novelty. In other words, we're shaping our minds to work in shorter bursts, making sustained focus more challenging.

. . .

This phenomenon has implications beyond mere attention spans. Researchers have noted that frequent shifts in attention—like those we experience when switching between phone notifications, work emails, and social media updates—can lead to a phenomenon called **cognitive switching penalty**. Each time we shift from one task to another, our brain needs to recalibrate, which requires energy and effort. Studies estimate that, on average, it can take more than 20 minutes to fully regain focus after a distraction. When multiplied across an entire day, these interruptions can have significant impacts on productivity, mental clarity, and even emotional well-being.

## Screen Overexposure Impacts Brain Development and Cognitive Health

The concern is especially pronounced in younger generations who have never known a world without digital devices. Research on digital exposure in early life indicates that constant engagement with screens can interfere with critical stages of brain development. During these periods, the brain is exceptionally "plastic" and vulnerable to external stimuli, which can influence the formation of crucial neural pathways for attention, memory, and emotional regulation. This early and often excessive exposure to digital devices may set the stage for attentional issues and impairments in later life, as well as contribute to an overall decrease in cognitive flexibility—the ability to adapt to new information and shift perspectives easily.

The ubiquity of screens has led scientists to a startling prediction: that many of us may experience early cognitive decline or even **digital dementia**, a form of memory and focus impairment linked to prolonged digital overstimulation. Symptoms resemble those of early-stage dementia, including poor memory retention, decreased learning abilities, and impaired attention spans. Alarmingly, while dementia is typically associated with aging, digital dementia can affect people much earlier in life, altering cognitive functions that are essential for navigating the world with ease and confidence.

These challenges highlight a need to rethink how we engage with our digital world. By recognizing the toll that overstimulation takes on our brains, we can begin to implement strategies to protect our attention and cognitive well-being. Science shows us that the human brain is resilient and adaptable, capable of strengthening itself with the right mental "workouts" to counterbalance the digital distractions. In the following sections, we will delve into the science of attention, memory, and focus, exploring techniques that can help us reclaim control over our minds in this hyper-stimulated world.

This journey is about more than simply improving focus; it's about preserving our cognitive health and fostering a mind that can thrive amid the demands of the modern world.

**The Cognitive Cost of Overstimulation**

The age of digital technology has changed us. Over the last few decades, our average daily screen time has skyrocketed, embedding screens into nearly every aspect of our lives. The convenience and instant gratification they offer are undeniable, but science is beginning to unveil the hidden cost: our minds are paying a steep price. The gradual erosion of our ability to focus is only the start—overstimulation also carries profound implications for memory, learning, and even emotional stability.

One of the most concerning effects of excessive screen time is the impact on our attention spans. Studies from the early 2000s revealed that the average attention span of a human was around 12 seconds. Fast forward to the digital age, and this number has reportedly shrunk to around eight seconds—shorter than that of a goldfish. While this statistic has sparked debates, it draws attention to a larger trend: our collective struggle to focus. Constant digital interaction seems to encourage "bottom-up" attention—our brains are constantly responding to external stimuli rather than focusing from within. This shift weakens our ability to engage in sustained, "top-down" attention, where we consciously direct focus on a chosen task or thought.

When we engage in top-down processing, we actively decide what to concentrate on, aligning our attention with specific goals or tasks. This process is in contrast to "bottom-up" processing, where attention is driven by external stimuli—like a phone ringing or a flashing notification—that captures our focus without our conscious decision. Studies have shown that excessive engagement in bottom-up processing can weaken the brain's top-down control, leaving us more vulnerable to distractions and less able to stay focused on complex, self-directed tasks.

The danger extends far beyond momentary distractions. Emerging research warns of digital dementia, particularly among younger generations who have grown up with screens. The theory is that chronic exposure to fragmented information, such as what we encounter on social media, news feeds, or endless notifications, trains the brain to expect information in bite-sized, shallow snippets. This impairs our ability to think deeply, connect ideas, and retain information long-term.

**Memory is Attention**

Memory itself is intricately linked to attention. Neuroscientists explain that our ability to store information in long-term memory relies on how effectively we pay attention in the moment. When our focus is constantly being pulled away, our brain has less opportunity to encode information properly. The brain's memory centers, particularly the hippocampus, rely on focused attention to consolidate new information. Studies indicate that a constant influx of new stimuli prevents the brain from fully processing and storing experiences, leading to more frequent memory lapses and a diminished capacity for retaining knowledge.

For children and adolescents, the effects of overstimulation can be even more pronounced. Their brains are still developing, meaning that consistent digital engagement shapes neural pathways at a fundamental level. Key areas like the prefrontal cortex—the region responsible for decision-making, self-regulation, and complex thought—are particularly susceptible to the effects of overstimulation.

Research conducted by the American Academy of Pediatrics and other institutions has shown that prolonged screen exposure during early developmental years can lead to delays in executive functions such as problem-solving, emotional regulation, and impulse control. These children may find it harder to concentrate, retain information, or control their impulses, issues that can extend into adulthood and even increase their risk for conditions like ADHD.

**Stress, Sleep Disruption, and Cognitive Resilience**

Another dimension of this overstimulation is its impact on stress and mental health. Studies indicate that frequent shifts between tasks and screens, such as checking a phone during work or switching between apps, elevate cortisol levels, the body's primary stress hormone. The link between screen-induced overstimulation and anxiety is now well-documented, as the constant demand on our focus leaves us in a near-constant state of alert. Over time, this chronic activation of the brain's stress-response system can erode mental resilience, making us more susceptible to anxiety, depression, and cognitive fatigue.

This overstimulation also affects sleep, a critical factor for cognitive health. When we engage with screens before bed, the blue light emitted by devices suppresses the production of melatonin, a hormone essential for sleep regulation. Poor sleep quality has been shown to impair attention, memory, and overall cognitive function, leading to a negative feedback loop where overstimulation during the day contributes to sleep disruption, which in turn further hampers mental clarity and focus.

One of the most compelling insights into the cost of overstimulation comes from studies examining its effects on cognitive resilience, or the brain's ability to withstand and adapt to mental challenges. People who frequently switch between tasks or consume large amounts of digital media show diminished cognitive resilience, meaning they are less equipped to handle complex tasks and recover from mental fatigue. Neuroimaging studies reveal that the brain areas associated with cognitive resilience—the prefrontal cortex and anterior cingulate cortex—are less active in individuals who are constantly multitasking. This reduced resilience can have long-term consequences, especially as we age, potentially increasing our risk for cognitive decline and neurodegenerative diseases.

These findings underscore that the impact of overstimulation goes beyond simple inconvenience; it alters the very foundations of how our minds operate. When we lose the ability to focus deeply, our cognitive efficiency, memory, and mental health all suffer. But while the problem is significant, understanding the science behind it empowers us. By recognizing the toll that constant stimulation takes, we gain the knowledge to counteract these effects through mindful practices and deliberate, focused attention. In the sections that follow, we'll dive into actionable strategies to reclaim our focus, enhance memory, and preserve our mental well-being.

## Mechanisms Behind Attention and Memory Decline

Understanding the mechanics of how our brains process focus and memory sheds light on why overstimulation has such a profound effect on our cognitive health. Attention and memory are deeply intertwined; one cannot exist effectively without the other. Attention is the gateway to memory—it allows us to process and prioritize information in real-time, while memory enables us to store and recall that information when needed. Together, they form the basis for all learning and cognitive resilience. When attention is constantly disrupted, however, memory storage weakens, and our mental agility diminishes. Let's explore the science behind these processes and why overstimulation disrupts them.

At the center of our attention mechanism lies a network of brain regions known as the **fronto-parietal attention network**. This network coordinates our focus by controlling the intensity and direction of our attention. The prefrontal cortex, often called the "executive" part of the brain, plays a key role here, helping us suppress irrelevant stimuli and stay locked in on our chosen task. Imagine the prefrontal cortex as a mental "gatekeeper," sorting through sensory inputs and deciding which ones are worthy of attention and which are distractions. However, with persistent overstimulation, this gatekeeper becomes overwhelmed, unable to manage the constant flood of information. As a result, attention becomes fragmented, and our ability to concentrate steadily declines.

Another brain region heavily involved in focus and memory is the **hippocampus**, often referred to as the brain's "memory center." The hippocampus is essential for encoding and consolidating new memories, acting as a storage system where experiences and learned information are retained for later recall. Effective memory encoding relies on a few key factors: undivided attention, emotional engagement, and adequate processing time. When we're constantly interrupted by notifications, multitasking, or switching between tasks, we disrupt this encoding process, making it harder for information to stick.

This constant "attention residue" that builds up from rapid task-switching can linger long after we've moved on to a new task. Research suggests that the brain takes time to fully shift from one activity to another, and this delay creates what psychologists refer to as the cognitive switching penalty. Even short interruptions can reduce our performance on subsequent tasks. For instance, one study found that people who were interrupted during a complex task took, on average, 23 minutes to fully regain their focus. Each interruption isn't just a momentary lapse; it weakens our ability to retain information, solve problems, and even make effective decisions, as our brains are not fully present in any one task.

## How Overstimulation Disrupts Deep Learning

Memory encoding and recall are also closely tied to brain wave patterns, which change based on our mental state. When we're in a focused, relaxed state, our brains exhibit theta waves, which are crucial for deep learning and information retention. However, in states of distraction or overstimulation, the brain shifts to higher-frequency beta waves, associated with alertness and stress. This state is useful in short bursts—such as when facing an immediate challenge—but harmful when sustained over long periods. In a state of high-beta frequency, the brain has difficulty with deep processing and is less likely to create stable, long-term memories. Over time, this reliance on quick, surface-level processing, rather than deeper cognitive engagement, can erode our memory retention and make it more difficult to retrieve information.

A crucial but often overlooked aspect of focus is the brain's ability to exercise cognitive control, or the capacity to regulate attention in alignment with long-term goals. Each time we focus on a task and resist distractions, we activate neural pathways that strengthen cognitive control. This process relies on neurotrophic factors, such as Brain-Derived Neurotrophic Factor (BDNF) and Nerve Growth Factor (NGF). These molecules play a pivotal role in neural health, supporting the growth, maintenance, and plasticity of neurons, especially in brain regions associated with learning and memory. BDNF, for example, has been shown to increase in response to sustained mental effort, particularly in tasks requiring prolonged concentration. It essentially "feeds" the neurons, keeping them resilient and adaptable. However, when we fail to sustain attention, these neurotrophic factors decrease, making it harder for the brain to develop new neural connections essential for learning and mental agility.

## Emotional Toll of Overstimulation

Finally, the impact of overstimulation on the brain isn't just limited to the cognitive domain; it affects our emotional regulation as well. Chronic overstimulation and fragmented attention disrupt the balance of neurotransmitters like dopamine, which is associated with reward and motivation. Many digital platforms exploit this dopamine response to keep us engaged, offering constant rewards in the form of likes, notifications, or new content. Over time, our brains start to crave these small bursts of pleasure, leading to a cycle of dependency on external stimuli for satisfaction. This dopamine-driven loop can make everyday activities feel dull or unfulfilling, as our brains become conditioned to need constant novelty to feel rewarded. In other words, the same chemical that's essential for motivation can also trap us in a loop of superficial engagement, leaving us less able to focus on activities that require sustained effort and deeper thought.

When we understand these mechanisms—how attention works, how memory is encoded, and how overstimulation disrupts them—we gain a clear perspective on why reclaiming focus is so essential. It's not simply a matter of productivity; it's about protecting our cognitive foundation and mental resilience. Our brains are built for deep, sustained focus, but they need the right conditions to thrive.

The path forward involves intentional practices that can help us rebuild our cognitive control and, ultimately, create a mind capable of withstanding the pressures of an overstimulated world.

. . .

## Reclaiming Focus: Evidence-Based Strategies

In our overstimulated world, regaining control over our focus isn't simply about willpower; it requires deliberate techniques rooted in cognitive science. Fortunately, research provides a number of strategies that can help us reclaim our attention, reduce mental fatigue, and build resilience against the distractions that surround us. In this section, we'll explore scientifically validated practices like meditation, the Attention Training Technique (ATT), the benefits of exercise with an external focus, and the profound effects of long-term mindfulness. Each approach offers a unique pathway to restoring our cognitive strength, nurturing mental flexibility, and fostering a healthier, more resilient brain.

## Meditation: Building Mental Fortitude

Meditation, especially practices that focus on sustained attention, is one of the most well-studied methods for enhancing focus and reducing the impact of overstimulation. By training the mind to concentrate on a single point of focus—whether it's the breath, a word, or an image—meditation helps us build attentional endurance, a kind of mental stamina that makes it easier to resist distractions. The power of meditation lies in its ability to strengthen the brain's "attentional network"—the interconnected areas responsible for sustaining focus and filtering out unnecessary information.

Short-term meditation can yield remarkable results. A study conducted by neuroscientist Yi-Yuan Tang demonstrated that even five days of integrative body-mind training (IBMT), a form of mindfulness meditation, led to improved attention, reduced anxiety, and lowered cortisol levels, a stress hormone. Cortisol is closely linked to the brain's fight-or-flight response, and chronically elevated levels can impair cognitive function. By reducing cortisol, meditation helps clear the mental clutter that often contributes to distracted thinking.

. . .

Beyond short-term gains, long-term meditation can lead to profound structural changes in the brain. Research led by neuroscientist Sara Lazar at Harvard University found that consistent meditation practice increases the cortical thickness in regions related to attention and sensory processing. This cortical thickening essentially adds "processing power" to the brain, allowing for improved focus and quicker recovery from distractions. Additionally, long-term meditators exhibit increased gray matter density in the hippocampus, the brain's memory center, suggesting that meditation supports memory retention and cognitive clarity.

## Attention Training Technique (ATT): Redirecting the Mind's Focus

The Attention Training Technique (ATT) is a method specifically designed to strengthen cognitive control by training individuals to shift their focus outward, away from internal thoughts and anxieties. Developed by clinical psychologist Adrian Wells, ATT helps practitioners manage cognitive anxiety by using auditory cues to shift attention toward the external environment, breaking the cycle of self-focused thinking that can contribute to mental fatigue and anxiety. It's particularly effective for people who struggle with overthinking or are easily distracted by their own thoughts, as it promotes a more flexible approach to attention.

ATT exercises usually involve listening to audio tracks that guide the listener to notice different sounds or sensations in their environment. This directed, outward focus reduces the mind's tendency to ruminate on internal concerns and instead trains it to pay attention to what is happening in the present. Studies have shown that ATT can significantly reduce symptoms of anxiety, improve attentional flexibility, and help individuals better manage intrusive thoughts. In a world full of mental distractions, ATT offers a way to reclaim mental space by reorienting focus to what's around us, reducing cognitive load and strengthening our overall capacity to concentrate.

. . .

## Exercise with an External Focus: Enhancing Physical and Mental Performance

While it may seem surprising, the way we focus during physical exercise can have significant impacts on both cognitive and physical endurance. Research in sports psychology suggests that directing attention externally—focusing on the environment or the desired outcome rather than the movement itself—leads to enhanced physical performance and can also improve mental resilience. This concept is known as "external focus of attention," and it's been shown to reduce mental effort, allowing the brain to process tasks more efficiently.

One study published in *Psychology of Sport and Exercise* found that athletes who focused on the movement's effect (e.g., the path of a basketball) rather than their body (e.g., arm motion) experienced improved performance, faster learning, and even greater physical stamina. From a cognitive perspective, focusing externally during exercise reduces the mental load placed on the brain, which enhances endurance and allows for more sustained attention. The benefits extend to non-athletes as well; applying an external focus in physical activities like running, hiking, or yoga can reduce the perceived effort and boost our ability to concentrate.

This approach also stimulates the release of endorphins and dopamine—neurotransmitters associated with pleasure, motivation, and cognitive resilience. These "feel-good" chemicals can enhance mood and focus, counteracting the fatigue that often accompanies overstimulation. By practicing external focus during exercise, we not only improve physical performance but also reinforce our capacity for sustained attention, helping us stay more present and resilient in other areas of life.

. . .

## Long-Term Meditation and Mindfulness: A Deeply Transformative Practice

While short-term meditation offers rapid benefits, long-term, intensive meditation and mindfulness training can result in profound, enduring changes in brain function. One landmark study led by Clifford Saron at the University of California, Davis, involved a group of participants in a three-month meditation retreat, during which they practiced mindfulness for up to five hours each day. The results were astounding: participants showed significant improvements in sustained attention and an increase in perceptual sensitivity. This means that their ability to focus for prolonged periods improved, as did their capacity to notice subtle details in their environment.

From a neurological perspective, these changes reflect increased neural efficiency and connectivity within the brain's attentional networks. Long-term meditation has been shown to enhance the connectivity between the prefrontal cortex, which is responsible for executive control, and the default mode network (DMN), which is active during mind-wandering and self-referential thought. Strengthening this connection allows for better regulation of the DMN, effectively helping meditators quiet "mental noise" and remain grounded in the present.

Moreover, intensive meditation has been associated with an increase in gamma wave activity, a type of brain wave linked to high-level cognitive functioning, clarity, and even states of heightened awareness. Gamma waves are thought to promote the binding of sensory experiences into a coherent "whole," supporting cognitive integration and memory consolidation. This means that long-term meditators may be better equipped to handle multiple sources of information without feeling overwhelmed, an invaluable skill in today's fast-paced, overstimulated world.

. . .

These scientifically backed strategies—ranging from meditation and ATT to exercise with an external focus—provide powerful tools for strengthening focus and protecting cognitive health. By integrating these practices into our daily routines, we create mental habits that not only improve attention but also build a brain that is more adaptable, resilient, and capable of thriving in the face of distraction.

**Nurturing Attention to Prevent Cognitive Decline**

In the quest to build a resilient, healthy mind, nurturing our ability to focus is as critical as regular exercise or a balanced diet. Recent research underscores that attention not only helps us perform day-to-day tasks but also serves as a buffer against cognitive decline, potentially lowering our risk for neurodegenerative diseases like Alzheimer's and other forms of dementia. Just as physical activity strengthens muscles and cardiovascular health, mental practices that enhance focus and cognitive control help reinforce the brain's neural networks, building resilience that protects against age-related decline.

Our attention spans and memory are not static; they are constantly shaped by the habits we cultivate and the ways we engage with our environment. Scientists studying cognitive aging have found that sustained focus is key to maintaining **cognitive reserve**—the brain's ability to compensate for damage and maintain function despite aging or disease. Cognitive reserve operates much like a mental buffer, with those who have greater reserves demonstrating a lower risk of cognitive impairment even in the face of brain changes typically associated with aging.

One study, published in *Neurology*, highlighted that people who regularly engage in mentally stimulating activities, such as reading, problem-solving, or practicing mindfulness, exhibit higher levels of cognitive reserve, which correlates with a reduced risk of dementia. The mechanisms behind this protection are both structural and functional. Structural changes include an increase in gray matter density, which supports memory and learning, while functional changes refer to the brain's improved ability to recruit alternative neural pathways when faced with cognitive challenges. Essentially, a brain that has been "exercised" through sustained focus and mental engagement is better equipped to handle the challenges that come with aging.

This cognitive reserve model highlights the importance of consistency. Practicing focus-enhancing activities doesn't merely provide temporary mental clarity; it builds up a reservoir of cognitive health that can protect the brain over time. Cognitive resilience—our mind's ability to adapt and maintain performance under stress or fatigue—relies on this reserve. Studies show that people who frequently engage in focus-intensive activities demonstrate higher cognitive flexibility, allowing them to switch tasks more effectively and recover from distractions more quickly. This adaptability is crucial for staving off the cognitive slowdown that often accompanies aging.

## Attention-Focused Practices

In addition to increasing cognitive reserve, attention-focused practices also help regulate emotional well-being, which is another critical factor in maintaining cognitive health. The relationship between attention and emotion is a two-way street; each affects the other. When we practice focus, we're training our brains to stay present, a state that's less vulnerable to rumination or worry, both of which are linked to stress and depression. Chronic stress has been shown to accelerate cognitive decline by shrinking the hippocampus and weakening neural connections in the prefrontal cortex, which is essential for decision-making and attention. By cultivating habits that reduce stress—such as meditation or even structured screen-free activities—we are not only enhancing focus but also protecting the brain from these damaging effects.

These focus-enhancing practices are essential not just for cognitive endurance but also for neuroplasticity, the brain's ability to rewire itself in response to new experiences. Neuroplasticity declines with age but can be sustained or even revitalized through certain mental exercises. Practices like mindfulness meditation and mental focus training stimulate the production of Brain-Derived Neurotrophic Factor (BDNF), a protein that promotes the growth and maintenance of neurons. BDNF is sometimes called "Miracle-Gro for the brain" due to its profound impact on mental flexibility, learning, and memory. In a series of studies, individuals who practiced focus-intensive activities exhibited higher levels of BDNF, suggesting that these activities can help the brain remain adaptable and healthy well into older age.

As stated in previous chapters, the fascinating aspect of BDNF production is its role in neurogenesis, the process by which the brain creates new neurons. For decades, scientists believed that adults could not produce new neurons, but recent studies have shown that neurogenesis does indeed occur, particularly in the hippocampus. However, this process slows down with age and is highly susceptible to lifestyle factors. Mentally engaging activities, such as meditation, cognitive games, and even focused exercise, have been shown to stimulate neurogenesis, effectively "growing" new neurons that enhance memory and attention. This discovery highlights that the more we engage in activities that demand focus and mental engagement, the more we protect our brain's structure and function in the long term.

## Digital Hygiene: A Daily Routine for Attention Health

In an age where screens are ubiquitous and interruptions are constant, practicing digital hygiene has become essential for maintaining our mental well-being and cognitive clarity. Digital hygiene refers to the intentional habits we build around our technology use—practices that help us avoid overstimulation, reduce stress, and improve our focus. Just as brushing our teeth is a daily ritual to protect our oral health, digital hygiene can serve as a daily safeguard for our mental and cognitive health.

·  ·  ·

The science behind digital hygiene shows that small adjustments in our technology use can have profound effects on our brain. When we establish boundaries with our digital devices, we reduce the brain's cognitive load, allowing it to rest and recharge. Constant digital engagement, particularly with social media and rapid notifications, keeps the brain in a state of heightened alertness. This state, while useful in short bursts, becomes problematic when sustained, as it prevents the mind from entering periods of calm that are crucial for memory consolidation, emotional regulation, and creativity. By introducing tech-free routines, we essentially provide the brain with "quiet time" that supports cognitive function and emotional balance.

One foundational practice of digital hygiene is setting specific limits around screen time. Studies show that excessive screen time is associated with higher levels of anxiety, depression, and stress. Limiting screen exposure allows our minds to decompress, reducing these negative effects. For example, creating "technology-free" zones in the home, like the dining room or bedroom, can reinforce boundaries and help establish a healthier relationship with screens. Research from the University of Pittsburgh found that participants who used social media less frequently showed greater improvements in mood and lower levels of anxiety, likely because they were less exposed to social comparison, constant updates, and information overload.

Another simple yet effective practice is to schedule dedicated "tech-free" hours each day. This could be the first hour after waking up or the hour before bed—times when mental clarity and focus are most beneficial. Starting the day without immediately checking a phone or email gives the brain a chance to wake up naturally, fostering a calm and focused mindset that can set a positive tone for the rest of the day. The blue light emitted by screens suppresses melatonin production, the hormone responsible for sleep, and checking our phones just before bed can lead to poorer sleep quality.

. . .

**Enhancing Focus, Productivity, and Mental Clarity**

Studies show that people who avoid screens at least one hour before bed fall asleep faster and report more restful sleep, which in turn supports better focus and memory the following day.

An additional layer of digital hygiene involves structuring our interaction with devices during the day. The Pomodoro Technique, a popular productivity strategy, aligns well with the principles of digital hygiene. This technique suggests working in focused 25-minute intervals followed by short breaks, a structure that supports sustained attention while minimizing mental fatigue. By focusing intensely on a task for a set period and then stepping away—even for five minutes—we allow the brain to rest, which can enhance productivity and prevent burnout. Additionally, this technique reinforces cognitive control, training our attention to stay on one task without the urge to multitask or check our devices.

Another highly beneficial habit is to engage in "deep work" periods—uninterrupted blocks of time dedicated to complex or creative tasks. Cal Newport, author of *Deep Work*, describes this as a period of focused, undistracted effort that allows for a flow state, a mental condition in which people feel deeply immersed and productive. During deep work, the brain's attentional networks are intensely active, allowing for a level of focus that is both satisfying and mentally rejuvenating. Studies show that those who regularly engage in deep work experience improved productivity and report a greater sense of fulfillment from their work, as well as enhanced mental resilience and cognitive flexibility.

Aside from setting boundaries and practicing deep work, engaging in screen-free activities that require sustained focus is another powerful aspect of digital hygiene. Reading a book, practicing a hobby, or spending time in nature offers the brain a break from digital overstimulation. These activities activate different cognitive pathways, giving our attention networks a chance to rest and reset. A study published in *Environmental Health Perspectives* found that spending time in nature reduces cortisol levels and increases alpha brain waves, which are associated with relaxation and focus. Even a short daily walk outside can help reduce mental fatigue, enhance mood, and sharpen focus by giving the brain a natural break from digital stimuli.

Finally, it's important to actively manage notifications on devices. By default, our phones and computers are designed to interrupt us frequently with pings, banners, and vibrations. While notifications may seem like minor interruptions, they activate our brain's alert system, diverting our focus from the task at hand. Every time we're interrupted, we experience a "switch cost," the cognitive penalty of shifting our attention from one task to another. Turning off non-essential notifications or setting devices to "Do Not Disturb" mode during work hours can help minimize these interruptions, allowing for deeper, more sustained focus. In a 2015 study by Gloria Mark at the University of California, Irvine, participants who turned off their email notifications for a few days reported feeling significantly less stressed and were able to complete their tasks more efficiently.

The cumulative effect of these digital hygiene practices is a mind that is less reactive, more present, and better equipped to handle the demands of modern life. Practicing digital hygiene empowers us to engage with technology in a way that supports, rather than detracts from, our mental well-being and cognitive health. In our fast-paced digital world, cultivating these habits isn't just about reducing distractions; it's about safeguarding the brain from overstimulation and fostering a balanced, resilient mind.

By integrating digital hygiene into our daily routines, we create a sustainable framework for mental clarity and focus. These small but consistent practices enable us to reclaim our attention, nurture our cognitive reserves, and lay the groundwork for a healthy, resilient mind well into the future. Embracing digital hygiene as part of a broader focus-centered lifestyle allows us to thrive in the digital age without sacrificing our cognitive health—a choice that is increasingly essential as technology continues to evolve.

# chapter 11 summary: cultivating focus in the age of overstimulation

**The Modern Attention Crisis**

- Attention has become a valuable commodity, targeted by companies and social platforms designed to hold our focus.
- Features like notifications, endless scrolling, and recommendations create a cycle of constant engagement.
- This environment undermines our ability to sustain focus and alters brain function through neuroplasticity.

**Impact on Brain and Behavior**

- Frequent shifts in attention lead to a "cognitive switching penalty," requiring significant time and energy to regain focus.
- Younger generations face unique risks as excessive screen exposure during developmental years impacts attention, memory, and emotional regulation.
- Digital overstimulation has been linked to "digital dementia," a decline in memory and focus resembling early-stage dementia, but occurring earlier in life.

**Attention and Memory Interplay**

- Attention is essential for encoding information into long-term memory.
- Fragmented attention prevents the brain from properly consolidating experiences, leading to memory lapses and weakened learning capacity.
- The hippocampus and prefrontal cortex—key regions for memory and decision-making—are particularly vulnerable to overstimulation.

**Emotional and Cognitive Toll**

- Overstimulation elevates cortisol levels, creating chronic stress that impairs cognitive resilience.
- Blue light from screens disrupts melatonin production, reducing sleep quality and further harming focus and memory.
- Reduced cognitive resilience and multitasking habits weaken the brain's ability to adapt and recover from mental fatigue, increasing susceptibility to long-term cognitive decline.

**Mechanisms of Focus and Overstimulation**

- Overstimulation shifts brain activity toward bottom-up processing (reacting to external stimuli) rather than top-down focus (intentional attention).
- Rapid task-switching creates attention residue, making sustained focus on complex tasks difficult.
- Over-reliance on shallow, quick information processing inhibits the creation of long-term memories.

**Reclaiming Focus: Key Strategies**

1. **Meditation:** Builds attentional endurance and improves cortical thickness and gray matter density in memory-related regions.
2. **Attention Training Technique (ATT):** Guides focus outward to reduce internal distractions, improving attentional flexibility.
3. **External Focus in Exercise:** Directing attention to the environment or outcome during physical activities boosts cognitive resilience and endurance.
4. **Deep Work Practices:** Engaging in uninterrupted, focused work sessions strengthens neural networks and enhances productivity.

**Nurturing Attention to Prevent Cognitive Decline**

- Sustained focus increases cognitive reserve, a buffer against age-related decline and neurodegenerative diseases.
- Practices that stimulate neuroplasticity, such as mindfulness and mental exercises, promote the production of BDNF, supporting neuron growth and memory retention.
- Mental engagement through reading, problem-solving, and hobbies helps protect against cognitive decline.

**Digital Hygiene: Protecting Attention**

- Limiting screen exposure, creating tech-free routines, and managing notifications reduce cognitive load and distractions.
- Techniques like the Pomodoro method and structured "deep work" sessions help maintain focus and prevent burnout.
- Screen-free activities and time in nature reduce cortisol levels, enhance mood, and allow for mental recovery.

- Turning off non-essential notifications minimizes interruptions, reducing the cognitive costs of task-switching.

# afterword

Reclaiming our attention goes beyond boosting productivity; it is a crucial aspect of maintaining long-term brain health and emotional well-being. By adopting focus-centered habits and practicing digital hygiene, we can safeguard our cognitive reserves and cultivate a brain that is both resilient and adaptable. These strategies empower us to navigate the challenges of the digital age while preserving mental clarity and enhancing our overall quality of life.

# neuro-insights

"The brain is like a muscle; the more you use it, the stronger it gets. Protect it, nourish it, and it will carry you throughout your life." – Dr. Daniel G. Amen, Psychiatrist and Brain Health Expert

"The health of your brain should be your number one priority. Every thought, every action, and every decision you make comes from it." – Dr. David Perlmutter, Neurologist and Author

# alcohol and brain health – a balancing act

ALCOHOL HAS LONG HELD a celebrated place in human culture. It is a staple of social gatherings, a way to mark celebrations, and, for many, a tool to relax at the end of a long day. Yet beneath its social appeal lies a complex and often misunderstood relationship with our most vital organ: the brain. While a glass of wine or a pint of beer may seem harmless, alcohol's effects on the brain extend far beyond the fleeting buzz or relaxation it provides.

As a psychoactive substance, alcohol alters the brain's chemistry almost immediately. These changes can range from subtle shifts in mood and perception to profound disruptions in memory, judgment, and behavior. But the effects don't stop there. Over time, alcohol can reshape the brain's physical structure and neural pathways, leading to lasting impacts on cognition, emotional health, and even aging. The brain is an incredibly adaptive organ, but alcohol's pervasive influence can challenge its resilience in ways that are often underestimated.

This chapter isn't about demonizing alcohol or promoting abstinence for everyone. Instead, it's about uncovering the science behind alcohol's interactions with the brain, offering insight into how it works and why its effects are so pervasive. From its immediate influence on neurotransmitters to its long-term impact on stress, memory, and aging, understanding alcohol's role in brain health equips you with the knowledge to make choices that align with your goals.

We'll start by exploring the unique chemistry of alcohol—what makes it capable of crossing the brain's natural defenses and disrupting its delicate systems. From there, we'll delve into how it affects your mood, habits, and resilience over both the short and long term. By the end, you'll have a clearer picture of how alcohol fits into the larger story of your health, and the tools to decide what's right for you.

**The Chemistry of Alcohol: A Brain-Penetrating Toxin**

Alcohol is a fascinating substance—not because of what it does, but because of how it does it. Unlike most substances we consume, alcohol has an uncanny ability to permeate nearly every part of the body. From the moment it enters your bloodstream, it begins a journey that few other compounds can match, crossing barriers and infiltrating tissues that are normally off-limits. Chief among these is the blood-brain barrier, a specialized shield designed to protect the brain from harmful substances. For alcohol, however, this barrier is no obstacle.

At the heart of alcohol's unique power is its molecular structure. Ethanol, the active ingredient in alcoholic beverages, is both water-soluble and fat-soluble. This dual solubility allows it to slip seamlessly through cell membranes, which are composed of fatty lipids, and into the brain. Unlike drugs that bind to specific receptors on the surface of cells to produce their effects, alcohol enters cells directly, exerting its influence from within. This is why its effects can feel so immediate and widespread.

. . .

Once in the brain, alcohol begins to alter the delicate balance of neurotransmitters—the chemical messengers that control everything from mood and memory to coordination and impulse control. It enhances the activity of gamma-aminobutyric acid (GABA), the brain's primary inhibitory neurotransmitter, while simultaneously suppressing glutamate, its main excitatory counterpart. This dual action slows brain activity, creating the familiar sensations of relaxation and sedation. At the same time, alcohol stimulates the release of dopamine, a neurotransmitter associated with pleasure and reward, which explains the initial feelings of euphoria that often accompany drinking.

But the brain isn't the only organ affected by alcohol. The liver, tasked with metabolizing ethanol, transforms it into a highly toxic compound called acetaldehyde. Acetaldehyde is so damaging that the body must quickly convert it into acetate, a less harmful substance. While most of this process occurs in the liver, small amounts of alcohol are metabolized directly in the brain, exposing its delicate tissues to the harmful effects of acetaldehyde. This exposure, combined with alcohol's ability to generate free radicals—unstable molecules that damage cells—contributes to oxidative stress and inflammation, two key drivers of brain damage.

Even a single episode of drinking disrupts brain function in profound ways, but the cumulative effects of regular alcohol use are far more concerning. Over time, the brain adapts to alcohol's presence by rewiring its neural pathways. These changes are not random; they reflect the brain's attempt to maintain balance in the face of repeated disruptions. Unfortunately, this adaptation often leads to tolerance, dependence, and a host of long-term consequences, including memory problems, emotional instability, and reduced cognitive flexibility.

Alcohol's ability to cross the blood-brain barrier and infiltrate neurons is both its allure and its danger. While it can create moments of joy, relaxation, or sociability, its chemical properties ensure that the brain pays a price. To truly understand alcohol's impact, it's essential to move beyond its chemistry and explore its immediate and long-term effects on the brain's most critical systems.

**Acute Effects on Brain Function: The Pleasure-Pain Balance**

The effects of alcohol can be both seductive and deceiving. In the short term, alcohol often feels like a social enabler, a stress reliever, or even a mood booster. But beneath the surface, alcohol is creating a cascade of chemical changes in your brain that can have both immediate and lasting consequences. To understand these effects, we must look at the interplay between alcohol and the brain's reward system—a delicate balance of pleasure and pain.

When alcohol first enters the brain, it stimulates the release of dopamine, a neurotransmitter often called the brain's "feel-good" chemical. This dopamine surge activates the brain's reward pathway, the same system that responds to natural pleasures like food, social connection, and physical intimacy. This explains the initial feelings of euphoria, confidence, and relaxation that many people experience after a drink or two. Alcohol also increases serotonin levels, another neurotransmitter associated with mood regulation, which adds to its calming and uplifting effects.

But alcohol's pleasant effects are fleeting. As the body begins to metabolize the ethanol, dopamine and serotonin levels quickly drop, leaving behind a void. This is the "crash" that often follows the initial high—a subtle but persistent sense of unease, irritability, or low mood. This dip in mood can drive a person to drink more, chasing the fleeting pleasure alcohol initially provided. The more frequently this cycle occurs, the more the brain begins to associate alcohol with reward, setting the stage for habitual or compulsive drinking.

. . .

## Short-Term Effects on Brain Balance

Beyond the reward system, alcohol also disrupts the balance between excitatory and inhibitory neurotransmitters in the brain. By enhancing the activity of gamma-aminobutyric acid (GABA), the brain's main inhibitory neurotransmitter, alcohol slows neural activity, creating a sedative effect. This is why alcohol can make you feel relaxed or drowsy. At the same time, alcohol suppresses glutamate, the primary excitatory neurotransmitter responsible for stimulating brain activity. This combination dampens overall brain function, affecting memory, coordination, and decision-making.

This dual action on GABA and glutamate explains many of alcohol's classic effects. As GABA floods the brain, it suppresses activity in the prefrontal cortex, the region responsible for decision-making and impulse control. This is why people often become more talkative, uninhibited, or impulsive after drinking. At higher doses, alcohol's suppression of glutamate can interfere with the hippocampus, the brain's memory center, leading to blackouts—periods of time where memories are not properly encoded and later cannot be recalled.

While alcohol slows brain function in some areas, it paradoxically increases activity in others, such as the amygdala, the brain's emotional processing center. This can lead to heightened emotional reactivity, making people more prone to laughter, tears, or anger when intoxicated. The emotional highs and lows of drinking can leave a person feeling emotionally unbalanced, even after the alcohol has worn off.

For all its acute effects, the brain's response to alcohol is not just about what happens in the moment. With repeated exposure, the brain begins to adapt to these chemical disruptions, reshaping its neural pathways to accommodate alcohol's presence. Over time, these changes can make the brain less responsive to natural rewards and more reliant on alcohol to achieve a sense of pleasure or normalcy.

. . .

Alcohol's ability to manipulate the brain's pleasure-pain balance is at the heart of its allure—and its danger. It offers a brief respite from stress or discomfort but often leaves behind a heightened sensitivity to both. Understanding these short-term effects is essential for appreciating the deeper, long-term changes alcohol can create in the brain.

**The Long-Term Impact: Neural Circuitry and Habit Formation**

While the immediate effects of alcohol are fleeting, its long-term influence on the brain is anything but. Over time, repeated exposure to alcohol doesn't just disrupt the brain's chemistry—it rewires its neural circuits, reshaping the way it processes pleasure, manages impulses, and handles stress.

These changes are both a survival mechanism and a vulnerability. The brain adapts to alcohol in an attempt to maintain balance, but this adaptation often comes at a cost: the reinforcement of habits and behaviors that can be difficult to break.

**How Alcohol Rewires the Brain**

At the heart of the brain's adaptability is neuroplasticity—the ability to form new connections and reshape existing ones in response to experience. Neuroplasticity is essential for learning, memory, and recovery from injury, but it is also the mechanism through which alcohol entrenches itself in the brain's reward pathways.

The first area of the brain affected is the mesolimbic dopamine system, often referred to as the brain's "reward center." With repeated drinking, this system becomes hypersensitive to alcohol. Each time you drink, the brain releases a burst of dopamine, reinforcing the association between alcohol and pleasure. Over time, these bursts become harder to achieve naturally, leading to a phenomenon known as "reward system blunting." In this state, the brain's response to natural rewards like food, social interaction, or achievement diminishes, while its craving for alcohol intensifies.

In addition to altering the reward system, alcohol also affects the prefrontal cortex, the region of the brain responsible for decision-making, impulse control, and self-regulation. Chronic alcohol use weakens the prefrontal cortex, reducing its ability to override urges or consider long-term consequences. This creates a feedback loop: as the prefrontal cortex becomes less effective, the basal ganglia—the part of the brain that governs habitual behaviors—gains more influence. This shift explains why drinking can become automatic or compulsive, even in situations where it is no longer enjoyable or beneficial.

**From Habit to Dependence**

At first, drinking may feel like a conscious choice—a way to relax, celebrate, or socialize. But as alcohol reshapes the brain's circuitry, it shifts from being a deliberate act to an ingrained habit. The basal ganglia, which store routines and habits, play a central role in this process. Once drinking becomes habitual, it is less about pleasure and more about meeting an ingrained expectation. This is why even casual drinkers may find themselves reaching for a drink in specific situations, like after work or during social gatherings, without consciously deciding to do so.

For those who drink heavily, this transition from habit to dependence is marked by further changes in the brain. The amygdala, which regulates emotions like fear and stress, becomes hyperactive in the absence of alcohol. This heightened activity creates feelings of anxiety or discomfort, which drinking temporarily alleviates. Over time, the cycle of drinking to escape these negative emotions reinforces dependence, making it increasingly difficult to quit.

. . .

**Cognitive and Emotional Consequences**

Chronic alcohol use doesn't just affect the brain's reward and habit systems—it also takes a toll on cognitive and emotional health. Some of the most common long-term effects include:

- **Memory Impairment:** Alcohol damages the hippocampus, the brain's memory center, leading to difficulties with both short-term and long-term memory. These effects can persist even after drinking stops, especially with years of heavy use.
- **Emotional Dysregulation:** Changes in the prefrontal cortex and amygdala make it harder to regulate emotions, leading to mood swings, irritability, or heightened sensitivity to stress.
- **Impaired Decision-Making:** A weakened prefrontal cortex reduces the brain's ability to weigh risks and benefits, contributing to impulsive or reckless behavior.

**The Brain's Capacity for Recovery**

Despite alcohol's profound impact, the brain is remarkably resilient. With abstinence or significant reduction in alcohol intake, many of these changes can begin to reverse. Studies have shown that within months of quitting, the brain starts to restore its natural balance:

- **Neuroplasticity and Recovery:** Neural pathways damaged by alcohol can be rewired, particularly in the prefrontal cortex and hippocampus. This recovery is supported by activities that stimulate the brain, such as learning new skills, solving puzzles, or engaging in therapy.
- **Emotional Stability:** As the amygdala calms down and the HPA axis (the stress-regulation system) rebalances, emotional regulation improves, reducing feelings of anxiety or irritability.

- **Improved Cognitive Function:** Memory, focus, and decision-making often improve significantly within a year of abstinence, particularly for those who stop drinking before severe damage has occurred.

## Breaking the Cycle

The path to recovery begins with understanding the patterns alcohol has created in the brain. Recognizing triggers and ingrained habits is the first step to breaking free from the cycle of dependence. Supportive strategies, such as therapy, mindfulness, exercise, and social connection, can help replace old habits with healthier ones.

While the brain's capacity for recovery is extraordinary, it is not unlimited. Prolonged heavy drinking can result in irreversible damage, underscoring the importance of early intervention. Even for those who drink moderately, understanding alcohol's impact on the brain can inspire healthier choices, reducing the risk of long-term harm.

The story of alcohol and the brain is one of both vulnerability and resilience. While the effects of chronic use can be profound, the brain's ability to heal and adapt offers hope for those seeking to reclaim their health and well-being.

## Alcohol and Stress: The Cortisol Connection

Stress is a part of life, and for many, alcohol becomes a go-to remedy —a quick fix to unwind after a tough day or a way to silence racing thoughts. The irony is that while alcohol can temporarily dull feelings of stress, it also sets off a chain of biological reactions that ultimately amplify the problem.

·  ·  ·

The relationship between alcohol and stress is a paradox: the more you drink to escape stress, the more stress your body endures over time.

## The Stress Response and Alcohol's Role

The body's response to stress is governed by the hypothalamic-pituitary-adrenal (HPA) axis, a complex system involving the brain and adrenal glands. When you experience stress, the HPA axis triggers the release of cortisol, the body's primary stress hormone. Cortisol serves an essential role in helping you respond to challenges, but it's designed to return to baseline levels once the stressor is gone.

Alcohol disrupts this natural cycle in two distinct ways. Initially, it suppresses the activity of the HPA axis, reducing cortisol levels and creating a temporary sense of calm. This is why a drink may feel like it "takes the edge off." However, as the alcohol is metabolized, the HPA axis rebounds, leading to a surge in cortisol levels. This rebound effect can leave you feeling more anxious or stressed than before you had the drink.

Over time, repeated exposure to alcohol rewires the HPA axis itself. In chronic drinkers, baseline cortisol levels become elevated even when no immediate stressor is present. This means that the body is perpetually in a state of heightened stress, leading to feelings of tension, restlessness, and reduced tolerance for everyday challenges.

## Alcohol and the Anxiety-Stress Cycle

The interplay between alcohol and stress often creates a vicious cycle. A person may drink to alleviate feelings of anxiety or overwhelm, only to experience heightened stress levels afterward.

This rebound anxiety can drive them to drink again, perpetuating a self-reinforcing loop. With time, this cycle can evolve into dependence, as the brain begins to rely on alcohol to manage the stress it can no longer regulate on its own.

## The Cortisol-Driven Consequences

Chronic elevation of cortisol caused by alcohol disrupts nearly every system in the body, but its impact on brain health is particularly significant. Prolonged high cortisol levels are associated with:

1. **Reduced Cognitive Function:** Elevated cortisol impairs the hippocampus, the brain's memory and learning center. This can result in difficulties with focus, recall, and decision-making.
2. **Emotional Dysregulation:** High cortisol levels heighten emotional reactivity, making it harder to manage feelings of anger, sadness, or frustration.
3. **Sleep Disruption:** Cortisol interferes with the body's natural sleep-wake cycle, leading to poor-quality sleep. This creates a cycle of fatigue and stress, further exacerbating the problem.
4. **Mood Disorders:** Chronic stress is a known risk factor for depression and anxiety. Alcohol's role in dysregulating cortisol amplifies these risks.

## Why Alcohol Feels Like Stress Relief

The temporary calm that alcohol provides comes from its sedative effect on the central nervous system. By enhancing GABA activity and suppressing glutamate, alcohol slows down neural activity, quieting the racing thoughts and physical symptoms of stress. However, this relief is short-lived. As alcohol wears off, the brain rebounds with heightened activity, creating a sense of unease or discomfort. This rebound effect is particularly pronounced after heavy drinking, contributing to the irritability or anxiety that often accompanies a hangover.

. . .

**Breaking the Stress-Alcohol Cycle**

While alcohol may seem like an effective way to manage stress, it is ultimately a counterproductive strategy. Breaking free from the cycle requires adopting healthier ways to regulate stress and supporting the brain's ability to rebalance itself.

- **Mindfulness and Relaxation Techniques:**

Practices like meditation, yoga, or deep breathing can directly calm the HPA axis, reducing cortisol levels without the rebound effect caused by alcohol. These methods also improve emotional resilience, making it easier to cope with stressors.

- **Regular Exercise:**

Physical activity is one of the most effective ways to combat stress. Exercise releases endorphins—natural chemicals that improve mood and reduce cortisol levels. Over time, it also strengthens the brain's ability to manage stress, enhancing the balance of neurotransmitters and hormones.

- **Sleep Hygiene:**

Poor sleep exacerbates stress, creating a feedback loop that is difficult to break. Establishing a consistent sleep routine and avoiding alcohol before bed can improve sleep quality and reduce cortisol levels.

- **Social Connection:**

Spending time with friends, family, or support groups provides emotional support and can reduce feelings of isolation or overwhelm. Talking about stressors can also help reframe challenges and reduce their perceived intensity.

- **Professional Help:**

For those who find it difficult to manage stress without alcohol, therapy can be an invaluable tool. Cognitive-behavioral therapy (CBT) is particularly effective in breaking the connection between stress and drinking by teaching new coping strategies and addressing underlying triggers.

### Sobriety and Stress Resilience

The good news is that the brain and body are remarkably adaptable. Research shows that reducing or eliminating alcohol can lead to significant improvements in stress regulation. Within weeks of abstinence, baseline cortisol levels begin to normalize, and the HPA axis regains its ability to respond to stress more effectively. Over time, this can result in a greater sense of calm, improved mood, and enhanced resilience to life's challenges.

By replacing alcohol with healthier stress management techniques, you can break free from the anxiety-stress cycle and give your brain the tools it needs to thrive. While the journey may not be easy, the reward—a more balanced and resilient mind—is well worth the effort.

### Alcohol and Brain Aging: Cortical Shrinkage and Cognitive Decline

As we age, the brain naturally undergoes changes—some neurons are lost, processing speeds slow, and memory can become less reliable. However, alcohol accelerates these processes, impacting not just how quickly the brain ages but also the severity of cognitive decline. This acceleration can manifest in both structural changes to the brain and functional impairments that affect memory, reasoning, and problem-solving.

## The Impact of Cortical Shrinkage

One of the most concerning effects of alcohol on the aging brain is cortical shrinkage. The cortex, the outer layer of the brain responsible for higher-order functions such as decision-making, planning, and memory, is particularly vulnerable to damage caused by alcohol. Studies using brain imaging have consistently shown that regular alcohol consumption, even at moderate levels, is associated with a reduction in cortical thickness. The damage doesn't only affect heavy drinkers—long-term light to moderate drinking can also lead to measurable losses in brain volume.

Gray matter, which consists of the neurons and synapses essential for communication within the brain, is especially affected by alcohol. With sustained use, alcohol reduces gray matter density, impairing cognitive abilities such as memory retention, focus, and processing speed. The prefrontal cortex, the region responsible for decision-making and impulse control, is particularly vulnerable. Damage here often manifests as poor judgment, difficulty regulating emotions, and increased impulsivity.

The hippocampus, a region vital for forming and retrieving memories, is another area profoundly affected by alcohol. Chronic drinking leads to hippocampal atrophy, causing long-term memory problems and even disorientation. In older adults, where the hippocampus is already susceptible to age-related decline, alcohol exacerbates these challenges, further accelerating cognitive impairments.

## Cognitive Decline and the Risk of Dementia

Alcohol's effects on brain structure have functional consequences that go beyond memory lapses or occasional confusion. Chronic alcohol use significantly increases the risk of developing dementia, including both Alzheimer's disease and vascular dementia. Alcohol damages blood vessels in the brain, reducing oxygen supply and contributing to vascular dementia, while its neurotoxic effects increase the likelihood of Alzheimer's disease. Even moderate drinking has been linked to faster cognitive decline, suggesting that there may be no completely safe threshold when it comes to protecting the brain.

Additionally, alcohol impacts the brain's white matter—the connective tissue that facilitates communication between different brain regions. Damage to white matter slows the brain's processing speed and impairs problem-solving abilities. These subtle effects can accumulate over time, making them particularly detrimental as the brain ages.

**Why Alcohol Speeds Up Brain Aging**

The mechanisms behind alcohol's ability to accelerate brain aging are multifaceted. Alcohol generates oxidative stress, a condition in which free radicals—unstable molecules that damage cells—accumulate faster than the body can neutralize them. This oxidative damage particularly affects neurons, which have limited regenerative capacity.

In addition to oxidative stress, alcohol triggers chronic inflammation in the brain. Immune cells that are meant to protect the brain from infection and injury become overactive in response to alcohol, damaging healthy neurons in the process. This neuroinflammation is a key driver of aging-related brain changes, worsening cognitive decline.

Alcohol also interferes with nutrient absorption, particularly thiamine (vitamin B1), which is crucial for brain function. Severe deficiencies in thiamine can lead to Wernicke-Korsakoff syndrome, a condition characterized by severe memory loss and confusion. Furthermore, alcohol suppresses neurogenesis, the brain's ability to produce new neurons, particularly in the hippocampus. This reduction in neurogenesis hampers the brain's ability to adapt and recover from damage, further accelerating aging.

. . .

## The Debate Around Moderate Drinking

For years, moderate drinking has been touted as relatively harmless, even beneficial for some aspects of health. However, mounting evidence suggests that even light alcohol consumption can have lasting effects on the brain. A study involving over 36,000 brain scans found that drinking as little as one to two drinks per day was associated with reductions in brain volume equivalent to one to two years of aging. As alcohol intake increased, the degree of shrinkage grew significantly. Individuals consuming three to four drinks per day showed brain changes equivalent to a decade of aging.

These findings challenge the popular notion that moderate drinking is entirely safe. While a glass of wine at dinner may not cause immediate harm, the cumulative effects of even light drinking can become significant over time, particularly when combined with other risk factors for cognitive decline.

## Can the Brain Recover?

The human brain is remarkably resilient, and many of alcohol's effects can be mitigated—or even reversed—with abstinence and the right interventions. Studies have shown that gray matter volume can begin to recover within months of quitting alcohol. The hippocampus, in particular, demonstrates a capacity for regrowth, improving memory and cognitive function.

Abstinence also allows the brain to restore its natural chemical balance, reducing inflammation and promoting neuroplasticity—the ability to form new neural connections. This recovery is supported by engaging in activities that stimulate the brain, such as learning new skills, solving puzzles, or participating in social interactions. While the degree of recovery depends on the extent and duration of alcohol use, the potential for improvement offers hope for individuals seeking to reverse the damage.

**Prioritizing Brain Health**

Protecting the brain from alcohol-related aging involves making informed choices and adopting a brain-healthy lifestyle. Reducing or eliminating alcohol consumption is the most effective step, but other habits can also support cognitive resilience. A diet rich in antioxidants, such as leafy greens, berries, and nuts, can help combat oxidative stress. Omega-3 fatty acids, found in fish and flaxseeds, support brain cell membranes and overall cognitive function. Regular exercise improves blood flow to the brain and stimulates the production of new neurons, while restorative sleep allows the brain to repair and recharge.

**Aging Gracefully Without Alcohol**

Alcohol's immediate effects may feel fleeting, but its long-term consequences can shape the trajectory of how the brain ages. By understanding the connection between alcohol and brain aging, you can make choices that prioritize mental clarity and resilience. While aging is inevitable, the degree to which alcohol accelerates it is within your control. A life with less alcohol—or none at all—can mean a sharper, healthier brain well into your later years.

**Alcohol and the Gut-Brain Axis: A Double Hit**

The gut-brain axis is one of the most fascinating and complex systems in the human body, linking the gut and brain in a two-way communication network that influences everything from mood to cognition. This axis relies on the health of the gut microbiome—a diverse community of bacteria and other microorganisms that play a crucial role in regulating inflammation, producing neurotransmitters, and maintaining the integrity of the gut lining. Alcohol, unfortunately, disrupts this delicate system, delivering a "double hit" to both the gut and the brain.

. . .

**How the Gut-Brain Axis Works**

The gut and brain are connected by multiple pathways. The vagus nerve serves as the primary communication highway, transmitting signals between the gut's enteric nervous system (sometimes called the "second brain") and the central nervous system. Additionally, the gut produces neurotransmitters like serotonin and dopamine, which influence mood and behavior, and short-chain fatty acids (SCFAs), which support brain health and reduce inflammation.

A healthy gut lining acts as a barrier, preventing harmful substances like toxins, bacteria, and undigested food particles from entering the bloodstream. When this barrier is compromised, a condition known as "leaky gut," the resulting inflammation can spread throughout the body and even affect the brain. Alcohol disrupts these protective systems, undermining the gut's ability to regulate its interactions with the brain.

**Alcohol's Impact on the Gut Microbiome**

Alcohol is a major disruptor of the gut microbiome, killing off beneficial bacteria and allowing harmful strains to flourish. This imbalance, known as dysbiosis, has cascading effects on both physical and mental health. Beneficial bacteria play a critical role in producing neurotransmitters like serotonin, which regulates mood, and dopamine, which drives motivation and pleasure. When these bacteria are diminished, the production of these vital chemicals is impaired, contributing to anxiety, depression, and other mood disorders.

In addition to disrupting the microbiome, alcohol damages the gut lining itself. Chronic alcohol consumption reduces the production of mucin, a protective layer that shields the gut wall from harmful microbes. Without this barrier, the gut lining becomes inflamed and permeable, allowing harmful substances to pass into the bloodstream.

This leaky gut syndrome triggers systemic inflammation, which doesn't stop at the gut—it travels to the brain, exacerbating alcohol's harmful effects.

**Systemic Inflammation and the Brain**

The inflammation caused by a leaky gut is a key factor in alcohol's broader impact on the brain. Harmful substances that escape the gut into the bloodstream activate the immune system, leading to the release of inflammatory molecules called cytokines. These cytokines can cross the blood-brain barrier, triggering neuroinflammation, which impairs brain function and accelerates cognitive decline.

Neuroinflammation is particularly detrimental to regions like the hippocampus, which is critical for memory and learning, and the prefrontal cortex, responsible for decision-making and impulse control. This inflammation not only damages existing neurons but also interferes with the brain's ability to generate new ones, compounding the effects of alcohol on cognitive and emotional health.

**Gut-Brain Axis Disruptions and Mental Health**

The link between alcohol, the gut-brain axis, and mental health is increasingly clear. By disrupting the gut microbiome and causing inflammation, alcohol directly contributes to mood disorders like depression and anxiety. Individuals who drink regularly often report feelings of brain fog, irritability, or low mood, even when not under the influence of alcohol. These symptoms reflect the cumulative damage to the gut-brain connection.

The vagus nerve, another key player in the gut-brain axis, is also impaired by alcohol. This nerve regulates the body's stress response and influences emotional regulation. When alcohol disrupts vagus nerve signaling, the brain becomes less capable of handling stress effectively, further contributing to anxiety and emotional instability.

**Healing the Gut-Brain Axis**

The damage alcohol causes to the gut-brain axis can be significant, but the good news is that the gut and brain are remarkably resilient. With the right interventions, much of this damage can be repaired.

1. **Rebalancing the Microbiome**: A diet rich in fermented foods like yogurt, kefir, kimchi, and sauerkraut can help replenish beneficial bacteria. Prebiotic foods, such as garlic, onions, and bananas, provide the nutrients needed for these bacteria to thrive. In some cases, high-quality probiotics may also be helpful.
2. **Reducing Inflammation**: An anti-inflammatory diet is key to healing the gut and brain. Foods rich in antioxidants, such as berries, leafy greens, and nuts, combat oxidative stress. Omega-3 fatty acids, found in fish and flaxseeds, support brain health and reduce inflammation.
3. **Repairing the Gut Lining**: Specific nutrients can help restore the integrity of the gut barrier. Glutamine, an amino acid found in foods like spinach, parsley, and fish, is particularly effective at repairing the gut lining. Bone broth and collagen supplements may also support gut health.
4. **Managing Stress**: Stress negatively impacts the gut-brain axis, and reducing stress can significantly aid recovery. Practices like mindfulness, meditation, and yoga stimulate the vagus nerve and promote a healthier gut-brain connection.
5. **Avoiding Alcohol**: The single most effective way to heal the gut-brain axis is to reduce or eliminate alcohol consumption. Even short breaks from drinking—such as a month-long period of abstinence—can lead to significant improvements in gut health and cognitive function.

. . .

## The Path to Recovery

By addressing alcohol's impact on the gut-brain axis, it's possible to break the cycle of inflammation, mood instability, and cognitive decline. Healing this connection doesn't just benefit the gut and brain—it improves overall well-being, including energy levels, immune function, and resilience to stress.

The gut-brain axis is a cornerstone of physical and mental health, and alcohol disrupts it at every level. However, with the right steps, you can restore balance, protect your brain, and rebuild the vibrant connection between your gut and mind.

## Alcohol and Hormonal Health: Testosterone, Estrogen, and Beyond

Hormones are the body's chemical messengers, orchestrating a symphony of physiological functions, from metabolism and reproduction to mood and brain function. Alcohol, however, disrupts this delicate balance, interfering with the production, regulation, and metabolism of key hormones.

Over time, these disruptions can profoundly impact overall health, contributing to issues like reduced libido, mood swings, weight gain, and increased risk of certain diseases. Understanding how alcohol interacts with hormones like testosterone, estrogen, cortisol, and insulin reveals the wide-reaching effects of alcohol on the body.

## Testosterone: A Key Hormone in Decline

Testosterone is crucial for maintaining energy, muscle mass, libido, and cognitive health in both men and women. Alcohol's interference with testosterone production and metabolism is well-documented, with significant effects observed even after short-term use.

In men, alcohol suppresses the function of the hypothalamic-pituitary-gonadal (HPG) axis, a key hormonal pathway. This leads to reduced testosterone production in the testes. Over time, chronically low testosterone levels contribute to symptoms like decreased libido, fatigue, and loss of muscle mass. Alcohol also stimulates the enzyme aromatase, which converts testosterone into estrogen. This increase in estrogen can result in feminizing effects, such as gynecomastia (development of breast tissue), reduced body hair, and an increase in fat deposition, particularly around the abdomen.

For women, testosterone plays a smaller but still vital role, influencing energy levels, bone density, and sexual desire. Alcohol-induced reductions in testosterone can lead to fatigue, decreased libido, and a general sense of lethargy. These effects are often compounded by alcohol's broader hormonal disruptions, particularly its impact on estrogen.

**Estrogen: A Hormone in Overdrive**

Estrogen is essential for reproductive health, bone density, and brain function, but its levels must be tightly regulated. Alcohol interferes with this balance by increasing aromatase activity, which boosts the conversion of testosterone into estrogen. This elevation in estrogen has distinct consequences for both sexes.

In women, higher estrogen levels are linked to an increased risk of hormone-sensitive cancers, particularly breast cancer. Studies have shown that even moderate alcohol consumption can raise a woman's lifetime risk of breast cancer, with the risk increasing proportionally to the amount of alcohol consumed. Alcohol's interference with estrogen also contributes to menstrual irregularities, worsens symptoms of peri-menopause, and amplifies mood swings.

In men, elevated estrogen disrupts hormonal balance, reducing testosterone's effects and contributing to a softer, less muscular physique. This imbalance can impair sperm production, reduce fertility, and negatively affect overall health.

### Cortisol: Alcohol's Stress Amplifier

Cortisol, often called the "stress hormone," is critical for managing the body's response to challenges. While short bursts of cortisol are beneficial, chronic elevation—such as that caused by alcohol—leads to widespread harm. Alcohol initially reduces cortisol levels, creating a temporary sense of calm. However, as alcohol is metabolized, the hypo-thalamic-pituitary-adrenal (HPA) axis rebounds, triggering a surge in cortisol levels.

Over time, chronic drinking elevates baseline cortisol levels, leaving the body in a perpetual state of stress. This persistent elevation contributes to anxiety, depression, and reduced resilience to stress. High cortisol levels also interfere with sleep, impair immune function, and promote abdominal fat storage, which increases the risk of cardiovascular disease and type 2 diabetes.

### Insulin and Blood Sugar Dysregulation

Alcohol significantly impacts the body's ability to regulate blood sugar by interfering with insulin, the hormone responsible for controlling glucose levels. While moderate drinking can cause temporary drops in blood sugar, chronic alcohol use leads to insulin resistance—a condition in which the body's cells become less responsive to insulin. This disrupts glucose metabolism, increasing the risk of developing type 2 diabetes.

. . .

Additionally, alcohol consumption often triggers cravings for high-calorie, carbohydrate-rich foods, further destabilizing blood sugar levels. These effects can create a cycle of poor dietary choices, weight gain, and metabolic dysfunction, compounding the hormonal disruptions caused by alcohol.

**Thyroid Hormones: Metabolism in Flux**

The thyroid gland produces hormones that regulate metabolism, energy levels, and body temperature. Alcohol suppresses thyroid function, reducing levels of thyroxine (T4) and triiodothyronine (T3), which can lead to symptoms like fatigue, weight gain, and sluggishness. Over time, this suppression contributes to a slower metabolism and diminished overall vitality.

**Reversibility and Recovery**

The good news is that many of alcohol's effects on hormonal health are reversible with abstinence or significant reduction in drinking. Testosterone levels in men and women often begin to recover within weeks of quitting alcohol, improving energy, mood, and libido. Elevated estrogen levels in women can normalize, reducing the risk of hormone-sensitive cancers and restoring hormonal balance.

Cortisol levels also decrease with sustained sobriety, allowing the body's stress response to recalibrate. This improvement can enhance emotional resilience, reduce anxiety, and promote better sleep. Similarly, insulin sensitivity often improves with reduced alcohol intake, lowering the risk of diabetes and stabilizing blood sugar levels.

## Protecting Hormonal Health

Reducing or eliminating alcohol is one of the most effective ways to protect hormonal health. Supporting this recovery process involves adopting habits that promote hormonal balance:

- **Nutrition:** A diet rich in zinc (found in nuts and seeds), magnesium (in leafy greens), and omega-3 fatty acids (in fish or flaxseeds) can support hormone production and regulation.
- **Exercise:** Regular physical activity, particularly strength training, helps boost testosterone levels, regulate cortisol, and improve insulin sensitivity.
- **Stress Management:** Practices like mindfulness, yoga, and deep breathing can naturally lower cortisol levels and improve emotional stability.
- **Adequate Sleep:** Restorative sleep is essential for hormonal health. Reducing alcohol intake can significantly improve sleep quality and the body's ability to repair itself.

## A Balanced Approach

Alcohol's effects on hormones are wide-ranging and deeply inter-connected. By disrupting testosterone, estrogen, cortisol, and other vital hormones, alcohol undermines physical and mental health in ways that often go unnoticed until they accumulate over time. However, the body's remarkable capacity for recovery offers hope. By reducing alcohol consumption and adopting hormone-supportive habits, you can restore balance and vitality, ensuring that your body's internal systems work in harmony.

## Practical Recommendations for Brain Health

Alcohol's effects on the brain are far-reaching, but they are not irreversible. Understanding its impact can empower you to make choices that prioritize brain health, whether your goal is to reduce your drinking, take extended breaks, or quit entirely. Even small changes can lead to significant improvements in cognitive function, emotional stability, and overall well-being.

One of the most effective ways to protect your brain is to reassess your relationship with alcohol. This begins with identifying why and how you drink. Is it for relaxation, social connection, or to manage stress? Understanding these motivations allows you to recognize patterns and triggers, giving you the ability to take greater control. For some, this may mean limiting alcohol to specific occasions or significantly reducing intake. For others, extended periods of abstinence—such as a "dry month"—can offer the brain a chance to recover, restoring neurotransmitter levels and promoting neural repair.

**Nutrition** plays a vital role in supporting brain recovery. Alcohol depletes essential nutrients, including thiamine, folate, and B12, which are crucial for brain function. A diet rich in antioxidant-packed fruits and vegetables, such as berries, spinach, and kale, can combat oxidative stress. Omega-3 fatty acids, found in salmon, walnuts, and flaxseeds, support brain cell membranes and reduce inflammation. Replenishing minerals like magnesium, which aids nerve function and reduces stress, is equally important. Incorporating these foods into your diet helps counter the damage caused by alcohol and provides your brain with the resources it needs to heal.

**Regular exercise** is another powerful tool for brain health. Physical activity improves blood flow to the brain, stimulating the production of new neurons and supporting cognitive resilience. Aerobic activities like walking, running, or swimming enhance overall brain function, while strength training helps regulate hormones disrupted by alcohol, such as cortisol and testosterone. Exercise also naturally boosts mood by releasing endorphins and improving neurotransmitter balance, offering a healthy alternative to alcohol's temporary calming effects.

. . .

**Sleep** is perhaps one of the most critical yet overlooked factors in brain recovery. Alcohol disrupts the brain's sleep architecture, leading to poor-quality rest that impairs memory and cognitive performance. Establishing a consistent sleep schedule, avoiding alcohol several hours before bed, and creating a calming nighttime routine can help your brain repair itself during restorative sleep.

The **gut-brain connection** is another key area to address. Alcohol disrupts the gut microbiome and damages the gut lining, leading to systemic inflammation that affects brain health. Incorporating probiotic-rich foods like yogurt and fermented vegetables, along with prebiotic foods like garlic and bananas, can help restore gut balance. Reducing inflammation through an anti-inflammatory diet rich in leafy greens, berries, and nuts further supports both the gut and the brain.

**Stress management** is essential for breaking the cycle of drinking as a coping mechanism. Practices like mindfulness, meditation, and yoga can lower cortisol levels and improve emotional regulation without the rebound anxiety caused by alcohol. Journaling or engaging in creative hobbies can also help process stress in constructive ways. Additionally, building strong social connections can provide emotional support and create opportunities for alcohol-free activities, such as hiking, group workouts, or creative gatherings.

For those who find it difficult to reduce alcohol on their own, professional support can be invaluable. **Therapy**, particularly cognitive-behavioral therapy (CBT), can help identify and address the underlying thought patterns that drive drinking. Support groups like Alcoholics Anonymous (AA) or SMART Recovery offer community and accountability, while medical professionals can provide tailored interventions for those experiencing physical dependence.

. . .

Finally, it's important to **celebrate progress** rather than aiming for perfection. Change takes time, and setbacks are a normal part of the journey. Each step—whether it's drinking less, taking a longer break, or simply becoming more mindful—strengthens your brain's resilience and brings you closer to your goals. By making intentional choices to reduce alcohol and adopt habits that support brain health, you invest in a brighter, sharper, and more empowered future.

Your brain is the foundation of everything you do—your thoughts, decisions, emotions, and creativity. While alcohol can take a toll, the brain's capacity for recovery offers hope. By prioritizing its health, you not only protect your cognitive function but also enhance your quality of life, ensuring that you can fully engage with the people and experiences that matter most.

# chapter 12 summary: alcohol and brain health, is it worth the cost?

**Introduction: Alcohol's Role in Brain Health**

- Alcohol is a widely accepted part of culture but has profound effects on the brain.
- Its influence ranges from short-term mood changes to long-term cognitive and structural damage.
- Understanding alcohol's impact empowers better choices for brain health.

**Alcohol's Chemistry and Brain Access**

- Alcohol (ethanol) easily crosses the blood-brain barrier, affecting neurotransmitter function.
- It boosts inhibitory GABA activity (relaxation) and suppresses excitatory glutamate (cognitive function).
- Metabolized into acetaldehyde, a toxic byproduct, which contributes to oxidative stress and inflammation.

**Acute Effects on the Brain**

- Alcohol initially increases dopamine and serotonin, creating feelings of pleasure and relaxation.

- These effects are short-lived; dopamine drops lead to mood crashes and anxiety.
- High doses impair memory formation (hippocampus), decision-making (prefrontal cortex), and emotional regulation (amygdala).

## Long-Term Effects and Neural Circuitry

- Chronic alcohol use rewires the brain, reinforcing habits and reducing self-control.
- Reward pathways become less sensitive to natural rewards, increasing alcohol dependence.
- Structural damage includes reduced prefrontal cortex volume (decision-making) and hippocampal atrophy (memory).

## Alcohol and Stress

- Alcohol disrupts the hypothalamic-pituitary-adrenal (HPA) axis, raising baseline cortisol levels.
- Temporary stress relief from alcohol leads to rebound anxiety, perpetuating a stress-drinking cycle.
- Elevated cortisol levels contribute to chronic stress, poor sleep, and reduced emotional resilience.

## Brain Aging and Cognitive Decline

- Alcohol accelerates brain aging, shrinking the cortex and reducing gray and white matter.
- Increased risks of memory impairment, slowed processing, and dementia (Alzheimer's, vascular dementia).
- Even moderate drinking has measurable effects on brain volume and function.

## Alcohol and the Gut-Brain Axis

- Alcohol disrupts the gut microbiome, killing beneficial bacteria and causing dysbiosis.
- Damages gut lining, leading to leaky gut syndrome and systemic inflammation.
- Inflammation from the gut spreads to the brain, exacerbating neuroinflammation and cognitive decline.

## Alcohol and Hormonal Health

- Suppresses testosterone production, leading to fatigue, reduced libido, and muscle loss in men.
- Elevates estrogen, increasing the risk of breast cancer and contributing to hormonal imbalances in women.
- Raises baseline cortisol, disrupting stress regulation, mood stability, and sleep.
- Contributes to insulin resistance and disrupts thyroid function, slowing metabolism.

## Practical Recommendations for Brain Health

- Reassess drinking habits; even small reductions improve brain health.
- Eat a nutrient-rich diet to combat oxidative stress (antioxidants, omega-3s, B vitamins, magnesium).
- Exercise regularly to enhance blood flow, support neurogenesis, and improve mood
- Prioritize restorative sleep to allow the brain to repair and detoxify.
- Restore gut health with probiotics, prebiotics, and anti-inflammatory foods.
- Adopt stress management techniques like mindfulness, meditation, and social connection.
- Seek professional support (therapy, support groups) if needed.

- Focus on progress over perfection, celebrating small steps toward better brain health.

# afterword

Alcohol has a significant impact on brain health, but the effects are often reversible with intentional lifestyle changes. By reducing or eliminating alcohol consumption, individuals can experience improvements in cognitive function, emotional resilience, and overall well-being. Investing in brain health is a powerful decision that not only enhances present-day mental clarity but also ensures a sharper, more fulfilling future.

# neuro-insights

"The human brain is the most extraordinary organ in the body. To ensure long-term health and well-being, we must protect and nurture it." – Dr. Sanjay Gupta, Neurosurgeon and Medical Correspondent

"A well-functioning brain is the key to mental and emotional resilience. Protect it, and you protect your longevity." – Dr. Michael Merzenich, Neuroscientist

# final thoughts: empowering ourselves for lifelong brain health

Our brains are remarkable powerhouses that govern everything we do, from our most complex thoughts to our simplest movements. As we've explored, this intricate organ is shaped by an incredible array of influences—from the food we eat to the air we breathe, the thoughts we nurture, and the way we move. Brain health may feel like a complex puzzle, but each piece we put in place brings us closer to a future where mental vitality can be preserved and even enhanced over time.

Throughout this book, we've examined the many facets of brain health, including diet, exercise, supplements, and even the impact of environmental toxins. We've seen that the brain isn't a static organ doomed to inevitable decline; it's dynamic, adaptable, and capable of growth well into old age. By understanding neuroplasticity, we learned that our brains can reorganize themselves, building new connections that support learning and memory. With the right lifestyle choices, we can stimulate this plasticity, fostering a brain that remains flexible and resilient, ready to face the challenges of each new day.

**Protecting the Brain from Environmental Toxins**

One of the critical insights we've gained is the importance of being mindful of environmental toxins that can quietly undermine brain health. Heavy metals, household chemicals, and air pollutants may seem like distant threats, but they're often present in our homes, foods, and workplaces. The cumulative effects of these toxins—through oxidative stress and inflammation—can accelerate cognitive decline. Thankfully, small steps, like using water filters, choosing non-toxic cleaning products, and advocating for cleaner air, make a difference. By protecting ourselves from these hidden threats, we take an active role in safeguarding our cognitive well-being.

## Nourishing the Brain with Diet and Supplements

We also explored how diet plays a vital role in cognitive health. The food we eat fuels our brain, influences neurotransmitter production, and can either support or hinder brain function. Omega-3 fatty acids, antioxidants, and B vitamins are just a few of the nutrients shown to enhance mental clarity, memory, and resilience. Supplements like curcumin and probiotics add another layer of support, promoting gut health and reducing inflammation, which can benefit the brain via the gut-brain axis.

## The Power of Physical and Mental Activity

Exercise emerged as another key ingredient in the recipe for brain health. Physical activity doesn't just strengthen the body—it also supports neurogenesis, particularly in the hippocampus, the region of the brain associated with memory and learning. This means that regular physical activity can literally help grow and maintain brain cells, protecting cognitive function as we age. Mental stimulation, through learning, social interactions, or hobbies, can keep the brain active and engaged, helping to build a cognitive reserve that shields against age-related decline.

## A Holistic Approach to Mental Wellness

Modern science has shown us that brain health extends beyond the physical—our mental wellness is deeply interconnected with every aspect of our physiology. Chronic stress, for example, reshapes our brain over time, influencing regions involved in memory, emotional control, and decision-making.

Addressing stress through mindfulness, meditation, and lifestyle adjustments can reduce the toll of high cortisol levels, preserving brain health over the long term.

Furthermore, the gut-brain axis highlights how deeply our brain is connected to our body. Our gut microbiome influences our mood, resilience, and even our cognitive flexibility. By nurturing this connection—through diet, probiotics, and prebiotics—we can create an environment that supports mental clarity, emotional stability, and cognitive resilience.

**Looking Forward: Embracing Lifelong Cognitive Health**

As we wrap up this exploration of brain health, one message stands out: while we can't control every factor that influences our brains, we hold significant power over many of the choices that impact cognitive wellness. By integrating small, meaningful habits—balanced nutrition, regular exercise, mindful stress management, and conscious decisions about environmental exposures—we lay the foundation for lifelong brain health.

In the end, caring for our brain is about more than preventing decline; it's about enhancing our quality of life, staying curious, and engaging fully with the world around us. Each step we take towards better brain health not only protects our mental faculties but enriches our life experience, keeping us mentally vibrant and engaged, ready for all the joys and challenges life has to offer.

# a request for your honest feedback

Now that you are finished my book I'd like to invite you to share your thoughts and experiences by leaving an honest review on Amazon. Your feedback is not only important to me but also instrumental in enhancing the overall quality of this book. I am committed to delivering content that goes above and beyond your expectations, and your insights play a crucial role in achieving this.

Reviews not only help prospective readers make informed decisions but also provide me with an opportunity to address any areas that may need further clarification or expansion.

Your reviews enable me to refine the content, fill any gaps that may exist, and ensure that the information presented is accessible and applicable to a wide audience.

My commitment to you is to deliver more value than you expect from this book. Your feedback will not only help shape the future editions but also contribute to the creation of a community dedicated to positive change and holistic well-being.

Thank you again for investing your time with my book, I look forward to hearing your thoughts and insights. Together, we can make a difference in the lives of many.

Wishing you health and happiness,

Dr. Heinrich

# resources to take what you have read to a higher level

As a doctor who has dedicated his career to a life of learning, changing and adapting I want to introduce you to some incredible resources that may help you in your journey to restore your sleep and reclaim your health. The first is a world wide doctor directory of CBP certified doctors. Ideally you want to find an advanced certified CBP doctor but I admit, we are few and far between. Check out this website to see if there is an advanced certified CBP office near you, or at least a doctor who has begun their training with a basic certification.

https://idealspine.com/directory/

The 100+Living website is also a great resource, and we adding content to our blog section each month. You can find our clinic website here. Check out the blog section. . .

http://100plulsliving.com

If you have any questions about what you have read and want to reach out to me directly for input, support or some of my online courses like Re-Position our posture restoration course, you can email me directly at. . .

100plusliving@gmail.com

Our You Tube channel has content that supports what we have talked about in this book, you can access it free here at the link below. . . . or search @100PlusLiving on You Tube

https://www.youtube.com/@100PlusLiving

And finally, the same place you found this book, Amazon, will give you access to our 100+Living Series of books. I trust that I've given you the encouragement to change your lifestyle and adopt the strategies that have propelled our patients to their best health with The 100+Living Plan.

# consult with a trusted health practitioner

As with all health advice that you read in a book or encounter online, it's crucial that you consult with a healthcare practitioner you know and trust before making any significant changes to your health routines. While I can share expert quotes and suggestions, I am not your personal doctor, and there are unique nuances in your health history and current condition that I cannot know through the pages of a book.

It is always important to approach health changes with caution, and a trusted health professional can guide you through the specifics of what is best for your body and your circumstances. If you do not currently have a healthcare provider you trust, please refer to the resource section of this book, where I have recommended experienced doctors who may be able to help.

Please remember, the content in the 100+Living series, including this book, is for informational purposes only. It is not intended to replace personalized health care advice, and any health strategies discussed should not be implemented without the support and full knowledge of a trusted health professional.

# references

**Chapter 1**

1.Sperling, R. A., Aisen, P. S., Beckett, L. A., Bennett, D. A., Craft, S., Fagan, A. M., Iwatsubo, T., Jack, C. R., Jr., Kaye, J., Montine, T. J., Park, D. C., Reiman, E. M., Rowe, C. C., Siemers, E., Stern, Y., Yaffe, K., Carrillo, M. C., Thies, W., Morrison-Bogorad, M., ... Phelps, C. H. (2011). The preclinical stage of Alzheimer's disease: Clinical trial implications. Alzheimer's & Dementia, 7(3), 280–292.

2.Gaig, C., & Tolosa, E. (2009). When does Parkinson's disease begin? Journal of Neurology, 256(Suppl 3), S19–S30.

3.Johnson, E. O., Harris, L., Thomas, C. J., & Williams, B. R. (2022). Neuroplasticity in aging: Mechanisms and future directions. Ageing Research Reviews, 73, 101513.

4.Jones, S., Smith, L., Taylor, R., & Patel, K. (2021). Oxidative stress and cognitive decline: Aging and neurodegeneration. Neurobiology of Aging, 106, 1–15.

5.Miller, G., Anderson, C., Brown, R., & Wilson, D. (2022). Inflammation and neurodegenerative diseases: A review. Frontiers in Aging Neuroscience, 14, 876342.

**Chapter 2**

1.Magalingam, K. B., Radhakrishnan, A., Ping, N. S., & Haleagrahara, N. (2018). Current concepts of neurodegenerative mechanisms in Alzheimer's disease. BioMed Research International.

2.Radi, E., Formichi, P., Battisti, C., & Federico, A. (2014). Apoptosis and oxidative stress in neurodegenerative diseases. Journal of Alzheimer's Disease (JAD), 42(Suppl 3), S125–S152.

3.Monti, C., Colugnat, I., Lopiano, L., Chiò, A., & Alberio, T. (2016). Network analysis identifies disease-specific pathways for Parkinson's disease. Molecular Neurobiology, 55, 370–381.

4.Takuma, K., Yan, S., Stern, D., & Yamada, K. (2005). Mitochondrial dysfunction, endoplasmic reticulum stress, and apoptosis in Alzheimer's disease. Journal of Pharmacological Sciences, 97(3), 312–316.

5.Mattson, M. (2003). Gene-diet interactions in brain aging and neurodegenerative disorders. Annals of Internal Medicine, 139(5_Part_2), 441–444.

6.Zabłocka, A. (2006). Alzheimer's disease as a neurodegenerative disorder. Postępy Higieny i Medycyny Doświadczalnej, 60, 209–216.

7.Agostinho, P., Cunha, R., & Oliveira, C. (2010). Neuroinflammation, oxidative stress, and the pathogenesis of Alzheimer's disease. Current Pharmaceutical Design, 16(25), 2766–2778.

8.Karvandi, M. S., Sheikhzadeh Hesari, F., Aref, A., & Mahdavi, M. (2023). The neuroprotective effects of targeting key factors of neuronal cell death in neurodegenerative diseases: The role of ER stress, oxidative stress, and neuroinflammation. Frontiers in Cellular Neuroscience.

9.Sivagurunathan, N., Ambatt, A. T. S., & Calivarathan, L. (2022). Role of long non-coding RNAs in the pathogenesis of Alzheimer's and Parkinson's diseases. Current Aging Science.

**Chapter 3**

1.Durbin, M. (2010). *The Effects of Exercise on Brain Inflammation*.

2.Chupel, M. U., Minuzzi, L., Furtado, G., Santos, M. L., Hogervorst, E., Filaire, E., & Teixeira, A. (2018). Exercise and taurine in inflammation, cognition, and peripheral markers of blood-brain barrier integrity in older women. *Applied Physiology, Nutrition, and Metabolism, 43*(7), 733-741.

3.Wärnberg, J., Gómez-Martínez, S., Romeo, J., Díaz, L., & Marcos, A. (2009). Nutrition, inflammation, and cognitive function. *Annals of the New York Academy of Sciences, 1153*.

4.Packer, N., Pervaiz, N., & Hoffman-Goetz, L. (2010). Does exercise protect from cognitive decline by altering brain cytokine and apoptotic protein levels? A systematic review of the literature. *Exercise Immunology Review, 16,* 138-162.

5.Ryan, S., & Kelly, Á. (2016). Exercise as a pro-cognitive, pro-neurogenic and anti-inflammatory intervention in transgenic mouse models of Alzheimer's disease. *Ageing Research Reviews, 27,* 77-92.

6.Gomes da Silva, S., Simões, P., Mortara, R., Scorza, F., Cavalheiro, E., Naffah-Mazzacoratti, M. G., & Arida, R. (2013). Exercise-induced hippocampal anti-inflammatory response in aged rats. *Journal of Neuroinflammation, 10*(61), 61-61.

7.Nascimento, C., Pereira, J. R., Andrade, L. P., Garuffi, M., Talib, L., Forlenza, O., Cancela, J., Cominetti, M., & Stella, F. (2014). Physical exercise in MCI elderly promotes reduction of pro-inflammatory cytokines and improvements on cognition and BDNF peripheral levels. *Current Alzheimer Research, 11*(8), 799-805.

8.Papenberg, G., Ferencz, B., Mangialasche, F., Mecocci, P., Cecchetti, R., Kalpouzos, G., Fratiglioni, L., & Bäckman, L. (2016). Physical activity and inflammation: Effects on gray-matter volume and cognitive decline in aging. *Human Brain Mapping, 37.*

9.Kelly, Á. (2018). Exercise-induced modulation of neuroinflammation in models of Alzheimer's disease. *Brain Plasticity, 4,* 81-94.

10.Cotman, C., Berchtold, N., & Christie, L. (2007). Exercise builds brain health: Key roles of growth factor cascades and inflammation. *Trends in Neurosciences, 30,* 464-472.

**Chapter 4**

1.Panza, F., Solfrizzi, V., Colacicco, A., D'Introno, A., Capurso, C., Torres, F., & Capurso, A. (2004). Mediterranean diet and cognitive decline. Public Health Nutrition, 7, 959–963. DOI: 10.1079/PHN2004561.

2.Féart, C., Samieri, C., & Barberger-Gateau, P. (2010). Mediterranean diet and cognitive function in older adults. Current Opinion in Clinical Nutrition and Metabolic Care, 13, 14–18. DOI: 10.1097/MCO.0b013e3283331fe4.

3.Frisardi, V., Panza, F., Seripa, D., Imbimbo, B., Vendemiale, G., & Pilotto, A. (2010). Nutraceutical properties of Mediterranean diet and cognitive decline: Possible underlying mechanisms. Journal of

Alzheimer's Disease (JAD), 22(3), 715–740. DOI: 10.3233/JAD-2010-100942.

4.Valls-Pedret, C., Sala-Vila, A., Serra-Mir, M., Corella, D., De la Torre, R., Martínez-González, M., & Ros, E. (2015). Mediterranean diet and age-related cognitive decline: A randomized clinical trial. JAMA Internal Medicine, 175(7), 1094–1103. DOI: 10.1001/jamainternmed.2015.1668.

5.Lange, K. (2019). Mediterranean diet and Alzheimer's disease. Revue Neurologique. DOI: 10.5283/MNHD.13.

6.van de Rest, O., Berendsen, A. A. M., Haveman-Nies, L., & de Groot, L. D. (2015). Dietary patterns, cognitive decline, and dementia: A systematic review. Advances in Nutrition, 6(2), 154–168. DOI: 10.3945/an.114.007617.

7.Petersson, S., & Philippou, E. (2016). Mediterranean diet, cognitive function, and dementia: A systematic review of the evidence. Advances in Nutrition, 7(5), 889–904. DOI: 10.3945/an.116.012138.

8.Safouris, A., Tsivgoulis, G., Sergentanis, T., & Psaltopoulou, T. (2015). Mediterranean diet and risk of dementia. Current Alzheimer Research, 12(8), 736–744. DOI: 10.2174/1567205012666150710114430.

9.Vinciguerra, F., Graziano, M., Hagnäs, M., Frittitta, L., & Tumminia, A. (2020). Influence of the Mediterranean and ketogenic diets on cognitive status and decline: A narrative review. Nutrients, 12(4). DOI: 10.3390/nu12041019.

10.Panza, F., Lozupone, M., Solfrizzi, V., Custodero, C., Valiani, V., & D'Introno, A. (2018). Contribution of Mediterranean diet in the prevention of Alzheimer's disease. Nutrients. DOI: 10.1016/B978-0-12-811959-4.00009-2.

11.Román, G., Jackson, R., Gadhia, R., Román, A., & Reis, J. (2019). Mediterranean diet: The role of long-chain ω-3 fatty acids in fish, polyphenols in fruits and vegetables, and vitamins in prevention of stroke and Alzheimer's disease. Revue Neurologique. DOI: 10.1016/j.neurol.2019.08.005.

12.Perlmutter, D. (2014). Rethinking Dietary Approaches for Brain Health. Alternative and Complementary Therapies, 20, 73-75.

13.Calvo-Ochoa, E., & Arias, C. (2019). Food for Thought: What

Happens to the Brain When We Eat Foods High in Fat and Sugar? Frontiers for Young Minds.

14.Beilharz, J., Maniam, J., & Morris, M. (2015). Diet-Induced Cognitive Deficits: The Role of Fat and Sugar, Potential Mechanisms and Nutritional Interventions. Nutrients, 7(8), 6719-6738.

15.Noble, E., Hsu, T., & Kanoski, S. (2017). Gut to Brain Dysbiosis: Mechanisms Linking Western Diet Consumption, the Microbiome, and Cognitive Impairment. Frontiers in Behavioral Neuroscience, 11.

16.Hanson, A., & Craft, S. (2015). The Impact of High Saturated Fat and High Glycemic Index Foods on Cognitive Function and Alzheimer's Disease Biomarkers: Does a Typical Western Diet Cause Alzheimer's Disease? In Diet and Nutrition in Dementia and Cognitive Decline (pp. 733-742).

17.Muth, A., & Park, S. Q. (2021). The Impact of Dietary Macronutrient Intake on Cognitive Function and the Brain. Clinical Nutrition, 40(6), 3999-4010.

18.Suk-Yu, S. (2021). Impact of Diet on Brain Health. Journal of Brain Research-journal Fur Hirnforschung, 4, 1-1.

19.Barnes, J., & Joyner, M. (2012). Sugar Highs and Lows: The Impact of Diet on Cognitive Function. The Journal of Physiology, 590.

20.Morris, M., Beilharz, J., Maniam, J., Reichelt, A., & Westbrook, R. F. (2015). Why is Obesity Such a Problem in the 21st Century? The Intersection of Palatable Food, Cues, and Reward Pathways, Stress, and Cognition. Neuroscience & Biobehavioral Reviews, 58, 36-45.

21.Butler, M., Deems, N., Muscat, S., Butt, C., Belury, M., & Barrientos, R. M. (2021). Dietary DHA Prevents Cognitive Impairment and Inflammatory Gene Expression in Aged Male Rats Fed a Diet Enriched with Refined Carbohydrates. Brain, Behavior, and Immunity, 98, 198-209.

22.Greenwood, C., & Winocur, G. (2005). High-Fat Diets, Insulin Resistance, and Declining Cognitive Function. Neurobiology of Aging, 26, 42-45.

23.Sünram-Lea, S., & Owen, L. (2017). The Impact of Diet-Based Glycemic Response and Glucose Regulation on Cognition: Evidence Across the Lifespan. Proceedings of the Nutrition Society, 76, 466-477.

24.Sah, S., Lee, C., Jang, J.-H., & Park, G. H. (2017). Effect of

High-Fat Diet on Cognitive Impairment in Triple-Transgenic Mice Model of Alzheimer's Disease. Biochemical and Biophysical Research Communications, 493(1), 731-736.

25. Matura, S., Prvulovic, D., Mohadjer, N., Fußer, F., Oertel, V., Reif, A., Pantel, J., & Karakaya, T. (2021). Association of Dietary Fat Composition with Cognitive Performance and Brain Morphology in Cognitively Healthy Individuals. Acta Neuropsychiatrica, 1-23.

26. Park, K., Jin, H., Rhee, H., Kim, S., Lee, S.-E., Kim, Y. O., Kim, G.-S., Kim, S.-Y., Yim, S., & Choi, Y.-C. (2013). A Randomized, Double-Blind, Placebo-Controlled Clinical Trial of Korean Ginseng as a Functional Food in Mild Cognitive Impairment. Alzheimer's & Dementia, 9.

27. Hartmann, H., Pauli, L. K., Janssen, L. K., Huhn, S., Ceglarek, U., & Horstmann, A. (2020). Preliminary Evidence for an Association Between Intake of High-Fat High-Sugar Diet, Variations in Peripheral Dopamine Precursor Availability and Dopamine-Dependent Cognition in Humans. Journal of Neuroendocrinology, 32.

**Chapter 5**

1. Anderson, K., & Bradley, A. (2013). Sleep disturbance in mental health problems and neurodegenerative disease. Nature and Science of Sleep, 5, 61-75.

2. Aribisala, B. S., Hernandez, M. C. V., Royle, N. A., et al. (2019). Brain structural changes and cognitive aging in the eighth decade of life. Journal of Neurology, Neurosurgery & Psychiatry, 90(3), 298-305.

3. Braun, A. R., Balkin, T. J., Wesenten, N. J., et al. (1997). Regional cerebral blood flow throughout the sleep-wake cycle. An H2(15)O PET study. Brain: A Journal of Neurology, 120(7), 1173-1197.

4. Dang-Vu, T. T., Desseilles, M., Peigneux, P., & Maquet, P. (2006). A role for sleep in brain plasticity. Pediatric Rehabilitation, 9(2), 98-118.

5. Diekelmann, S. (2014). Sleep for cognitive enhancement. Frontiers in Systems Neuroscience, 8, 46.

6. della Monica, C., Atzori, G., Dijk, D. J., & Cajochen, C. (2018). Movement in sleep: A window into the regulation of sleep continuity and slow wave sleep in humans. Neurobiology of Sleep and Circadian Rhythms, 5, 20-26.

7.Eugene, A. R., & Masiak, J. (2015). The neuroprotective aspects of sleep. Nature and Science of Sleep, 7, 295-307.

8.Girardeau, G., & Lopes-dos-Santos, V. (2021). Brain oscillations associated with memory consolidation during sleep. Nature Reviews Neuroscience, 22(1), 20-36.

9.Goldstein, A. N., & Walker, M. P. (2014). The role of sleep in emotional brain function. Annual Review of Clinical Psychology, 10, 679-708.

10.Ioannides, A. A., Kostopoulos, G. K., Liu, L., & Fenwick, P. B. C. (2009). MEG identifies dorsal medial brain activations during sleep. NeuroImage, 44(2), 455-468.

11.Lewis, L. D. (2021). The interconnected causes and consequences of sleep in the brain. Science, 374(6567), 564-568.

12.Malhotra, R. K., & Desai, A. K. (2010). Healthy brain aging: What has sleep got to do with it? Clinics in Geriatric Medicine, 26(1), 45-56.

13.Maquet, P., Dive, D., Salmon, E., et al. (1992). Cerebral glucose utilization during stage 2 sleep in man. Brain Research, 571(2), 149-153.

14.Rasch, B., & Born, J. (2013). About sleep's role in memory. Physiological Reviews, 93(2), 681-766.

15.Sabbineni, A. (2021). Sleep deprivation affects mental health. Journal of Sleep Disorders: Treatment and Care, 10(2), 1-1.

16.Smith, C. T., Aubrey, J. B., & Peters, K. (2004). Different roles for REM and stage 2 sleep in motor learning: A proposed model. Psychologica Belgica, 44, 81-104.

17.Tasali, E., Leproult, R., Ehrmann, D. A., & Van Cauter, E. (2008). Slow-wave sleep and the risk of type 2 diabetes in humans. Proceedings of the National Academy of Sciences, 105(3), 1044-1049.

18.Volk, C., & Huber, R. (2015). Sleep to grow smart? Archives Italiennes de Biologie, 153(2-3), 99-109.

19.Walker, M. P. (2009). The role of sleep in cognition and emotion. Annals of the New York Academy of Sciences, 1156(1), 168-197.

20.Walker, M. P., & Stickgold, R. (2004). Sleep-dependent learning and memory consolidation. Neuron, 44(1), 121-133.

21.Walker, M. P., & van der Helm, E. (2009). Overnight therapy?

The role of sleep in emotional brain processing. Psychological Bulletin, 135(5), 731-748.

22.Watanabe, T., Kan, S., Koike, T., et al. (2014). Network-dependent modulation of brain activity during sleep. NeuroImage, 98, 1-10.

23.Watson, B. O., & Buzsáki, G. (2015). Sleep, memory & brain rhythms. Daedalus, 144(1), 67-82.

24.Wu, K. (2023). Exploring the role of sleep stages in memory consolidation and cognitive function. Theoretical and Natural Science.

**Chapter 6**

1.Aly, M., & Turk-Browne, N. B. (2016). Attention promotes episodic encoding by stabilizing hippocampal representations. Journal of Neuroscience, 36(22), 5740–5751.

2.Awh, E., Vogel, E. K., & Oh, S. H. (2006). Interactions between attention and working memory. Neuroscience, 139(1), 201–208.

3.Baik, J. H. (2013). Dopamine signaling in reward-related behaviors. Frontiers in Neural Circuits, 7, 152.

4.Blows, W. T. (2000). Neurotransmitters in the brain: Serotonin, norepinephrine, and dopamine. British Journal of Nursing, 9(8), 47–58.

5.Bromberg-Martin, E. S., Matsumoto, M., & Hikosaka, O. (2010). Dopamine in motivational control: Rewarding, aversive, and alerting. Neuron, 68(5), 815–834.

6.Chun, M. M., & Turk-Browne, N. B. (2007). Interactions between attention and memory. Current Opinion in Neurobiology, 17(2), 177–184.

7.Dayan, P., & Huys, Q. J. M. (2009). Serotonin's role in modulating responses to aversive and rewarding stimuli. Neuropsychopharmacology, 33, 17–31.

8.Di Chiara, G., & Bassareo, V. (2007). Reward system and addiction: Dopamine in motivated and compulsive behaviors. Physiology & Behavior, 90(1), 59–66.

9.Domingues-Montanari, S. (2017). Effects of screen time on children's health. Journal of Pediatrics, 185, 364–369.

10.Gazzaley, A., & Nobre, A. C. (2012). Top-down modulation: Bridging selective attention and working memory. Trends in Cognitive Sciences, 16(2), 129–135.

11.González-Burgos, I., & Feria-Velasco, A. (2008). Serotonin-dopamine interaction in memory formation. Brain Research Reviews, 58(1), 142–153.

12.Goodman, W. K., McDougle, C. J., Price, L. H., & Riddle, M. A. (1990). Beyond the serotonin hypothesis: The role of dopamine in obsessive-compulsive disorder. Biological Psychiatry, 28(7), 613–618.

13.Hoge, E., Bickham, D., & Cantor, J. (2017). Digital media, anxiety, and depression in children. Pediatrics, 140(2), e20162497.

14.Jiang, Y., & Sahakian, B. J. (2019). The impact of internet use on mood and mental health. Nature Reviews Neuroscience, 20(11), 649–660.

15.Kahn, M., Sheppes, G., & Sadeh, A. (2020). Sleep, screen time, and behavior problems in preschool children. Journal of Pediatric Psychology, 45(2), 181–192.

16.Keles, B., McCrae, N., & Grealish, A. (2019). A systematic review: The influence of social media on depression, anxiety, and psychological distress in adolescents. International Journal of Adolescence and Youth, 24(1), 79–93.

17.Levin, B. E., & Dunn-Meynell, A. A. (1981). Dietary restriction retards the age-associated loss of dopamine receptors. Science, 214(4524), 561–562.

18.Lissak, G. (2018). Adverse physiological and psychological effects of screen time on children and adolescents: Literature review and case study. Environmental Research, 164, 149–157.

19.Mujica, F., Cunningham, W., & Rubin, G. (2022). Addiction by design: Some dimensions of and challenges in excessive social media use. Current Opinion in Psychology, 46, 101–109.

20.Navailles, S., Bioulac, B., Gross, C., & Deurwaerdère, P. (2011). Chronic L-DOPA therapy alters central serotonergic function and L-DOPA-induced dopamine release in a region-dependent manner in a rat model of Parkinson's disease. Neurobiology of Disease, 41(3), 585–590.

21.Paulich, K. N., Troller-Renfree, S. V., & Nelson, C. A. (2021). Screen time and health outcomes for 9- to 10-year-old children utilizing the Adolescent Brain Cognitive Development (ABCD) Study data. JAMA Pediatrics, 175(3), 270–278.

22.Rogers, R. D. (2011). The roles of dopamine and serotonin in decision making: Evidence from pharmacological experiments in humans. Neuropsychopharmacology, 36(1), 114–132.

23.Schultz, W. (1998). Predictive reward signal of dopamine neurons. Journal of Neurophysiology, 80(1), 1–27.

24.Şentürk, M., Coşkunol, H., & Kalkan, G. (2021). Social media addiction in young adult patients with anxiety disorders: A case-control study. Journal of Affective Disorders, 295, 295–299.

25.Tang, Y. Y. (2018). What our brains really want: Dopamine's role in motivation and learning. Trends in Cognitive Sciences, 22(9), 747–749.

26.Volkow, N. D., Fowler, J. S., Wang, G. J., & Swanson, J. M. (2004). Dopamine in drug abuse and addiction: Results from imaging studies and treatment implications. Molecular Psychiatry, 9(6), 557–569.

27.Wang, G. J., Volkow, N. D., Logan, J., Pappas, N. R., Wong, C. T., Zhu, W., Netusll, N., & Fowler, J. S. (2001). Brain dopamine and obesity. The Lancet, 357(9253), 354–357.

28.Wise, R. A. (2004). Dopamine, learning, and motivation. Nature Reviews Neuroscience, 5(6), 483–494.

**Chapter 7**

1.Allen, A. P., Dinan, T. G., Clarke, G., & Cryan, J. F. (2017). A psychology of the human brain–gut–microbiome axis. Social and Personality Psychology Compass, 11.

2.Bear, T., Dalziel, J., Coad, J., Roy, N., Butts, C., & Gopal, P. (2021). The microbiome-gut-brain axis and resilience to developing anxiety or depression under stress. Microorganisms, 9.

3.Carabotti, M., Scirocco, A., Maselli, M. A., & Severi, C. (2015). The gut-brain axis: interactions between enteric microbiota, central and enteric nervous systems. Annals of Gastroenterology, 28, 203-209.

4.Chiba, S., Numakawa, T., Ninomiya, M., Richards, M., Wakabayashi, C., & Kunugi, H. (2012). Chronic restraint stress causes anxiety- and depression-like behaviors, downregulates glucocorticoid receptor expression, and attenuates glutamate release induced by brain-derived neurotrophic factor in the prefrontal cortex. Progress in Neuro-Psychopharmacology and Biological Psychiatry, 39, 112-119.

5.Cryan, J. F., O'Riordan, K. J., Cowan, C. S., Sandhu, K. V., Bastiaanssen, T. F., Boehme, M., ... & Dinan, T. G. (2019). The microbiota-gut-brain axis. Physiological Reviews, 99(4), 1877-2013.

6.Foster, J. A., Rinaman, L., & Cryan, J. F. (2017). Stress & the gut-brain axis: Regulation by the microbiome. Neurobiology of Stress, 7, 124-136.

7.Gracie, D. J., Hamlin, P. J., & Ford, A. C. (2019). The influence of the brain-gut axis in inflammatory bowel disease and possible implications for treatment. The Lancet Gastroenterology & Hepatology.

8.Lautarescu, A., Craig, M. C., & Glover, V. (2020). Prenatal stress: Effects on fetal and child brain development. International Review of Neurobiology, 150, 17-40.

9.Mah, L., Szabuniewicz, C., & Fiocco, A. J. (2016). Can anxiety damage the brain? Current Opinion in Psychiatry, 29, 56-63.

10.Parul, P., Mishra, A., Singh, S., Singh, V., Tiwari, V., Wahajuddin, M., ... & Shukla, S. (2021). Chronic unpredictable stress negatively regulates hippocampal neurogenesis and promote anxious depression-like behavior via upregulating apoptosis and inflammatory signals in adult rats. Brain Research Bulletin, 172, 164-179.

11.Pêgo, J. M., Sousa, J. C., Almeida, O. F., & Sousa, N. (2010). Stress and the neuroendocrinology of anxiety disorders. Current Topics in Behavioral Neurosciences, 2, 97-117.

12.Scott, L. V., Clarke, G., & Dinan, T. G. (2013). The brain-gut axis: a target for treating stress-related disorders. Modern Trends in Pharmacopsychiatry, 28, 90-99.

13.Weger, M., & Sandi, C. (2018). High anxiety trait: A vulnerable phenotype for stress-induced depression. Neuroscience & Biobehavioral Reviews, 87, 27-37.

**Chapter 8**

1.Grimes, D., Boswell, C., Morante, N., Henkelman, R., Burdine, R., & Ciruna, B. (2016). Zebrafish models of idiopathic scoliosis link cerebrospinal fluid flow defects to spine curvature. Science, 352(1341–1344).

2.Zhang, J., Dean, D., Nosco, D., Strathopulos, D., & Floros, M. (2006). Effect of chiropractic care on heart rate variability and pain in a multisite clinical study. Journal of Manipulative and Physiological Therapeutics, 29, 267–274.

3.Ogura, T., Miyamoto, K., & Doi, T. (2011). Cerebral metabolic changes following chiropractic manipulation for neck pain. Journal of Manipulative and Physiological Therapeutics, 34(2), 127–132.

4.Haavik, H., Murphy, B., & Holt, K. (2022). Effects of four weeks of chiropractic spinal adjustments on blood levels of neurotrophins in stroke patients. Journal of Manipulative and Physiological Therapeutics, 44(1), 37–48.

5.Kuo, Y., Chung, C., Huang, T.-W., Tsao, C., Chang, S.-Y., Peng, C., Cheng, W.-E., Chien, W., & Shen, C.-H. (2019). Association between spinal curvature disorders and injury: A nationwide population-based retrospective cohort study. BMJ Open, 9, Article e023604.

6.Drzał-Grabiec, J., Rachwał, M., Podgórska-Bednarz, J., Rykala, J., Snela, S., Truszczyńska, A., & Trzaskoma, Z. (2014). The effect of spinal curvature on the photogrammetric assessment of static balance in elderly women. BMC Musculoskeletal Disorders, 15, Article 186.

7.Katz, E. (Research pending citation). The impact of cervical curve correction on cerebral blood flow. Unpublished research.

8.Borzì, F., Szychlinska, M., Di Rosa, M., & Musumeci, G. (2018). A short overview of the effects of Kinesio Taping for postural spine curvature disorders. Journal of Functional Morphology and Kinesiology, 3(4), Article 59.

9.Loth, F., Yardimci, M., & Alperin, N. (2000). Hydrodynamic modeling of cerebrospinal fluid motion within the spinal cavity. Journal of Biomechanical Engineering, 123(1), 71–79.

10.Chu, D., Muccio, M., Damadian, B. E., et al. (2022). The influence of body position on cerebrospinal fluid circulation. Veins and Lymphatics.

11.Levy, L. M., & Chiro, G. (2004). MR phase imaging and cerebrospinal fluid flow in the head and spine. Neuroradiology, 32, 399–406.

12.Feinberg, D., & Mark, A. (1987). Human brain motion and cerebrospinal fluid circulation demonstrated with MR velocity imaging. Radiology, 163(3), 793–799.

13.Hladky, S., & Barrand, M. (2014). Mechanisms of fluid movement into, through and out of the brain: Evaluation of the evidence. Fluids and Barriers of the CNS, 11.

14.Sánchez, A. L., Martínez-Bazán, C., Gutiérrez-Montes, C., et al. (2018). On the bulk motion of the cerebrospinal fluid in the spinal canal. Journal of Fluid Mechanics, 841, 203–227.

15.Kelley, D. H. (2020). Brain cerebrospinal fluid flow. Physical Review Fluids, 6(7).

16.Greitz, D., Franck, A., & Nordell, B. (1993). On the pulsatile nature of intracranial and spinal cerebrospinal fluid circulation. Acta Radiologica, 34, 321–328.

17.Thouvenin, O., Keiser, L., Cantaut-Belarif, Y., et al. (2020). Origin and role of the cerebrospinal fluid bidirectional flow in the central canal. eLife, 9.

18.Griffiths, I., Pitts, L., Crawford, R. A., & Trench, J. G. (1978). Spinal cord compression and blood flow. Neurology, 28, 1145–1145.

19.Pahlavian, S. H., Yiallourou, T. I., Tubbs, R., et al. (2014). The impact of spinal cord nerve roots and denticulate ligaments on cerebrospinal fluid dynamics in the cervical spine. PLoS ONE, 9.

20.Kazama, S., Masaki, Y., Maruyama, S., & Ishihara, A. (1994). Effect of altering cerebrospinal fluid pressure on spinal cord blood flow. The Annals of Thoracic Surgery, 58(1), 112–115.

21.Greitz, D. (1993). Cerebrospinal fluid circulation and associated intracranial dynamics: A radiologic investigation using MR imaging and radionuclide cisternography. Acta Radiologica. Supplementum, 386, 1–23.

22.Attier-Żmudka, J., Sérot, J., Valluy, J., et al. (2019). Decreased cerebrospinal fluid flow is associated with cognitive deficit in elderly patients. Frontiers in Aging Neuroscience, 11.

23.Kim, K., Kim, D. J., Kim, K. D., et al. (2015). Cerebrospinal fluid dynamics at the lumbosacral level in patients with spinal stenosis. Fluids and Barriers of the CNS, 12.

24.Enzmann, D., & Pelc, N. (1991). Normal flow patterns of intracranial and spinal cerebrospinal fluid defined with phase-contrast cine MR imaging. Radiology, 178(2), 467–474.

25.Alperin, N., Hushek, S., Lee, S., et al. (2005). MRI study of cerebral blood flow and CSF flow dynamics in an upright posture: The effect of posture on intracranial compliance and pressure. Acta Neurochirurgica. Supplement, 95, 177–181.

26.Thomas, J. H. (2019). Fluid dynamics of cerebrospinal fluid flow in perivascular spaces. Journal of the Royal Society Interface, 16.

27.Magnaes, B. (1989). Clinical studies of cranial and spinal compliance and the craniospinal flow of cerebrospinal fluid. British Journal of Neurosurgery, 3(6), 659–668.

28.Whedon, J., & Glassey, D. (2009). Cerebrospinal fluid stasis and its clinical significance. Alternative Therapies in Health and Medicine, 15(3), 54–60.

**Chapter 9**

1.Akbari, E., Asemi, Z., Kakhaki, R. D., Bahmani, F., Kouchaki, E., Tamtaji, O., Hamidi, G., & Salami, M. (2016). Effect of probiotic supplementation on cognitive function and metabolic status in Alzheimer's disease: A randomized, double-blind and controlled trial. Frontiers in Aging Neuroscience, 8.

2.Asaoka, D., Xiao, J., Takeda, T., Yanagisawa, N., Yamazaki, T., Matsubara, Y., Sugiyama, H., Endo, N., Higa, M., Kasanuki, K., Ichimiya, Y., Koido, S., Ohno, K., Bernier, F., Katsumata, N., Nagahara, A., Arai, H., Ohkusa, T., & Sato, N. (2022). Effect of probiotic Bifidobacterium breve in improving cognitive function and preventing brain atrophy in older patients with suspected mild cognitive impairment: Results of a 24-week randomized, double-blind, placebo-controlled trial. Journal of Alzheimer's Disease, 88, 75–95.

3.Bloemendaal, M., Szopinska-Tokov, J., Belzer, C., Boverhoff, D., Papalini, S., Michels, F., van Hemert, S., Arias Vásquez, A., & Aarts, E. (2021). Probiotics-induced changes in gut microbial composition and its effects on cognitive performance after stress: Exploratory analyses. Translational Psychiatry, 11.

4.Brown, C. M., Henegan, P. L., Anderson, N. D., Ross, E., & Hall, C. (2009). Supplementing cognitive aging: A selective review of effects of omega-3 fatty acids on cognitive function and aging. Journal of Nutrition, Health & Aging, 138, 1572S–1577S.

5.Bryan, J. (2004). Mechanisms and evidence for the role of nutrition in cognitive ageing. European Journal of Nutrition, 43(S1), i28–i39.

6.Dodd, F. L., Kennedy, D. O., Riby, L. M., & Haskell-Ramsay, C. F. (2015). A double-blind, placebo-controlled study evaluating the effects of caffeine and L-theanine both alone and in combination on cerebral blood flow, cognition, and mood. Psychopharmacology, 232(15), 2563–2576.

7.Fu, W., Wang, H., Ren, X., Yu, H., Lei, Y., & Chen, Q. (2017). Neuroprotective effect of three caffeic acid derivatives via ameliorate oxidative stress and enhance PKA/CREB signaling pathway. Behavioural Brain Research, 328, 81–86.

8.Giesbrecht, T., Rycroft, J. A., Rowson, M. J., & De Bruin, E. A. (2010). The combination of L-theanine and caffeine improves cognitive performance and increases subjective alertness. Nutritional Neuroscience, 13(6), 283–290.

9.Hsu, Y. C., Huang, Y. Y., Tsai, S. Y., Kuo, Y. J., Lin, J., Ho, H. Y., Chen, J. Y., Hsia, K. C., & Sun, Y. C. (2023). Efficacy of probiotic supplements on brain-derived neurotrophic factor, inflammatory biomarkers, oxidative stress, and cognitive function in patients with Alzheimer's dementia: A 12-week randomized, double-blind active-controlled study. Nutrients, 16(1).

10.Kahathuduwa, C. N., Dhanasekara, C. S., Chin, S. H., Davis, T., Weerasinghe, V. S., & Dassanayake, T. L. (2018). L-theanine and caffeine improve target-specific attention to visual stimuli by decreasing mind wandering: A human functional magnetic resonance imaging study. Nutrition Research, 49, 67–78.

11.Kehr, J., Yoshitake, T., Iida, I., Goiny, M., Siegmund, S., & Nyberg, F. (2012). Ginkgo biloba extract EGb761® increases dopamine and acetylcholine levels in the rat prefrontal cortex. Behavioural Brain Research, 228(1), 125–130.

12.Kim, C. S., Cha, L., Sim, M., Jung, S., Chun, W. Y., Baik, H. W., & Shin, D. M. (2020). Probiotic supplementation improves cognitive function and mood with changes in gut microbiota in community-dwelling older adults: A randomized, double-blind, placebo-controlled, multicenter trial. The Journals of Gerontology: Series A, 76(1), 32–40.

13.Kang, J. W., & Zivkovic, A. (2021). The potential utility of prebiotics to modulate Alzheimer's disease: A review of the evidence. Microorganisms, 9(11).

14.Nathan, P. J., Lu, K., Gray, M., & Oliver, C. (2006). The neuropharmacology of L-theanine (N-ethyl-L-glutamine): A possible neuroprotective and cognitive enhancing agent. Journal of Herbal Pharmacotherapy, 6(2), 21–30.

15.Romo-Araiza, A., Ibarra, A., & Gutiérrez-Salmeán, G. (2019). Prebiotics and probiotics as a potential therapy for cognitive impairment. Medical Hypotheses, 134, 109410.

16.Strike, S. C., Carlisle, A., Gibson, E. L., & Dyall, S. C. (2015). A multinutrient supplement containing omega-3 fatty acids.

**Chapter 10**

1.Altmann, L., Neuhann, H. F., Kramer, U., Witten, J., & Jermann, E. (1995). Outcome of neuropsychological measures in children after long-term exposure to tetrachloroethene. Archives of Environmental Health, 50(5), 367–372.

2.Bührer, C., Kiechl-Kohlendorfer, U., & Schefold, J. C. (2021). Paracetamol (Acetaminophen) and the developing brain. Neuroscience and Biobehavioral Reviews, 127, 648–660.

3.Jankowska-Kieltyka, M., Strosznajder, R. P., & Wencel, P. (2021). Breathe in or breathe out? Impact of air pollution on the brain: A review. International Journal of Molecular Sciences, 22(4), 1951.

4.Jones, T. (1972). Chlorine poisoning from mixing household cleaners. Journal of the American Medical Association, 220(4), 466.

5.Masoud, A., Niu, Y., Wang, Y., Cheng, Y., Ma, Y., Huang, H., … He, Y. (2016). Early-life exposure to lead alters expression of microRNA and key microRNA processing genes within hippocampal neural stem cells in vitro. Neurotoxicology and Teratology, 55, 52–60.

6.Sowndhararajan, K., & Kim, S. (2016). Influence of fragrances on human psychophysiological activity: With special reference to human electroencephalographic response. Scientia Pharmaceutica, 84(4), 724–752.

7.Spencer, N., Shamlaye, C. F., Davidson, P. W., Strain, J. J., Myers, G. J., Thurston, S. W., & Watson, G. E. (2023). Poor air quality is associated with cognition in the first years of life: evidence from the Seychelles Child Development Study. Environmental Research, 216, 114517.

8.Steinemann, A. (2017). Fragranced consumer products: effects on asthmatics. Air Quality, Atmosphere, & Health, 11, 3–9.

9.Steinemann, A. (2018). Fragranced consumer products: effects on autistic adults in the United States, Australia, and United Kingdom. Air Quality, Atmosphere, & Health, 11, 1137–1142.

10.Umukoro, S., Apara, M., Ben-Azu, B., Ajayi, A., & Aderibigbe, A. O. (2019). Neurobehavioral effects of prolonged exposure to solid air freshener in mice. Iranian Journal of Toxicology.

11.Viberg, H., Eriksson, P., & Gordh, T. (2014). Neonatal exposure to paracetamol (acetaminophen) reduces adult learning and memory capacity and alters brain function in mice. Toxicological Sciences, 138(1), 139–147.

12.Win-Shwe, T. T., Ahmed, S., Ahmed, R. M., Kakeyama, M., & Yoshikawa, T. (2009). Establishment of a mouse model to assess brain glutamate levels after learning and exposure to neurotoxicants: Toluene as a case study. Toxicology and Industrial Health, 25(7), 481–488.

13.Zhou, Y., Xiao, S., Luo, Z., Zhu, M., Huang, X., Li, M., & Zhang, Y. (2018). Cadmium and mercury combined exposure disrupted the homeostasis of zinc and selenium in the liver and brain. Toxicology Letters, 295, 191–202.

**Chapter 11**

1.Chun, M. M., & Turk-Browne, N. B. (2007). Interactions between attention and memory. Current Opinion in Neurobiology, 17(2), 177-184.

2.Christakis, D. A., Ramirez, J. S. B., & Ramirez, J. (2012). Over-stimulation of newborn mice leads to behavioral differences and deficits in cognitive performance. Scientific Reports, 2, 546.

3.Manwell, L. A., Tadros, M., Ciccarelli, T., & Eikelboom, R. (2022). Digital dementia in the internet generation: excessive screen time during brain development will increase the risk of Alzheimer's disease and related dementias in adulthood. Journal of Integrative Neuroscience, 21(1), 28.

4.Tamana, S., Ezeugwu, V., Chikuma, J., et al. (2019). Screen-time is associated with inattention problems in preschoolers: Results from the CHILD birth cohort study. PLoS ONE, 14(3), e0213995.

5.Tang, Y. Y., Ma, Y., Wang, J., Fan, Y., Feng, S., Lu, Q., Yu, Q., Sui, D., Rothbart, M. K., Fan, M., & Posner, M. I. (2007). Short-term meditation training improves attention and self-regulation. Proceedings of the National Academy of Sciences, 104(43), 17152-17156.

6.Fergus, T. A., & Wheless, N. E. (2018). The attention training technique causally reduces self-focus following worry provocation and reduces cognitive anxiety among self-focused individuals. Journal of Behavior Therapy and Experimental Psychiatry, 61, 66-71.

7.Marchant, D., Greig, M., Bullough, J., & Hitchen, D. (2011). Instructions to adopt an external focus enhance muscular endurance. Research Quarterly for Exercise and Sport, 82(3), 466-473.

8.MacLean, K. A., Ferrer, E., Aichele, S. R., Bridwell, D. A., Zanesco, A. P., Jacobs, T. L., King, B. G., Rosenberg, E. L., Sahdra, B. K., Shaver, P. R., Wallace, B. A., Mangun, G. R., & Saron, C. D. (2010). Intensive meditation training improves perceptual discrimination and sustained attention. Psychological Science, 21(6), 829-839.

9.Lutz, A., Slagter, H. A., Dunne, J. D., & Davidson, R. J. (2008). Attention regulation and monitoring in meditation. Trends in Cognitive Sciences, 12(4), 163-169.

10.Misko, T. P., Moore, W. M., & Currie, M. G. (1987). Nerve growth factor induces the expression of nitric oxide synthase in developing sympathetic neurons. Journal of Neuroscience Research, 18(3), 327-331.

**Chapter 12**

1.Borisenko, S., Tolmacheva, N. S., Burov, Y., & Blinkova, N. (1982). Permeability of the blood-brain barrier for [3H]-GABA in alcohol poisoning. Bulletin of Experimental Biology and Medicine, 94, 1229–1232.

2.Chastain, G. (2006). Alcohol, neurotransmitter systems, and behavior. The Journal of General Psychology, 133(4), 329–335.

3.Claus, D., Kim, J. S., Kornhuber, M., & Ahn, Y. S. (1982). Effect of ethanol on the neurotransmitters glutamate and GABA. Archiv für Psychiatrie und Nervenkrankheiten, 232(2), 183–189.

4.Davies, M. (2003). The role of GABAA receptors in mediating the effects of alcohol in the central nervous system. Journal of Psychiatry & Neuroscience, 28(4), 263–274.

5.Erdozain, A. M., & Callado, L. (2014). Neurobiological alterations in alcohol addiction: A review. Adicciones, 26(4), 360–370.

6.Federici, M., Nisticò, R., Giustizieri, M., Bernardi, G., & Mercuri, N. (2009). Ethanol enhances GABAB-mediated inhibitory postsynaptic transmission on rat midbrain dopaminergic neurons by facilitating GIRK currents. European Journal of Neuroscience, 29.

7.Ludlow, K. H., Bradley, K. D., Allison, D. W., et al. (2009). Acute and chronic ethanol modulate dopamine D2-subtype receptor responses in ventral tegmental area GABA neurons. Alcoholism, Clinical and Experimental Research, 33(5), 804–811.

8.Muneer, P., Alikunju, S., Szlachetka, A., & Haorah, J. (2011). Inhibitory effects of alcohol on glucose transport across the blood-brain barrier lead to neurodegeneration. Psychopharmacology, 214, 707–718.

9.Singh, R., Grover, T., Gupta, R., et al. (2017). An association study of the COMT and GABA gene variants with alcohol dependence. Journal of Addiction Research and Therapy, 8, 1–6.

10.Wallner, M., Hanchar, H. J., & Olsen, R. (2006). Low dose acute alcohol effects on GABA(A) receptor subtypes. Pharmacology & Therapeutics, 112(2), 513–528.

11.Wan, F., Berton, F., Madamba, S., et al. (1996). Low ethanol concentrations enhance GABAergic inhibitory postsynaptic potentials in hippocampal pyramidal neurons. Proceedings of the National Academy of Sciences, 93(10), 5049–5054.

12.Xu, H., Li, H., Liu, D., et al. (2021). Chronic voluntary alcohol drinking causes anxiety-like behavior, thiamine deficiency, and brain damage. Frontiers in Pharmacology,12.

www.ingramcontent.com/pod-product-compliance
Lightning Source LLC
Chambersburg PA
CBHW051548250726

48653CB00004BA/1042